Links Lizards:

The Continuing Adventures of 'The Grip', 'The Street', and 'The Kid'

Tom Hoch

By Tom Hoch

© 2016 Tom Hoch
All Rights Reserved.

No part of this publication may be reproduced, stored in a retrieval system, or transmitted, in any form or by any means, electronic, mechanical, photocopying, recording, or otherwise, without the written permission of the author.

First published by Dog Ear Publishing
4010 W. 86th Street, Ste H
Indianapolis, IN 46268
www.dogearpublishing.net

ISBN: 978-1-4575-4940-3

This book is printed on acid-free paper.

This book is a work of fiction. Places, events, and situations in this book are purely fictional and any resemblance to actual persons, living or dead, is coincidental.

Printed in the United States of America

To my brothers, Gene and Rick

and

son-in-law, Nate

Other works by author:

Chip Fullerton/Annie Smith Sports Series (under T. L. Hoch)

Chasing Normal (girls basketball)

Discovering Balance (girls softball)

Kat and the Bone (football)

Divot Dogs (golf)

Author web site—tlhochbooks.com <http://site—-tlhochbooks.com>

Author e-mail—thoch58@gmail.com

Acknowledgments

Thanks to all who were involved with this story.

The people at the Las Vegas National Golf Club and at the TPC at Deere Run were very accommodating. I'm sure they're used to seeing a ton of celebrities pass through their pro shops. They had no idea who I was when I showed up, but they gave me the royal treatment anyway.

Abby Smith did her usual superb job as a copy and content editor. She is absolutely terrific.

My manuscript readers were up to the task with their usual pertinent advice and comments. Arleta Vian always attacks her hard copy with an unbelievable understanding of what I'm trying to accomplish with my story telling. I am very fortunate to have her on my team.

Charlie Johnson was also instrumental with his insightful take on the story. He insists that I keep my three main characters in the game for at least one more gig. We'll see, Charlie.

Kathy Kelsey Holmes again lent her talents for the cover art. She is an amazing artist. I'm sure her former art students just smile when they see her work on my books. "Yup, that looks like something Ms. Holmes would draw." She definitely has the gift.

Tony Vegas is one of the three real people in **Divot Dogs** and **Links Lizards.** I always liked his bluesy rock tune, *Python Lee Jackson*. When I asked him if I could use it for the name of a Detroit pool hall, he said, "no problem". If you close your eyes when Tony is performing, you'd swear that Clapton or maybe Santana was up there on stage laying down the riffs. He's that good.

Scott Manninen was my gambling expert. He always had an answer when I had a technical question that involved a casino game.

Preface

I'm sure most authors get intensely involved with their characters when they're writing a story. When Ronnie and Eddie, and now Will, are on the course or just standing around talking, I'm standing right there with them. When a moment in the story becomes dramatic I get a little misty. I figure if I didn't, then something's amiss with the story telling or the writing thereof.

I've told several of my readers that if the second book or movie isn't better than the first, then it should stay on the drawing board until it is. I am confident that what follows will pass the test.

Tom Hoch

June 2016

CHAPTER ONE

—Setting The Hook

A golf buddy and I ran into Winston and Green a while back. We were all square after fourteen holes, then Green kicked it into second gear. We lost a hundred each to them. If you ask me, they're just a couple of two-bit hustlers that will never amount to anything.

—-Rodney Korver, realtor, part-time drug dealer

Deception can be a useful tool, depending on what you are trying to achieve. It's used in almost all sports. A "play-action" pass starts with a fake to a running back, hopefully making the linebackers stay home for a count or two, enabling a receiver to slip in behind them. Looking one way, and then passing the basketball to a different player without looking at them can be very effective if it's done right. A change-up in baseball will confuse even an experienced hitter if the wind-up and delivery resembles the pitcher's fastball. Like the ones stated above, some deceptions are simple. Others take a lot more thought, beforehand and during their execution.

Wayne bobbed his head backwards and appeared to have trouble focusing on his cards. Making his decision to call, he tossed a twenty on top of the small pile of bills in the center of the table. He looked up at the other players.

"I'm calling," he said in a slightly slurred voice as he turned over his hole cards. "Three kings, gents."

The man across from him grinned and exposed his diamond flush. Wayne nodded his head slowly in acceptance and leaned back in his chair.

"You know that old song about if it weren't for bad luck, I'd have no luck at all?" he asked no one in particular. "Well, tonight I think that tune was written with me in mind."

"I'm surprised a kid like you would know that old blues tune," responded Curly, a bald man in his late fifties.

"There are a couple of old guys that I play golf with once in a while," said Wayne, as he took the last sip from the flask he had been nursing for the past few hours, "and they love that old blues stuff. I probably heard about it from them."

"Well you certainly didn't learn about card playing from them," said his brother, Mack, as he sat across the table with a somewhat larger pile of bills sitting in front of him. "How much have you donated tonight, a couple a hundred?"

"Closer to three, but it ain't no big thing. I've been working a lot of overtime lately. Like I said, old lady luck is puttin' the hammer on me tonight. Now if we were playing golf, that would be a different story. There's a little luck playing small ball, but it's mostly skill, not like cards. Can't do much when all you're dealt is junk."

"Don't start in with that golf crap," said Mack with more than a little agitation in his voice. "Every time you get a little drunk, you start talking like you're God's gift to the sport."

The rest of the guys around the table were getting a kick out of the two young brothers that were sitting in on their weekly card game in the back of Bernie LaDuke's pro shop at a prestigious country club near Lansing, Michigan. The brothers heard the pro ran an honest game where the stakes didn't get out of hand. It took them a couple of months to wrangle an invitation, and when it came, they jumped at it. Three of the players at the table were members of the club and the other, in addition to the head pro, was one of his assistants.

"C'mon, bro, you're just pissed 'cause I can give you three a side and still spank you like a whiney little bitch," said Wayne. "Maybe I should let you play the reds next time, then you might be within shouting distance of my drives."

"You two don't look like brothers," commented Shaun, the assistant pro.

"Same mom, different dad," explained Mack. "I'm legit. He's the bastard."

Wayne stood up from the table and stared daggers at his half-brother. "So that makes you better than me? There's nothing you can do that I can't do better. My woman's better looking, and I make more money than you do."

"All right, all right," said the pro, attempting to diffuse the situation. "Easy, you two. Don't bring any family problems to my game. We're just here for a good time."

"Yeah," added Paul Champion, one of the club members. "A good time where there are no women involved. Hell, my wife thinks I'm at a Lion's Club meeting."

This little admission brought a round of chuckles from the players at the table.

"Mine thinks I'm meeting with the investment club I belong to," said Crandall Irwin. "Actually my time was invested wisely tonight, because I'm holding some of young Wayne's dough."

"Like I said, if we were playing golf, it would be a different story," said Wayne, sitting back down and digging into his pocket for some more bills.

"Can it, Wayno," said Mack, as he egged his brother on. "There are probably three guys at this table that would kick your butt out on the course. The last time you played you barely broke eighty. I'm sure the pro, his assistant there, and one of these members here would have no trouble with what you call a golf game."

Reason was thrown out the window, as Wayne got up and came around the table toward his half-brother. He threw an open-handed slap that grazed the side of Mack's head. Before any of the stunned observers could react, Mack stood and punched Wayne on the jaw with a quick right jab. There wasn't a lot behind the punch, but it still put Wayne back on his heels. The pro and his assistant jumped up and separated the two before any more punches were thrown.

"Sorry you guys had to see that," said Mack as he stood facing his brother. "He gets a little crazy when he's been drinking the hard stuff. Beer isn't a problem, but once he gets a little whiskey in him, he's a different person. I told him to leave that flask at home."

The assistant let Mack go, as it seemed he had no intention of continuing the altercation. Bernie held on to Wayne, who was still breathing hard and gave no indication of what he was going to do next.

"You know I don't like being called a bastard," wailed Wayne. "And you also know that I can beat any man in this room. I've got two grand to put up if there are any takers."

The pro, sensing an opportunity, let go of Wayne and stepped back. "Let me get this straight. You're willing to play Shaun here for two grand? Is that what you're saying?"

"That's what I'm saying," replied Wayne in a voice that sounded more like a little kid that was pouting. He reached into his pocket and pulled out a wad of bills. "And I ain't just talking either. My money and my golf swing do my talking for me."

"Don't do it, brother. It's the whiskey talking, and you know it. Shaun here played college golf, and he's won a few tournaments. You've never won a tournament in your life. Just because you work at a golf course doesn't mean you're an expert."

"I don't care," said Wayne as he took his jacket off the back of his chair preparing to leave. "I meant what I said. So what, now you're all concerned on my behalf, brother?"

"I just don't want to see Angie get all upset again because you've done something stupid. As soon as you do, she calls my wife, and then we're all involved in one of your delusional escapades. He's not going to play, Bernie—at least not for even money. That would be pure suicide."

"What are you saying?" asked Shaun. "He wants some sort of odds?"

"I'm saying he's not playing you even up for two G's, that's all," explained Mack. "C'mon hothead, let's go. You can fantasize about winning the U. S. Open on the way home—if you can stay awake that long. Sorry about the argument, guys. Y'all seem like a square bunch of fellas."

"Hold on a sec," said Bernie, taking Shaun by the arm and guiding him off to the side, where he spoke quietly to his assistant. "Look, Shaun. Let's assume you can beat this guy three out of four times. If you do, you would be two units up. You know, you're holding three and he's holding one. So, if you give him two to one, the odds say you will still come out ahead. If you beat him three out of four, you would still be one unit up. In this case, a unit is two grand."

"I hear what you're saying, but what if he's some kind of hustler trying to set us up?"

"Could be, but I doubt it," reasoned Bernie, looking over his assistant's shoulder at the two brothers. "What did you shoot yesterday?"

"I was minus two on both sides, a 68."

"Does that kid over there look like he can come in to your backyard and shoot those kind of numbers?"

"No, but I don't have that kind of dough to bet, even if it looks like a sure thing."

"Don't worry about that. I'm sure a couple of the members here would want some of the action. Let's offer him three to two. Maybe that will make his brother happy. He seems to be calling the shots."

As Will Green and Mitch Winston pulled out of the club's entrance, they gave each other a little fist bump in the dark.

"This isn't getting any easier, bro," said Will with an accent on the 'bro'.

"I know. We're straying farther and farther from home. Do you think they're suspicious?"

"Naw. Like you said—they seem like a square bunch of fellas. You injected the caddy angle at just the right time. Asking if you could carry my bag so I wouldn't do something stupid was pretty smooth. Maybe you should change your college major to acting."

"I'll stick with business. One more semester and I'm out of there, ready to take on the world. Speaking of taking on the world, what are you going to do when this area dries up? For a guy that doesn't want to travel, you're putting yourself in a spot where that will soon be your only alternative."

"I know," responded Will, looking out his window as they flew by dark Michigan farm fields. "It's not like we're living in a big city like Chicago or L. A., where you could probably hustle for years without seeing the same guys twice. I've been kicking something else around. Melissa and I have been discussing it for a couple of weeks now."

"What's that?"

"I'm keeping it under wraps for now, but I'll tell you when I've made my decision."

"You're the boss of this operation," said Mitch. "Same split tomorrow, 500 for me and you pocket the rest?"

"Yup. I studied the notes you got from your college buddy. It looks like he knows the course forwards and backwards."

"He should. He grew up playing the track, and his dad was the assistant greenskeeper for fifteen years. Nothing like getting some solid inside information. Sorry about the punch to the jaw. When you slapped me, I figured that would be a natural reaction. Why did you veer from the script? The plan was for you to grab me by the shirt."

"I know," said Will, feeling his jaw in the dark. "I guess I got caught up in my acting. I hope you didn't leave a mark. Melissa will be pissed if she thinks I was in a fight."

The next day Will and Mitch arrived at the club at 3:45, fifteen minutes before they were scheduled to tee off. Will thought about doing the poor starving golfer bit with the ragged bag and clothes but decided against it. He now considered himself a professional at what he did, and besides, there was no profit in making his mark, or marks, look foolish. Sticking to the principles that Grip and Street had taught him, he never lied about golf. Outside of that, like false names and pretending to be brothers, some minor factual adjustments were acceptable. Without putting on some sort of show, it would be hard for him to get a decent money game within a few hundred miles of home.

Unbeknownst to the guys at the club, he and Mitch stopped at a driving range they discovered on their first trip so he could warm up. To Shaun and his backers, it looked like he was going to get out of the car, hit a few practice putts, and then head for the first tee.

The pro and his assistant watched with interest as Mitch walked around the practice green tossing a few quarters here and there, making sure they were at different distances. Ignoring the holes, Will putted two balls going from coin to coin, getting a feel for the speed of the green. If the head pro was more experienced, and maybe a little more devious at this sort of arrangement, he might have made sure the practice green didn't reflect the speed of the greens out on the course. Maybe it was because he felt they had a sure thing going.

A few holes into the round the situation began to turn ugly. Will was walking beside his caddy discussing sports, politics, and music like they usually did. It was part of their normal routine, and it helped to keep them loose. Shaun also walked, but his clubs were on one of the carts. Mitch did pin duties for the both of them and worked his man's bag like a seasoned caddy. There were three carts following the play. One of the guys watching was staring intently at Will, especially when Mitch pulled out an index card with course notes on it. His expression turned more troublesome right after Will rolled in his third birdie on the front nine. Mitch was looking right at the skinny man in the cart, and the look that was returned sent a chill through him. Under different circumstances, Mitch would have chuckled at the man's bad hairpiece, but something told him this wouldn't be the smart thing to do. The guy was downright scary—like, shoot-you-in-the-back-of-the-head scary.

On the next tee, a medium length par three, Will hit his five-iron twelve feet right and hole high. As they stood watching Shaun prepare to hit, Mitch, standing behind his player, slowly ran his thumb down Will's spine from top to bottom. Will froze for an instant. Without looking around, he whispered, "Who?"

"The skinny guy with the bad hair," whispered Mitch. "He just closed up his phone and from the look on his face it was a serious conversation. I'm guessing we were the main topic of the conversation."

Even though Will had never been in a casino, he knew Mitch's gesture was the international sign that they had been "made". It's usually reserved for when casino security spots a cheater and wants to get him off the floor without too much fanfare. A simple thumb down the back was a way of saying, "I know what you're up to, and we need to have a little talk".

"So what?" commented Will as they walked off the tee. "They would have figured it out sooner or later. Let's stick with the plan. I go into the last hole two strokes up and give one of them back. That way it'll look like I barely beat him."

"I don't like the way he was looking at us," cautioned Mitch. "The dude just looks mean. I don't know how much he has invested in this match, but whatever it is, he's not going to part with it on friendly terms."

"I'll think of something when we make the turn," said Will. "Hopefully they will just be pissed and won't take their loss personal."

With nine holes under their belts, Will was two strokes up on Shaun. They all walked into the bar and grill to get something to drink before heading out to the back side. Will excused himself and made his way toward the restrooms. Once inside, he went into a stall and whipped out his phone. Ronnie Green, aka Ronnie Costas, answered his grandson's call on the second ring.

"What's up?" asked Ronnie as he and Eddie Davis, aka Eddie Ferguson, were riding down the eighth fairway at Stonehedge South.

"Hey, Grip, Mitch and I might have a situation up here in Lansing. I've got the assistant pro on the hook for three large, and it looks like one of his backers is not real happy. He's a scary looking guy, and something tells us he won't part with his share of the purse without a fight. You got any suggestions?"

"Give me a sec," answered Ronnie as he signaled for Eddie to stop the cart. He explained the situation to his fellow hustler, and they discussed the boys' options.

"Okay," said Ronnie. "If you feel you're in any physical danger, you'll have to dump. It's a judgment call, but you don't want to do any hospital time over three lousy grand."

"Actually it's only two grand. He's giving me three to two. Not bad, huh?"

"Not bad if you walk away healthy. Listen, I'll give Herman a call. Maybe he's got somebody in the area that will pull security duty for a few bucks. I'll text you if it's a go. How much time do we have, and what course are you at?"

"We're at the turn, so I'd say two hours max. Let me know as soon as you can. I hate to give up my hard earned dough if I don't have to. The course is..."

With two holes to go, Will was five under and Shaun was minus three. It was exactly where he and Mitch wanted to be. The man with the hairpiece drove back to the clubhouse when the players finished fifteen. Will just shrugged and proceeded to pound his tee shot 295 yards down the middle of the fairway.

"Nice ball," said Shaun. He had figured out early that Will was no slouch, and this probably wasn't going to be the big payday he was expecting. He only had $200 of the action, but it was still a substantial amount for a guy that was only making $375 a week.

"Thanks, man," responded Will as he felt his pocket vibrate. He walked over and stood behind Mitch, so he could use him as cover and looked down at his phone. He read, *help will arrive shortly*. "No worries," he said to his caddy as they walked down the seventeenth fairway.

Shaun and Will shook hands on the eighteenth green. Will had just three-putted, but still held a one-shot advantage. It could have easily been more, but one shot was as good as five in a situation like this. They all went into the pro shop to settle up. After the money exchanged hands, the guy with the bad hair offered to buy everyone a drink. Will looked at Mitch and shrugged his shoulders. Maybe it would buy more time for the security team to arrive.

"Two Michelob Ultras, unopened," said Mitch to the waitress. When the others at the table looked at him, he gave them a sheepish grin. "It's just a superstition," he explained. "I'm pretty sure one of my ex-girlfriends spit into my beer after a nasty breakup."

"What kind of girls do you date?" asked Shaun grinning. He was down $200 but was taking it well.

"I didn't find out that she was a psycho until about a month into the relationship. She was pretty good at hiding it."

"I told you I was a better judge of women than he is," added Will as he held up his bottle to toast Shaun. "You can really play, man. You thinking about taking the next step and maybe playing some mini-tour events?"

"Yeah, I'm heading south when we close up here. I'll practice hard all winter, and then maybe take a shot at it if I feel I'm ready. What about you?"

"Naw, I'm pretty happy just mowing roughs and playing for a few dollars now and then. I'd probably crumble under all that pressure."

"So, the last time you played, you barely broke 80, like Mack said?" asked the pro.

"That's true. We never lie about golf. He forgot to mention that I was only using a 4-iron, a wedge, and my putter. I'm pretty good at it, but there's one old boy that I refuse to play even up with anything less than a full bag. You ever hear of Eddie Davis?"

"Hell, yes, I've heard of him," responded Bernie with a painful look. "Played him way back when, and I don't mind telling you that I was taken to the cleaners. So that's where you got your moves. I should have known better. What would you have done if Shaun here had shot a couple of strokes better?"

"I would have paid up, with no regrets," said Will, standing and extending his hand. "It was fun guys."

They shook hands all around, and the two visitors headed for the door. The guy with the hair was standing by the pro shop door. He gave Mitch an almost imperceptible nod as they passed.

"Man, I thought those guys would be sore, but they were pretty cool about it," said Mitch as they headed for their car. "I still don't like the way Mr. Hairpiece looked at us when we passed through the pro shop. Let's get in and head back to a friendlier environment."

Will opened the trunk of his Camry and stashed his clubs. Over the top of the car he could see a couple of richly dressed members messing around on the putting green. He laughed to himself thinking if he ever dressed like that, Mitch had permission to go upside his head with a 5-iron. The two were almost comical. They obviously had no idea what they were doing. *At least they have enough scratch to belong to a fancy club like this*, he thought. *Hopefully I'll be there some day. Melissa deserves the best. She's almost got her nursing degree and here I am out hustling nickels. Well, it's not exactly nickels, but it's getting tougher and tougher to make some real money playing single matches. Especially when I get carried away and put myself in a no-win situation like I did last week. Losing $500 to that yuppie-looking dude was hard to take. Like Street always says, 'crafting the bet was often more important than how well you played on a given day'. I should have been a little craftier on that one. Maybe I should take grandpa and Eddie up on their offer to sponsor me on the Tour. I don't know. I would feel like I'm selling out to all the commercialism. Melissa will be back here in Michigan working, and I'll be running all over the place pretending to be a Tour golfer. I do have to admit that times are different than when those two made all their golf money.*

Over to his right by one of the parking lot lights, he could see a couple of rough looking guys smoking cigarettes and talking quietly. He surmised that they must be the security dudes that Herman had contacted. They nodded at him when he gave them a little wave. It was nice to have connections in potentially dangerous situations like this. Herman, ex Special Forces turned private investigator, was a good guy to have in your corner.

Mitch reached over and hit the horn signaling for Will to stop standing there behind the car daydreaming. It was almost dark and time to hit the road. Will grinned and slammed the trunk. He took two steps when a hand grabbed his left arm from behind and spun him around.

"You look like a guy that's holding a lot of money," said a gravely voice. The owner of the voice didn't look like a golfer. He was more of a hard-core "biker" type with long scraggly hair and a beard. Tattoos ran up and down both arms. The guy standing next to him didn't look like country club material either. Will looked over the speaker's shoulder at the two guys who were practicing on the putting green. They were now standing by their car putting their clubs away, laughing and joking with each other. Mitch got out of the car and came around to see what was going on. The parking lot was almost deserted. The two smokers had vanished.

"Let's do this so nobody gets hurt, okay?" said the guy with the tattoos. He appeared to be about 225 pounds, with a sizable spare tire hanging over his belt. "Just hand over the five grand, and we'll be on our way."

"Are you kidding me?' asked Mitch. "These country clubbers get all that serious over a few bucks. This is insane."

The second guy stepped over and cuffed Mitch hard on the side of his head.

"Jeeze, dude, there's no need for that," said Mitch, reaching for his wallet. "I vote we give them the money, Will. I don't know where you got that five grand figure, buddy. We've only got about a hundred between us."

"Will? They said your name was Wayne."

"Whatever, man," said Will, as he dug out his money clip from his left front pocket.

One of the guys from the putting green approached the group. He had his hand out with what looked like a small white card in it. His putting partner was walking beside him with his right hand behind his back. "I saw that little slap, young man. If you need a lawyer, I'm your guy. I specialize in personal injury cases."

When he got close enough, the "lawyer" jammed his knee into the back of the biker dude's knee, then grabbed the back of his head and slammed his face into the trunk lid. His partner quickly stepped behind the slapper and brought a nightstick up under his chin.

"Hey, let's do this so no one gets hurt anymore than they already have," said the guy with the baton, mimicking the biker's first comment. "You move and I crush you throat."

"Bad move, little man," said the first biker as he staggered free with blood dripping from his nose. He stepped back and brought his fists up.

Before he could throw a punch, the "lawyer" moved in and delivered several quick blows to his body and face. Then he delivered a side kick to the larger man's stomach. They could hear the air rush out of him as he went down. He came up to his hands and knees on the concrete and just stayed there trying to suck in some badly needed oxygen. The guy with the baton did a quick one-hand frisk of his captive, then pushed him toward his accomplice.

"Go help fat boy up, and get out of here," he said laughing. "You two are an embarrassment to the enforcer business. Lay off the donuts and start working out for Christ's sake."

The two would-be collectors slunk off slowly into the night. Mitch and Will stood there with appreciative looks on their faces.

"So you're Robbie Green's son?" asked the fake lawyer with his hand out. "I met your dad once, and it was quite a thrill. His reputation as a soldier was beyond reproach."

"You talk like a lawyer," said Will, shaking the older man's hand, "but you move like Rambo."

"If anybody moved like Rambo, it was Lieutenant Green. Your dad was what we all were in our dreams, kid. I'm sorry about what happened to him. It was just shit luck, man. Anyway, I'm Barry Allison, and this is Chad Merkle. When I got the call from that private investigator in Chicago, I was about to take the wife out to dinner. All he had to do was mention your dad's name, and I told him I was his man. Chad here is always up for an adventure. He was a lowly Marine, but he'll do in a pinch."

After they shook hands all around, Will pulled out a few hundred-dollar bills. Barry put his hands up in refusal.

"No way, man. We were glad to do it for Robbie. You two should be more careful about the parking lots you hang around in. I don't know what you were up to, but the rich guys that frequent these places have ways of settling scores without getting their own hands dirty. Bunch of pussies, getting others to do their dirty work. Anyhow, take care guys."

The two hustlers stood and watched Barry and Chad walk across the parking lot to their car.

"Wow, your dad must have been really something," said Mitch as they got back in the Camry and pulled out of the lot.

"He was, partner. And like the man said, it was just shit luck that brought him down. Now let's get out of here before anyone else tries to lay claim to our hard-earned winnings. By the way, your share of the gas is twenty bucks."

"Write it off on your taxes, hotshot," said Mitch as he reached into the cooler that they kept in the back seat. He took out two cans of Pepsi and opened one for the driver. They clinked cans together as Will gunned the engine and steered for home. Another plan had come together. They needed a little help with this one, but they were leaving with more dough than they came with, and that was the name of the game—at least for the time being.

CHAPTER TWO

–Insanity Revisited

My boss is the best. I owe everything to him. The only bad thing about him is he's married. Men like him are hard to find in the city. The guys I know are always working some kind of angle, trying to get into your pants or your wallet—or both. Why are all the decent guys always taken?

—-Estelle Roseboro, secretary, Wakefield Investigations

Eddie was leisurely hitting balls at the Cedar Creek range when Bert, the shop manager, walked up on the elevated tee. His expression looked like a guy that had just lost his last two dollars pitching quarters.

"Hey, Eddie, we need to talk," said Bert in a concerned voice.

Eddie sat down on a bench and motioned for Bert to join him. Whatever it was, it was obviously bothering Bert.

"I got a call from Donaldson, one of the psychos that you and your partner dumped to last year."

Eddie grinned when Donaldson's name was mentioned. As Ronnie said right after paying Donaldson and his partner off, it was the most fun he ever had losing three grand. Once they found out that they were connected to a big New York City crime family, he and Ronnie did a calculated fold and vowed to never get involved with those two again. They told Bert to inform the two goodfellas, if they ever called again, that there were no takers in the area due to their superior skills on the short grass.

"I don't know how Greer and Donaldson found out, because you, Ronnie, and I are the only ones who knew about your throwing the match with them, but they did, and they want another game. I told them that you guys nor anyone else in the area were willing to play them, and that was when he got nasty. You should have heard that a-hole. He went into a deep east coast accent explicitly telling me how I better set something up or bad things would happen to me and to my family. The guy is nuts. Anyway, what should we do about it? I know you don't want to play them again."

"Let me think about it," responded Eddie, after hearing Bert's story. "There's got to be some way to get these guys off our backs without playing them again. I'll get with Ronnie and between the two of us, we'll come up with something. Damn crazies are a disgrace to the game."

The two hustlers sat just off the first tee at Bedford Valley and discussed their latest dilemma.

"What is it with these guys?" asked Ronnie. "They took our dough last time, so you'd think that would be the end of it. You don't think Bert ratted on us about throwing the match, do you?"

"No, I don't," responded Eddie. "I know it doesn't seem possible, but those two probably came to the conclusion that our well-disguised collapse wasn't just a case of nerves. What we need to figure out is how serious these guys are. On the surface they look like clowns with nice golf swings, but how far are they willing to go if they don't get what they want? They mentioned family to Bert, and that scares me a little."

"Dickheads," mused Ronnie as a twosome pulled up behind them. "Let's see if we can get a game with these two first, then I'll call Herman. Maybe he'll come up with something. If we have to, we'll just have the big guy shoot them both and dispose of the bodies. It'll be expensive, but it will be worth it."

"What if the family finds out, and it turns into a matter of honor for them?"

"I didn't think of that," answered Ronnie as two thirty-somethings got out of their cart and approached them with big smiles on their faces.

"Gentlemen," said the guy wearing the University of Michigan golf shirt. He extended his hand to Eddie. "I'm Hap, and this is Larry. You two interested in a little game?"

"You guys got a handicap?" asked Ronnie. "We're already at a huge disadvantage. What are you guys, still in college?"

"Hardly," laughed Hap. "We booth shoot around eighty. And before we go any further, we know who you are. Let's come up with something that puts us on a somewhat level playing field."

Eddie looked the two newcomers over. He pegged Hap to be a teacher, high school or maybe college. Larry's hands and demeanor said he had a job that was a little more physical. Whatever they did for a living, he took an instant liking to both of them.

"Okay, the bald guy and I are usually pretty close to par, unless he's been arguing with the wife, then he plays a totally different game."

"She messes with his head, huh?" asked Larry.

"Not like you think," answered Eddie. "When he's mad at her he flat crushes it, and he putts like he's got a laser sight on the flat stick. How about this: low ball, low total, and we play with only our irons, no woods? If the points are lopsided after nine, we'll make an adjustment."

Larry looked at his partner who responded with an affirmative nod.

"Is $20 a point too rich for guys that have reached legendary status around here?" asked Hap.

"We'll probably crumble under the pressure," said Ronnie, holding out a closed fist full of tees.

"Even," said Larry.

Ronnie opened his hand to show five tees. He pulled his 3-iron out of his bag and headed for the tee.

"One question before you hit," said Hap. "How are you getting along with the wife?"

Ronnie grinned and ripped his tee shot straight down the middle. "Let's just say we parted on amicable terms this morning."

"That means it's going to be up to me to keep us out of the poor house," said Eddie. His 2-iron landed next to Ronnie's ball and rolled fifteen more yards closer to the green. Larry and Hap both applauded. The two hustlers didn't know it, but their opponents were more than willing to lose some cash in exchange for the playing lesson they were about to get.

"You must have got a little this morning," observed Eddie as they sat in their cart waiting for their opponents to come out of the bar and grill at the turn. "You only made one putt outside of four feet."

"It's my favorite way to start the day," admitted Ronnie. "What are you bitchin' about? We're up four points. I wouldn't want it much more than that. They ask a lot of questions, but I like these guys."

"Yeah, me too. And you're right, they do ask a lot of questions. If I didn't know any better, I'd say they're getting their money's worth in golf advice."

Eddie was surprised when his phone started ringing in the middle of the tenth fairway. He looked at it and saw that it was his wife calling. She was deeply involved with an important case, and she rarely called when she was at work.

"Hey, Babe," answered Eddie. "Everything okay?"

"Street, did you pay the lawn boy for our last mowing?" asked Suzanne in a shaky voice.

"I'm pretty sure I did. Why?"

"Well, I needed a break, so I came home for a late lunch. When I went back out to the car, there was a dead cat lying on the hood."

"Whoa, that's weird. Jimmy's a good kid. I'm sure this isn't his work. What did you do with it? Do you want me to come home?"

"No. I pushed it off with a broom. It's still there on the side of the driveway. I'll leave it up to you to dispose of it. Who would do something like that? It was gross."

"What time will you be finished at the office tonight?"

"We're knocking off at seven, why?"

"I'll be in the lot waiting. I actually do have a hunch who might be behind this. Let me talk it over with Ronnie. Stay on your toes, and I'll see you at seven."

Eddie closed his phone and looked over at his partner. Ronnie flipped his phone shut and gave Eddie a strange look.

"Let me guess," said Eddie. "Dead cat on the hood of the car?"

"Yeah. One of her employees came into the store and told her about it. I told her that I'd be there when she got off work. Same thing with Suzanne?"

"Yup. The question is: how far will these nuts go to get us to play them again? And, if we play them and beat them, how will they respond? This is getting out of hand. It looks like Donaldson and Greer have seen *The Godfather* one too many times. I hope Herman can come up with a solution that puts this whole thing to rest. Damn, those dudes are creepy."

* * *

Approximately 150 miles west in downtown Chicago, Herman Wakefield closed his phone and sat back in his office chair. The oversized chair groaned under the big man's weight. His 6'4" frame carried his 240 pounds with a grace that came from athletics and intense physical training in the military. Ever since high school, he had figured on a military career. It was one of the only ways for him to escape the projects where he witnessed the drug trade and the crime that went along with it on a weekly basis. College and maybe professional sports were other options, but he couldn't wait for any future income, no matter how large those checks might have been. He needed to earn cash as soon as possible to help out his family.

He changed his mind about making the military his life's work when Robbie Green was killed by an Iraqi sniper. He and Ronnie's son were inseparable after they had finished their Special Forces training and were assigned to the same unit. It was as if they each recognized the other's abilities and had complete trust in each other when the action became intense, which was pretty much on a daily basis.

The Chicago private detective had worked for Ronnie and Eddie on several occasions, and no doubt, would do so in the future. For two guys that were trying to live the normal life of retired businessmen, they seemed to get themselves into a lot of dicey situations where his assistance was needed. He chuckled to himself. Why did it not surprise him that the two old guys were at odds with some mafia types? He looked over at his secretary, Estelle, who was busy typing on her computer.

"Hey, Stell, I need a couple of things."

She stopped her work and looked up from her screen, waiting for her boss to continue.

"First, a plane ticket to New York City, and then all the information you can get me on a crime family named Trenton. There should be all sorts of stuff on them on the Internet. What I'm looking for is names and responsibilities of the family members. I need a contact guy to present my case to. Our two favorite golfers have become involved with these guys, and I need to figure out a way to make peace."

Estelle Roseboro spun her chair to a different computer and went to work. Herman smiled to himself. Five years earlier he had discovered his future secretary on a street corner in the middle of the city. She was standing there sobbing softly into her hands. He stopped to see if he could be of assistance, and after hearing her story, he decided that she would be a worthwhile project. The teen had graduated at the top of her class. A short year later, after working a few dead end jobs, her youthful enthusiasm for the world beyond high school had slowly been sucked out of her by the harsh reality of fending for herself in the big city. She had nowhere to go and no prospects. The motivation behind his act of humanitarianism was known only to his wife and to Ronnie Green. The question, "What would Robbie do?" entered his mind on occasions like this. Late one evening he explained to his wife, Charise, that helping others in need from time to time was one of the ways that he could honor his fallen comrade, the finest man he had ever been associated with.

Four days later, Herman sat at a high-end restaurant in midtown Manhattan. A man with thick, curly black hair and the bushiest eyebrows he had ever seen, approached and sat down at his table. Herman guessed that his suit cost as much as courtside seats at a Bulls playoff game when Jordan and Pippen roamed the floor. Over his shoulder, the private investigator noticed another man dressed in a similar fashion loitering by the door. Anthony Trenton was the youngest of three brothers. He wasn't happy about this meeting, but he was intrigued as to why a private dick from Chicago wanted to talk with someone from the family. Maybe there was an angle that he could financially exploit to gain some points with the old man. After introductions, he ordered one of the most expensive steaks on the menu and stared expectantly across the table at Herman.

"You were right when you said you would be easy to spot. What do you go, about 250?"

"Two-forty, but it ain't easy. If I don't stay on top of it I could easily shoot up to 275. That wouldn't be good for business."

They made small talk until the food arrived—East coast sports teams versus Midwest. New York politics versus the Chicago way of running things. A twenty-something waitress sat their plates in front of them and gave them her best seductive smile, waiting to see if they needed anything else. Anthony waved her away.

"You notice those two dames over there at the table by the door giving you the eye? They must think you're some rich, sports star."

"Yeah, I see them. Hopefully, they will just stay put and won't bother us."

"Could be your loss," said Anthony as he dug into his rib-eye. "All right, big man, what do you want from the Trentons?"

Herman laid the situation out for the mob underling as the guy wolfed down his meal. The guy across from him had the manners of a cave man. He was wearing a suit that cost a couple of month's wages to a working man, but he ate like he was in a frat house. Juice dripped from his mouth onto the cloth napkin that he had tucked into his shirt. Herman wasn't sure if the guy was trying to be funny or if he was just a pig. He almost laughed out loud when he pictured the whole family eating dinner together in a similar fashion. When he was done, Anthony pushed his plate away and let out with a loud belch. The two women that were eyeing Herman earlier were on their way to the guys' table, but thought better of it when his burping skills were demonstrated. The men both laughed when the women did an abrupt about face.

"When I first got your secretary's call, I thought you were working some sort of scam on us," remarked Anthony. "And I think you know that that would be an extremely stupid move on your part. But I like you, Chicago, so I'll give it to you straight. The two guys you are referring to are my cousins, and I wish to God they weren't, but fate plays some dirty tricks on us at times. We know they're total fuck-ups. The old man told them they needed to use different names when they were out trying to fleece some poor schmucks doing whatever they do. They have orders not to disgrace the family any more than they already have. At least they're doing that right. The bottom line is, as long as they keep the family name out of their business, we don't give a shit what they're up to. So, it sounds like it's your problem and not ours. Hey, thanks for lunch."

With that, Anthony rose and waved his cohort to the door. The meeting was over. Herman sat there and watched them go. *That was one expensive lunch. Fly here and back home for a twenty-minute conversation with a guy straight from "Animal House". Hell, I could have done that over the phone. And now, he knows what I look like.*

Herman leaned back in his first-class seat as his plane leveled off and headed west to the Second City. He racked his brain for a solution to the hustlers' problem. He could put the hammer on the two mobster lunatics, but who knows what the repercussions would be? Down deep the family insiders would probably be grateful, but there was always the matter of saving face with the rival families. Like Eddie and Ronnie, theirs was a business where you never wanted to show your ass. Dealing from a position of strength was paramount, which included disguising or down right covering up your weaknesses. The big man closed his eyes and went into his half asleep stage where his mind tuned out everything around him, but was still able to focus on his objective. Using the Socratic method, he asked himself a series of logical questions. He had been trained to use this strategy when solving serious problems in Iraq, and it had served him well. This situation was much different than leading a unit of highly trained men where death was constantly part of the equation.

Since he had exposed himself to a member of the Trenton family, he would be a suspect if anything violent were to happen to Greer and Donaldson. He felt an unknown presence near him, which caused him to go into immediate assessment mode. His whole body became tense as his eyes opened wide, his open hands flashing up in front of his face in a defensive position. His actions startled the flight attendant who was standing next to him. She almost dropped the gin and tonic that she was preparing for the guy across the aisle. She relaxed when he gave her a big smile and requested the same.

Halfway through his drink, he had formed a strategy. The solution was simple. The guys needed to ingratiate themselves with the Trentons. What could Ronnie and Eddie do to make the family beholding to them—beholding enough to call the dogs off? In this case, the dogs were more like Schnauzers, and so far all they had done was piss on Ronnie's and Eddie's leg. They needed to be stopped before the pissing turned into serious biting or worse. He opened his phone to call his secretary. This was going to take some detailed research. There had to be something he or the two golfers could do for the family. He doubted if they had military connections, but if that was the case, he was prepared to call in any favors that he had at his disposal. And, as the owner of a Distinguished Service Cross, the second highest medal that a U. S. soldier could be awarded, his connections were considerable. One thing in his favor was Estelle's dogged efforts to dig up any information, no matter how minute, on a subject that they were investigating. Once she got her teeth into a case, she became obsessed. He figured that she came by her relentless research techniques by watching countless episodes of NCIS.

CHAPTER THREE

Connie's Gig

Eddie Davis? He's the king, man—the absolute king. When you see him on the street, grab hold of your wallet and get to steppin'. That dude can smell money like a dog sniffin' out fresh table scraps through a garbage bag.

—-Elliot "Magic Man" Murphy, card sharp, con man, currently hiding out from a long list of criminal types

We are definitely in the "look at me" era. For some reason there are an inordinate number of citizens that want others to see them on the Internet or on television. A teacher once asked a class of thirty students how many wanted to be on television. Twenty-five of them raised their hands. When asked why they wanted to be seen on TV—to display a special skill or to share their expertise with the viewers, they answered that they simply wanted others to see them. This goes a long way in explaining the strange behavior exhibited by seemingly normal people whenever a camera is in their vicinity. This could be the result of having been told one too many times by their parents that they are so very special.

It was U. S. Open week as the three hustlers sat at the GLV bar and grill eating sandwiches while they discussed their new dilemma. The head pro walked up with a concerned look on his face. As he approached, Ronnie covered up their scorecard with his forearm. Normally, the guys didn't need a card to see how close they were to par, but it was a necessary scorekeeping tool when there where a multitude of side bets to keep track of. Today's round was memorable for several reasons. The main reason was the scores on the card. Will's ace on thirteen was the deciding factor on this unforgettable day. The pro saw Ronnie's little maneuver with the scorecard, so he gently reached down and slid it out. He met no objection, but knowing these three, he knew Ronnie's gesture meant he should keep what he saw to himself. He held it up close to his face and looked the numbers over. The pro laid the card back down and shook his head with a wry smile. The totals on the card read: S-64, G-63, K-62. He turned to walk away, then did an about face. The three of them just sat there grinning like they had just gotten off with a warning instead of a speeding ticket.

"I'm guessing there will be no further mention of the ace or the scores on that card?" asked the pro in a quiet voice.

"You got it," answered Ronnie. "The only thing that happened here today was the kid took us for $60 each."

"What the hell are you three doing here? There's huge money out there for guys with your skills."

"We like it here," said Eddie. "You know you would miss us if we weren't here to brighten up your dreary life. We've got no interest in being on television or YouTube. Our operation would have serious difficulties if Ronnie's face was showing up on Sports Center every time he shot a good round or threw one of his ridiculous tantrums out on the course."

"Exactly," added Ronnie. "If our faces were plastered all over the place, people would always be bothering us more than they do now. And, we'd have to fill our shirts up with company logos. Hey, Eddie could have 'Viagra' in huge letters across the back of his shirts. He'd be a big hit with the older crowd."

"Right. Seeing those scores made me almost forget why I came over in the first place. Some guy was in the shop earlier asking about you, Eddie. My guy behind the counter knew you were out on the course, but played dumb as to your whereabouts. We figured you would want to see him, or not, on your own terms. I saw him leave with another guy that looked somewhat familiar, but I couldn't place him."

"Thanks, pro. I appreciate it. I will tell you that Ronnie and I have a situation going on, and it's best that we keep an even lower profile than we usually do around here."

"No problem. I'll let my staff know."

Eddie got up and walked out into the hall to use the restroom. He looked through the glass into the pro shop and saw a face that brought back old memories—Connie Canier. What the hell was he doing here? Putting off his immediate needs, he turned back to the grill in full "sting" mode. He had taken Connie and his bunch for a bundle back in Detroit. Canier was a solid two-handicapper way back then, but his numbers and his ability to create advantageous situations were lacking when it came to making a lot of dough in the business of golf hustling. He was lucky in one respect—he had married into big money. Unlike the others that they both hung around with, there was always a lot less pressure on Connie to make the crucial shot that decided who was going to be pocketing the cash. He never had to worry about food or rent money like the rest of the regulars.

In the short time it took Eddie to get back to the table, he had formed a plan. Canier was obviously here at GLV asking for him because he had some sort of angle figured out. The guys that they used to hang around with always had something going and had no problem taking cash off one of their own if times were slow. They knew that if they weren't successful most of the time they would have to go into the work force, and that was something that they were trying to avoid at all costs. A regular nine-to-five job punching a clock was the stuff of nightmares to his old hustling buddies. There were times when each of them had to stoop to actually working, but they exited the work force as soon as they had a big enough stake to do what they felt they were destined to do. Relieving the lesser skilled of their hard earned funds was their goal in life. Selling clothes or insurance wasn't their idea of gainful employment. Eddie was the exception to their rule. He didn't mind working a few hours in the pro shop every week. It gave him a sense of respectability, and it was good for lining up gigs. On several occasions, by just making small talk with the golfers, he would structure a money game to his liking. After a while, some of the guys he had taken previously would want to partner up with him when they brought a fresh player to the club looking to take a few dollars off some unsuspecting pro shop worker. Eddie loved it when some other guy was willing to bring a mark to him. He was like a shark just sitting there with a napkin tied around his neck, waiting for his dinner to be served.

Eddie figured that Canier's partner, the guy that the pro said looked somewhat familiar, was probably a real talent. Maybe even a regular satellite tour player that had, on occasion, some experience playing at the next level. As usual, Eddie was a couple of steps ahead of Connie.

"Quick, Will," ordered Eddie. "Pull your shirt out and start bussing tables."

Will stood and did as his mentor instructed. He knew better than to question Eddie's methods.

"Hey, come back here first," said Eddie in a low voice. When Will got close, Eddie messed up his hair and splashed what was left of his ice tea on Will's shirt. Ronnie just sat there taking it all in with a smug look on his face. He loved it when his partner was working on a gig, which was apparently about to take place. Pam started to walk over, but turned around when Eddie motioned her away.

The stage was set when Conrad and his buddy, Cliff, strode into the room. Connie stood about a head shorter than his partner. He had blond wavy hair that he was obviously very proud of. Every dyed and pampered strand was in its place. A slender build, similar to Eddie's, coupled with a dark tan, was proof that he still spent most of his time out in the sun. From a distance, because of his build and fluid mannerisms, it appeared that he was around forty years old, but up close it was obvious that the man had a few more years than that on him. The dude's face looked tight like his skin was stretched over his skull. Eddie wondered if there was any cosmetic surgery involved—no doubt funded by his old lady. Connie made a beeline for Eddie's table with Cliff in tow. He had been waiting for this for a long time. He owed Eddie one, and once he got word of the ex Detroiter's whereabouts, he worked out a plan that would transfer a wad of Eddie's cash straight into his pocket. Finding out that Eddie was still among the living was somewhat of a shock, but once that information was verified, he immediately went to work on what he considered to be a foolproof gig. This was going to be one sweet payback. So sweet that he had to focus on not drooling in front of everyone.

Cliff looked every bit the professional golfer. He had perfect white teeth with an ingratiating smile coupled with an athletic body. Today's pro spent more time keeping fit than the game's trailblazers did decades ago. The superb competition from within the states and from overseas made this an absolute necessity. Even the tour pros that appeared to be overweight were usually in decent physical condition. A round of golf on the courses they were used to playing usually consisted of at least a five-mile walk. One had to put some real effort into being out of shape after strolling up and down the hilly terrain that they had to traverse week in and week out.

"Well, if it ain't Eddie Davis!" exclaimed Connie, with his hand extended. "What are you doing here away from the big city and all the action? The guys back in Detroit said that you were dead. Some dame's husband came home unexpectedly and caught you in the sack with her. Wasted the both of you on the spot. That was the story anyway. Apparently you had enough warning to slip out the window. Hey, I want you to meet my nephew, Cliff Barnes."

Eddie stood and shook hands with the two of them, then he introduced Ronnie. He motioned for the two visitors to sit down.

"You boys are a long way from home," said Eddie as he got Pam's attention. "How about a drink?"

"If you're buying, then we're drinking," answered Connie.

Pam approached and asked, "What can I get your friends, Mr. Davis?" She was one of the few people at GLV that knew Eddie's real name. Ronnie tried to hold back a snicker when Eddie's guests ordered what he considered to be an inferior whiskey. Will's efforts to look like he knew what he was doing as he attempted to clean off a nearby table, added to the amusing situation. The clang of plates and glassware drew some strange looks from some of the other diners.

"I'll come right to the point, Street," offered Connie in a low voice. "For a while I held a grudge against you. I always thought you were the luckiest son-of-a-bitch that I ever played against. In my older years, I've come to the conclusion that maybe most of it wasn't luck. Anyway, I've been practicing, and my nephew here has played some college golf. We're looking for a little excitement away from home, and I'll be damned if one of the locals said you were a member here. What do you say we reenact old times with a little friendly competition? Say a little low ball/low total for a grand a point? You can pick anyone you want if you don't have a regular guy. You can't go callin' Speith or Fowler though. You don't know them, do you?"

"Nope, never talked to either of those guys in my life. I usually play with Ronnie here, and we trade a few dollars back and forth. Nothing serious. I'm more of a recreational golfer in my old age."

"Don't tell me the king of the Detroit hustlers doesn't play for a little scratch now and then. For you, a grand a point is probably chicken feed. C'mon, man. Give me a chance to win back some of the cash that I've lost to you over the years."

Pam sat their drinks down and gave Eddie her sweetest smile. He thanked her and returned the smile. She gave the guys a little more hip sway than she normally did as she walked away. The swing wasn't lost on Canier.

"I suppose you've been bangin' her," said Connie as he watched Pam walk away. "You sly dog. He's probably got a whole string of them here, Cliff. I told you this guy was something, didn't I?"

Eddie refused to be baited and remained silent.

"I thought you said he was a real swashbuckler," remarked Cliff. "If he's afraid to play us, let's go find a couple of little old ladies who are lookin' for some action. Let's not waste our time on an old has-been."

"Easy, Tiger," cautioned Eddie. "I didn't say I wouldn't play. What are you, about twenty-five? I don't mind dropping a few skins once in a while, but givin' it away is for rich philanthropists. What do you say, Ronnie? You want to take Connie and this young buck on?"

Connie's pulse was racing, but he kept his expression calm at the thought of two fifty-somethings going up against him and Cliff. He had an ace up his sleeve, and it looked like his old nemesis was going to walk right into a situation that would prove quite lucrative for him and his partner.

"I don't know," answered Ronnie, right on cue. "My wrist is still giving me some trouble. You don't want me holding you back. Besides this dude looks like he hits it a mile. Why don't you ask my grandson over there cleaning tables? He's not too bad, and he beat me by a stroke the last time we played. He'll probably play if he doesn't have to put up any money. Bussing tables is not a rich man's occupation."

"Alright, if you don't think you're up to it. Hey, Will, come over here a minute. I want you to meet an old friend of mine."

Will walked over with a dull expression on his face. His grandfather turned away feigning interest in some other activity that was going on in the room. This was about as sweet as the business gets. Marks coming up and sitting down with offers to play for decent cash were few and far between. Normally, a guy had to work extremely hard to get something going that would return something more than cigar and whiskey money.

The game was agreed upon, and the money arrangements were made. Each side was to give the pro $10,000 to hold before the match started. Connie lobbied for $12,000 but finally agreed that ten was acceptable. He also wanted the stipulation that if both teammates birdied the same hole, and won the hole, an extra point was to be awarded. Eddie agreed but countered with a birdie and an eagle should also get the extra point. He got a funny look from Cliff when he proposed the addition. Connie was too excited to give Eddie's addition a second thought. They all shook hands, and after Eddie called over to Stonehedge for the tee time, they agreed to meet on the first tee of the North course at noon the next day. Connie was juiced, as he and Cliff had just played the North course and Cliff had birdied three of the six par fives.

"Wait until Mr. Lucky sees you drive the ball," said Connie, as he and Cliff walked through the parking lot. "That, my friend, is how you arrange a match. I can't believe that the famous Eddie "The Street" Davis has never heard of you. He must be losing his touch. How many regular tour events have you played in, ten?"

"Six," answered Cliff. "And by the way, I have talked to Speith and Fowler. Never played with either of them, but we said "hello" in the parking lot once. I hope this guy and his friend's grandson show up tomorrow. If they don't, you drug me halfway across the state for nothing. Any chance you exaggerated a little on this guy's golfing exploits? He didn't look all that impressive to me."

"No exaggeration. In his day, he was probably the best in Detroit. I wasn't kidding about him being lucky though. Tomorrow, partner, all the luck in the world won't help him get his hands on our dough. We'll be holding a fist full of dollars at the end of the day. I've been waiting for this opportunity for a long time."

"You're lucky that I agreed to this. I need to make a quick five G's so I can settle up with some fellas back home. They take their loans seriously, and I need to focus on my game, not on trivial stuff like who owes who a few peanuts. Did you know that most tour events pay the winner close to a million dollars? Man, with that kind of scratch, I can tell just about anybody to get screwed, and they'd have to take it. Yep, having a boatload of money makes you a serious player in this man's world. Okay, I'm ready to take these hicks for a few grand and then head back to the real world. Hey, if I forget after we collect our winnings, thanks for setting this up.

You ain't gonna choke tomorrow, are you? I can probably handle them myself, but I might need a little assistance."

"Don't worry. Thanks to modern technology, I'm playing better than I ever have in my life. Now let's get some rest. Tomorrow's gonna be payday and payback day all rolled into one. They won't know what hit them when you start hitting those par fives in two. Street, you are going to crash and burn tomorrow, and I'll be sittin' in a front row seat enjoying the show. I hope you noticed how he disrespected us back there—asking the busboy if he wanted to play. Two-to-one he ain't that Ronnie dude's real grandson."

"Kinda like you ain't my real uncle, huh?" sneered Cliff. "You old-timers are past your prime in more ways than one. That old man and that skinny fuckin' kid better show tomorrow, or I'm gonna be pissed."

The GLV pro walked back into the grill as soon as the two visitors left.

"Hey, guys. I just Googled that Cliff Barnes guy. He's got a lot of satellite tour experience, and he's even played in a few regular tour events. He made one cut last year but finished last thanks to a final round 77. He's a big hitter but seems to be a little wild off the tee. It also sounds like he's got a little bit of an attitude. I watched a short video clip from his hometown TV station and cocky doesn't begin to describe him."

"This is getting better all the time," said Ronnie. "Kid, you were just complaining about how hard it is to get gigs, and now one walks right up to you and all but sits on your lap. Is this a great country or what?"

Later that evening, when Eddie walked through the front door, his wife was sitting on the couch with a worried look on her face.

"Street, somebody has been calling my cell phone and hanging up. There have been five calls in the past hour. What is going on? What sort of trouble are you and Ronnie in?"

Nothing had happened since the dead cats had shown up on the girls' cars two weeks prior. Herman had informed them that he had gotten nowhere with the Trentons in New York, so he was working on an alternative plan of his own. The guys had shown up when their wives got off of work for the last ten days. Since there were no further occurrences, they were hoping that the cat thing might be the end of it, and the two lunatics might have gone off in search of easier prey. They both knew that it was just wishful thinking on their part.

CHAPTER FOUR

—Financial Necessity

I was homeless for quite sometime. It was a combination of bad luck and, to be honest, bad decisions on my part. I used to hang out around this pool hall where this one guy spent a lot of time. Every time he saw me he would stop and talk to me about sports, the weather, whatever. Before he left, he would always slip me a twenty. Back then, I didn't even know his name. I think he was there to play poker in the back room. Now that I'm back on my feet, I realize that I should have shown him more gratitude. I heard that he passed away recently. He was a great guy and an unbelievable help to someone like me.

—-Greg Owens, tire store manager

Money quite often turns a reasonable person into a totally different animal. There appears to be no limit to what some people won't do to put a little cash in their pocket. Family members, friends, or strangers are not exempt from their greed. The source of their new found riches is immaterial to them. Sadly, many are willing to risk jail to acquire something that they do not have the skills, the creativity, the mentality, or the perseverance that other hard-working people do.

    Then there are the people that covet their money to such a degree that they fail to enjoy what they have. Enough is never enough with them. There is nothing wrong with wanting to acquire wealth in a capitalistic system like the United States. It has been proven to be the best set-up to reward the positive attributes mentioned above. That's why America is a leader in so many fields that provide a better quality of life for millions of people. Why are there so many foreign doctors working in U. S. hospitals and in private practices? It's simple. They like our way of doing business and the way we live. We are free to prosper at our own pace. The mechanism is there for those that have the wherewithal and common sense to use it.

Naysayers complain about the unequal wealth distribution in this country. Apparently, they don't understand the system well enough to form an educated opinion or to take any sort of constructive action to benefit their own situation. Capitalism never claimed to be a utopia. For those that understand it, it is a way to live comfortably without the constant fear of not being able to afford the necessities. It's also a way to be in a position to give back to those that are truly in need.

Will sat at the kitchen table discussing their financial situation with his beautiful wife. They had decided early on that they would do their best to make their own way. Melissa's parents were middle class, so they were willing to loan the young couple some start-up funds if they were in dire need. Will's grandfather, on the other hand, volunteered to front them Melissa's school money and any amount of cash that Will needed to make a go of it in the golf business, wherever that might lead. They turned both offers down, wanting to prove that they could be self-sufficient. Tomorrow's match with Eddie's friend was huge, as they had burned through the young hustler's substantial winnings faster than they had anticipated.

"Liss, something has to change, or we're going to be in way over our heads financially. I had no idea that things cost so much. Remember when our economics teacher back in high school warned us about digging too deep of a hole when it came to debt? The obvious facts are that we've been living way beyond our means. I know it doesn't seem like it, but we are. I remember him saying that if you make 60k you should live like you make 40k. He also said that you have to pay your dues before you get to a comfortable position in life. It doesn't happen automatically, unless your parents are super rich or you're some kind of royalty."

"It certainly doesn't seem like we're living the high life," observed Melissa. "But you're right. We do spend our money without thinking about the big picture. My car is new and yours is still in pretty good shape. I guess we should be driving a couple of old beaters until we can afford decent ones. When I get my degree and start working full time our income will go up substantially."

"True," said Will with wheels turning in his head. He was now an expert at setting up profitable gigs, but his overall approach to family finances was somewhat lax. That probably came from hanging around two guys that didn't have to worry about money.
"We will have more to put on our current bills, but if we start a family, will we be able to afford it? I hear that those little suckers are expensive beyond belief."

"Maybe we should ask Grandpa Ron for a little help," she suggested. "He's told us on several occasions that all we have to do is ask."

"I know, but that will make us look like we're just a couple of stupid kids that didn't follow the advice of the people that tried to educate us. I hate to fail at something as simple as this. There's tons of cash out there, and I need to figure out a way to get our hands on it. Maybe we can buy a house so I can fix it up and sell it for a big profit. Grandpa is an expert at that sort of thing."

"He made his money back in the big city, and he had an excellent contractor if I remember," added Melissa. "We don't have either of those advantages. Besides, you would be miserable, and you know it. Will, you are a golfer, and that's all there is to it. You love the game, and you are unbelievably skilled. Why don't you take a shot at the Tour?"

"We'd still have to borrow money from Ronnie and Eddie, and I don't want to do that. I feel bad enough about Eddie putting up the money for tomorrow's match with the two Detroit guys. You should have seen the setup. It was like a well-rehearsed play. Hey, maybe I should go into acting. There's got to be hundreds of good-looking babes that would want to play opposite me in an action thriller. I could be the next James Bond or maybe Batman."

Melissa smiled sweetly at her young husband. She thought back to when she first saw him hit a golf shot with her 5-iron. It was truly a thing of beauty that only another golfer would appreciate.

"Living with Bond or Batman would be exciting, but I think you should take a shot at one of the Tours," she said with conviction. "Let me ask you this: tomorrow when you play the two Detroit hotshots for big money, in a match that means more than just the money to Eddie, what are the chances of you not being on your game? What are the chances of you just tanking it?"

"You know what the numbers are," he mused. "Two-thirds of the time, I'll play my regular game. One-sixth of the time, I will play lights out, and one-sixth of the time I'll play worse. At least when I'm sleeping in my own bed, with an awesome woman I might add, and when I'm playing a course I'm familiar with."

"So Eddie's situation with these two guys won't affect your game one way or another? There's no extra pressure there that might cause you to mess up a shot?"

Will looked at her with a look that showed right to his inner core. It was a look that gave her goose bumps every time she saw it. A look that set him apart from other highly skilled young men who could play the game at its highest level. He locked eyes with her and spoke with a voice that could have come from a tenured college professor or any other acknowledged expert in their field.

"If I mess up a shot, it will be for one of three reasons: I didn't think it through, I didn't execute the proper mechanics for the particular shot, or I didn't believe in the shot in the first place. There are no other reasons. The situation, the money, the elements, they really don't enter in to it. I can stay in the moment, and I can block out everything. It was how I was trained. And you have to admit that I'm a pretty good student. It also helped to have two of the very best instructors in my corner."

"So if I were standing naked right by the pin, you could hit a 5-iron, say, fifteen feet short of the flag with absolute confidence?"

"Now you're talking crazy, woman. No real man could resist that gorgeous body and sweet temperament. You could stop a NASCAR race dead in its tracks, even if you were standing at the very top of the bleachers without anything on. Now you've got me thinking about other things. Let's take this discussion upstairs."

He stood and offered his hand to his high school sweetheart, and they headed for the privacy of their bedroom. His plan to attempt to qualify for the U. S. Open would have to wait for another year. The qualifying rounds were already underway when he finally convinced himself to give it a shot. Oh well, making stupid mistakes was just part of paying your dues. He watched Melissa walk up the stairs ahead of him and smiled to himself. At least she was one of the things he did right. Besides, he was playing with the famous Eddie 'The Street' Davis for big bucks tomorrow. Things weren't too bad in the Green household.

Eddie lay next to his wife, the attorney. He could hear her soft breathing which made him smile. He hoped Herman had come up with a solution to their dilemma. He would never forgive himself if anything ever happened to her. If the private detective came up empty, he would need some sort of a backup plan. He stared at the ceiling, running through his options. Finally, he turned over and rested on his side. Regardless of Herman's plan, he decided that he needed to contact his guy, Doc, back in Detroit. The Chicago investigator was a real bad ass, and he knew his stuff, but Doc had a particular set of skills that might come in handy before this was all over.

* * *

Eddie and Will met Connie and Cliff on the practice green at Stonehedge the next day at 11:40. At Eddie's request, the pro kept a half hour of blank times behind them. The pro said it wouldn't be a problem, since it was a slow day and there was a group of women scheduled to tee off around 12:30. Eddie figured his group would be a little slower due to Connie's looking at every putt from every possible angle. And if Canier was still true to form, he would get slower the farther he got behind in the match.

As they stood on the first tee on the North course, they decided that the two young bucks would play from the black tees, while the more experienced golfers would play from the green tees which made the track play about 450 yards shorter. Cliff was grinning from ear to ear as the terms were agreed upon. At a total of 6673 yards, this course was right up his alley. He couldn't remember playing for money on a course shorter than 7000 yards. It was time to fleece the "legend", if he ever was one and his busboy partner.

Connie guessed even and when Eddie opened his hand to show two tees; the match was on. Cliff stepped up and put a hellatious swing on the ball, which produced a drive of 295 yards. Right at the end of its flight, the ball curved left and nestled down in the left rough. Eddie made a comment to Will that it was going to be a long day if he couldn't keep up with Cliff. Will stepped up and out drove Cliff by ten yards, right down the waterline. Connie and Cliff looked at each other with stunned expressions. Their expressions didn't change when Will took out his 5-iron and carried his second shot to the front edge of the green.

Cliff did his part on the hole by hitting his second shot from the rough to about 50 yards short of the green. He then proceeded to get it up and down to match Will's two-putt birdie. The home team went one up when Eddie hit his 3-iron just short of the green, then chipped it to three feet. His birdie putt dropped in giving his team a total of eight. Connie's shaky par was the high ball on the hole. Will and Eddie were up two grand as they walked off the first green. They won the total and collected the bonus point as both of them made bird. Cliff didn't appear to be very happy as he stood next to Connie, watching their opponents hit their tee shots on the par three second.

Quality golf shots were struck by all four combatants as the match progressed. Connie settled down and played some decent golf, but it still wasn't enough to match Eddie's superior ball striking. Cliff, on the other hand, was flat getting outplayed. To his credit, he didn't get down on himself. Maybe it was because he was too stupid to see what he was up against. The locals were up by three units when they came to number seven. The seventh hole calls for a layup off the tee, as a big hitter can easily reach the pond that guards the front of the green. Cliff watched Will closely as the kid hit his 4-iron off the tee. He followed suit with a similar shot that came to rest on a downhill lie about 100 yards out.

Will stood over his ball, looking at the green. The cup was cut just over the front edge in a precarious position. If you didn't play the shot right, the results could be disastrous. Eddie and Connie were both on, facing birdie putts of about twenty feet on opposite sides of the hole. Will hit his pitching wedge with very little wrist action. Instead of hitting his normal crisp short iron, he felt like he was guiding the ball at the hole. The swing looked a touch awkward, but the result was ideal. The ball landed about six feet in front of the pin and then bounced up the slope leaving him a five-foot downhill birdie putt. After the shot, he showed disappointment as he walked back to the cart. He gave his partner a two-fingered salute, as if he knew what was about to happen. He knew that Cliff was watching his every move, and when Will feigned disgust because he left his ball above the hole, the Detroit pro played his shot accordingly.

Wanting to stay below the hole, Cliff hit his lob wedge with tons of backspin. The ball carried just past the pin, then spun back off the green into the front trap. He couldn't believe it! Why didn't the kid's ball react like that? When Eddie and Will both rolled in their birdie putts, an extra bonus point was tacked on per the pre-match agreement. They were now up six grand.

"Tell me the truth, Street," said Connie as they stood on the seventh tee. "Is this kid really your buddy's grandson?"

"Yup," answered Eddie. "He's a little rough around the edges, but he was the only one available last night."

"You're still a shifty son-of-a-bitch, aren't you?"

"You know that kind of talk hurts my feelings, Connie. And you also know that I never lie about golf."

"And I bet you don't feel bad about setting us up against a tour pro like Will, do you?"

"Will, a tour pro? Hell, the kid's never won a tournament in his life. He's just a recreational golfer like Ronnie and me."

"Save it for some other shmuck, man. I know how this game is played."

"You want to use some of your special knowledge of the game on the back side and double the bet?"

"Fuck you. Let's just play it out. Your luck can't hold out forever."

"You just keep telling yourself that it's all luck, Connie. I will admit that you are striking the ball better than you used to."

With that statement, Connie's demeanor totally changed. Even though the money was secondary in this match with his old nemesis, maybe he could come away with something just as valuable. Hell, the money was never that big of a deal after he married Lucille. She wasn't overly bright, but she was loaded, thanks to daddy's string of convenience stores and truck stops. Losing to Eddie again would damage his pride, but his wallet wouldn't suffer all that much. He even laughed about losing 20k at the racetrack a couple of weeks ago. He knew that he was in violation of the second rule of gambling by doing several shots with his buddies, but he hadn't seen them in a while, and he was trying to impress them with a show of cash.

"So, you think I'm better than when we used to play for nickels back in Detroit?" asked Connie.

"I do," answered Eddie. "Back there on five when you were in the right rough, you faded your second to the front edge. You wouldn't have even tried that shot fifteen years ago."

"Yeah, you're right. I've added that little shot to my repertoire. I've been working with a club pro back home. He's just a kid, but he really knows his stuff."

Eddie nodded in Will's direction. "I hear you. There's a lot of young talent out there today. It's too bad that fewer young people aren't taking up the game. There are a lot of courses closing due to lack of play. It's sad, man. Those courses have a lot of history, and they hold tons of memories for old guys like us."

From then on, Connie was much more congenial. It was as if he finally saw Eddie for what he was: a nice guy operating in a field where most of the guys were somewhat less than nice. Eddie played the game the way it was supposed to be played. No gamesmanship and no deceptions once the match started. Thinking back, he should have asked what Will's handicap was. If, as Eddie said, he never lied about golf, he would have told him how good the kid really was. He and Cliff were so confident that they had the edge, it didn't occur to them that Eddie had an ace up his sleeve. Now that he thought about it, Eddie never even asked what kind of scores Cliff usually posted. There was obviously a reason for that. *Shit, Street is sitting on a gold mine here! Why aren't they out in the real world playing for big bucks, instead of a few lousy grand here and there?* He decided to ask him once the round was over.

The four of them sat in the Stonehedge bar and grill drinking cold beers and discussing the round. With a few holes to go, Connie knew it was hopeless. His plan to get somewhat even with Eddie had backfired. The surprising thing was, he didn't feel bad about what had just transpired. His play improved on the back side, as he and Eddie reminisced about old times back in the Motor City. He looked the card over one more time to see if he had made any errors.

"Here are the numbers, gents: I was one over, Eddie and Cliff were four under, and Will was eight under. Dang, kid. Six birdies and an eagle. That was some pretty impressive golf out there. If you ever want to come to Detroit, I can set up a few matches that could turn into some big payoffs."

"Thanks, Connie, but I like it here just fine," said Will. "What are your plans, Cliff?"

The tour pro hadn't said much since they had walked off the thirteenth green. They were only five points down thanks to his birdie on the short par three eleventh. He and Connie had the honors, when he stepped up to the 192-yard par three. They were five points down with thoughts of turning the match around. His 6-iron settled in eight feet from the hole. He walked confidently back to the cart thinking his superb shot would rattle Will. Will responded by sticking his shot half way between Cliff's ball and the cup. Cliff then missed his putt after watching Eddie roll in a twenty-footer for a birdie. Three points were on the line when Will calmly stroked in his four-footer. He and Connie were now down to the tune of eight grand. There was no use getting pissed about the situation. Connie was bankrolling him on this venture, so he had nothing at risk. He'd just have to come up with another way to pay off his debts.

"I guess I'll just keep plugging away," answered Cliff. "I like playing golf, and I like seeing the country. It ain't a bad life, kid. You should think about it."

"I don't know. I've got a wife that's working on her nursing degree. I wouldn't feel right about leaving her alone, even though we've both got family here. Maybe some day."

"You're a real piece of work, Will," added Connie. "And I mean that in a good way. Somehow I get the feeling that today's round wasn't that much out of the ordinary for you. Eddie, can I talk to you in private for a second?"

While Eddie and Connie went over to another table, Cliff tried to impress Will with all the tour players he knew. He explained that he had never actually played with any of the big names, because they were always paired together for the first two rounds. The second and third tier players played with guys of equal notoriety. But, on the practice tee they were all treated the same. He recalled one tournament where he hit balls between a U. S. Open winner and a guy that had finished second in the P. G. A. His plan was to make that a more common occurrence if he could only make a few more putts. Out on the Tour, they all could putt.

Will remembered a comment from an older guy back when he was running the Stonehedge range. The guy said pros were pros because they could putt. He mentioned that to Ronnie and his grandpa laughed. Ronnie said pros were pros because they could putt for birdies. And, they were good at making that crucial par putt that would keep their momentum going. A good putter that shoots three or four over needs to improve his ball striking or maybe his course management.

Eddie and Connie came back to the table. Surprisingly, Connie was all smiles. Will thought that was rather odd for a man that had just lost ten grand. The guys shook hands all the way around, and the two visitors headed for the door and the two-hour drive east. Eddie went over to the pro shop counter and asked for the cash that was being held for them. He came back to the table and tossed one $10,000 bundle to Will, while dividing his own stake money into two halves, then stuffing the hundred dollar bills into the pockets of his cargo shorts. Will just stared at it.

"Listen, Will," he said in a low voice. "I know how tough it is when two people are just starting out. To me, this match wasn't about the money. I guess you could say it was about pride or just wanting to know if I still had it."

"Thanks, Eddie. I've learned that arguing with you or grandpa is useless in situations like this. You tied a guy with tour experience that's half your age. I guess that proves you've still got it. Tell me, were you surprised that I shot eight under against a guy that had competed on the big stage?"

Eddie leaned back in his chair wishing he could light up a Macanudo. Moments like this made his life all that more rewarding.

"Kid, I wouldn't have been surprised if you would have shot a couple of shots lower than you did. The shot you hit on seven with the dead hands approach was a thing of beauty. When that thing hit and took a little skip forward, I had to look away from Connie. Because of the way your ball came in there, I knew exactly what Cliff's would do. He's a fine ball striker, but he's lacking in course management. Maybe that will come some day and maybe it won't. I don't think he had anything at stake today. If he did, I think we would have seen another side of him. It doesn't pay to get worked up out on the course unless you can turn your frustration into something positive. Not many players can do that."

"What would you have done if the scores were reversed and you had to pay off a guy that was here to get a little revenge?" asked Will.

"I would have congratulated them, and then you and I would be sitting here discussing what we needed to do to improve our games and our thinking out there. Tour pros are a sharp bunch. At least the successful ones are. They're the ones that are always trying to learn from a given situation. This is a no excuses game, even with all the bad breaks golfers get. I learned that early on. Once, in a high school match, my opponent and I hit the same tree with our second shots on a par five. His bounced back into the fairway, and mine went further into the woods."

"What did you do?"

"After I quit laughing, I found my ball and chipped it back out onto the fairway. It took me four to get on, and when he three-putted, we walked away all square on the hole. The old saying about, 'it's not what happens to you in life, it's how you react to what happens to you' definitely holds true in golf. I think Cliff would be a much better player if his attitude improved."

"Can I ask what you and Connie talked about over at the other table?"

"He asked me what he needed to do to become a better golfer. He said he thought for sure that he could beat me or at least keep up with me. Then, even after a round where he putted reasonably well, I beat him by five strokes. I will say that his attitude has improved compared to what it used to be. I wish him well. He's not a bad guy. I think at times he just wants it too much. His reputation means a lot to him with the guys back home. He's won his share of matches, so he's got nothing to be ashamed of. Eddie looked down at his phone and read a text from Ronnie.

"Hey, your grandpa just got home, and he's about to fire up the grill. I hope Suzanne and Melissa get here soon. We need to get over there before he burns our steaks."

Connie and Cliff were loaded up and about to pull out of the lot when a '57 Chevy convertible pulled up. Two beautiful women, one in her early twenties and one in her middle fifties, got out and headed into the clubhouse.

"Look at that, Cliffie," said Connie. "You win a bundle out on tour and maybe someday you'll have a chance at something classy like those two. I wonder who the lucky bastards are that they're attached to?"

CHAPTER FIVE

Julian

I feel bad for my husband. He's got so much talent. He doesn't want to give the Tour a try because he's afraid to leave me alone. We both know it would be a long shot, but he'll never know if he won't take a chance. He wants to be just like his grandpa and his friend, Eddie. But times are different now. Hustling at golf is a tough business, and I'm afraid a disgruntled loser might someday decide to do something drastic.

—-Melissa Green, nursing student

Will and Melissa sat at their kitchen table discussing their finances for the umpteenth time. The ten grand from the match with the Detroit guys went mostly to bills. They couldn't believe how fast they spent their money, especially when Melissa watched it like a hawk. The conversation centered around starting a family and how much income they would need. Melissa was still in favor of her husband attempting to qualify for a tour event. If he did well in just one of them, it would take a lot of the pressure off. He didn't have to play the Tour full time—just enough to get them in to a stronger position financially.

"You don't have to play full time," observed Melissa. "Just go out and play a good qualifying round. Then finish in the top twenty and bring home some cash. How hard is that?"

"Now you're making fun of me. How hard is that? For every guy out there on tour, there are probably twenty, no a hundred guys, who think they have enough talent to do the same thing. And I'm not talking about scratch players or guys with plus handicaps. I'm talking about tournament-hardened players with a lot of game. I've never even played in a formal tournament. Hell, I probably wouldn't know how to act. Babbling like a fool and drooling all over myself."

"You didn't have any problem with that Cliff guy, and he has played some Tour events."

"Yeah, but like I said before, on one of my home courses and sleeping in my own bed."

"I still think you should give it a shot. It'll be tougher when we have little ones running around."

"I'll think about it. Let's go to bed and practice making some little ones. When the real time comes, I want to be on my game."

"Sweetheart, when it comes to that, you are always on your game."

* * *

Will sat on his rough mower and surveyed his work. He took great pride in doing his part to make the North and South courses at Stonehedge the best they could be. When he was satisfied, he headed for the maintenance shed. It took him fifteen minutes to clean his equipment, then park it in its spot. It was time to head to the practice tee. He used to love to hit practice balls, but lately, after about a half hour, he would find his attention wandering. Maybe he had too much on his mind: money, future babies, his wife's schooling, money, and his golf game. He wondered why some of the Tour players that had a good, or even a great season, would fall way back in the rankings or off the map altogether. It had happened to a lot of them. Was it more mental than physical? He'd never heard of an NBA player in his prime that averaged 25 points a game drop down to 10 the next season, unless he was nursing some sort of injury. Golf was totally different. A guy could swing the club the same way he had always swung it, but his scores would be nowhere near what they were the previous season. There was such a fine line between good golf and great golf. And out on the Tour, it took great golf to win any real money.

The young hustler hit a few short wedges to warm up, and then he went into his half hour routine. Today, it was the odd-numbered clubs. He pulled out his 9-iron and hit three standard shots. After that, he hit three knock-downs, three fades, and then three draws. He did the same with the seven, the five, and the three. The last 3-iron was more of a hook than a draw. Maybe next time he'd hit a few more, to make sure he had that club down. Tomorrow, he would hit shots out of bad lies. His mentors had instructed him to do that back when he was a teenager still learning the game. You never knew what to expect out there, and if something weird came up, it would be helpful if it wasn't the first time you had experienced it.

* * *

Mitch sat at the Cedar Creek bar having a few beers with his college buddies after a friendly round where he had just lost $20. He was a three-handicap, which meant that Will had to give him a boatload of strokes or make some outrageous concessions when they played for a few dollars. His favorite game with Will was "pull back". Anytime Will was inside ten feet in regulation, he had to pull it back to twenty feet. And Mitch got to choose the spot where his opponent had to putt from. If Will was between ten and twenty feet, the ball went back to forty feet, and it didn't have to stay on the green. When Will stuck his second shot on a par four between the flag and a trap about twelve feet from the hole Mitch picked up his ball and paced off forty feet from the cup and promptly dropped Will's ball in the sand. The hustler had a downhill shot to a green that sloped drastically away. Mitch calmly dropped his three-foot par putt, while bogey was the best Will could do. He enjoyed these games with his close friend, and the money was pretty much even over the past few years.

Mitch decided to stay for one more beer after his college buddies said their good-byes. He wondered what they would say if they knew that he was part of a hustling team where thousands of dollars sometimes changed hands. They knew that he had a friend that played pretty decent, but that was about it. For obvious reasons, Will rarely played outside of his close inner circle of family and friends. The less people knew what he was about, the better.

He was about to head home when he spotted Julian, the guy that mowed greens, sitting at the end of the bar nursing a beer. Julian looked a little out of sorts with himself, so Mitch walked over and plopped down next to him. The greens mower had dark leathery skin and a huge nose that took up most of his face.

"Hey, Jules, are you okay?" asked a concerned Mitch.

"Yeah, I guess," came the muffled response.

Mitch knew that Julian was around seventy years old, and the word was that he used to be a pretty fair golfer. According to the handicap sheet, he still shot around 80, making him one of the best senior golfers at the club. He was sometimes a stroke or two below and sometimes a stroke or two above. All in all, he was also one of the most consistent golfers at Cedar Creek. Mitch knew very little about him, except that the guy had lost his wife a few years ago and now pretty much kept to himself.

"It's obvious something's bothering you. What did you do, shoot a bogey round?"

Julian looked at Mitch with tears in his eyes.

"I don't like to talk about it, Mitch. I should be able to handle it, but it gets under my skin every time it happens."

"Somebody bothering you here? I've known the owner for years. We can tell him, and he'll put a stop to it."

"No, not here. I get invited over to the Battle Creek Country Club every couple of weeks to play, and there are a couple of guys over there that have it out for me. Normally, I'd just stay away from the course, but it's such a joy to play. You'd think at my age that sort of crap wouldn't happen, but it does. They're both about thirty-five, and they're obnoxious as hell. They come from old money in the B. C. area. Every time they see me, they start razzing me about being an old has-been that has to still mow greens for a living. They're just rich, spoiled assholes. Just once, I'd like to put them in their place. You know, take them on and whip their asses good. It would be like old times. Problem is, they're both pretty good golfers. I think one is a two, and the other is maybe a four. That's too much for me to handle. How well do you play, Mitch?"

"Sorry, man. I'm a solid three, so that wouldn't be much help. Tell you what. Let's have another round. Maybe we can come up with something."

For the next half hour, Mitch and the greens mower talked about golf, women, college, and life in general. It was the most Mitch had ever spoken to Julian, and in the end, he decided that he really liked the old guy. He had an obvious love for the game, and it seemed like he was getting a bad deal from a couple of creeps that needed to be put in their place. After two more beers, Mitch decided to propose what was on his mind since he heard Julian's predicament.

"How about this, Jules? What would you say if I could deliver one of the finest golfers in the state and probably the country?"

"What, you're on a first name basis with a top Tour pro? Hell, that wouldn't matter anyway. They'd never play against someone that makes their living playing golf. They may be rich jerks, but they're not stupid."

Mitch cautioned himself. Setting up gigs while drinking was not his team's usual way of doing things. And, when there was alcohol involved, one had to be careful not to be overconfident. It could lead to a situation that could end up costing them money. Normally, he had the authority to set up anything that he thought might be lucrative for the team. He decided that this was a situation where they could make a little money and, at the same time, help out a fellow golfer that appeared to appreciate the game as much as he and Will did.

"What if you were to challenge them to a little two-point match for, say $200 a point? A point for low ball and a point for low total."

Julian squinted his eyes as he looked at his drinking buddy. Was this kid serious, and who was this guy that he was trying to team him up with?

"You're serious, aren't you? C'mon, Mitch. These guys shoot pretty close to par on their home course, and the money is chump change to them, so there's not much of a chance that it will affect their game one way or another."

"The money is just a small part of it," countered Mitch. "I thought it was all about one-upping these dudes. My guy would gladly play for a grand a point, but that would probably scare your guys off. Anybody willing to come to a course he had never played before for that kind of money must be a real go-getter. Do you shoot the same scores at the Country Club that you do here?"

"Yeah, I usually make about ten pars and eight bogeys. That's from the forward tees, of course. From the reds, it's only about 5200 yards. I'm 68 years old. I just can't hit it as far as I used to. I make very few mistakes, and I've got a real good short game."

"You told me what the other two guys shoot. What I need to know is how they do it. Are they consistent like you, or are they big hitters that can balance their bad holes with birdies?"

"I'm told they're pretty consistent. Mostly pars, with a few bogeys and even fewer birdies. I'm sure they took lessons as kids, 'cause, as I said before, their parents are loaded. Why, what difference does it make how they play?"

"Well," explained Mitch, "if they can crank it out there and can make two or three birdies each, then my guy's birds would be neutralized."

"You think your guy can just show up an make five or six birdies?"

"Trust me, by the time he gets here, he'll know all about the course. And to answer your question, yeah, he can do that. How about this? You play for $200 a point and a flat extra $100 for every birdie. That way, even if you tie on the original game, you'll walk away with a few hundred in bird money. Would that be enough to shut these guys up?"

Julian appeared to be deep in thought. Mitch's offer sounded interesting. But, the kid was drinking, and he was still green. He decided to put off his decision until the next day.

"Tell you what, Mitch. I'll put out a little feeler with my buddies at the club, to see if it might be doable. Maybe these guys won't bite. Then, tomorrow, when both of us are sober, we'll make a decision."

"Good enough," said Mitch holding up his glass. "You just let me know, and I'll talk to my guy. I promise you that you have never seen anything like him."

Julian watched Mitch walk away. *It sure would be nice to be young again with all the new fangled equipment available,* he thought. *A whole bunch of Tour guys averaging over 300 yards on their drives. Hitting 5-irons 220. It was a different game for the young bucks, that's for sure. So he thinks he knows a guy that's good for five or six birdies at the Country Club? This could be interesting.*

"Hey, buddy," greeted Mitch as Will answered his cell phone. He knew when Will usually ate lunch over at Stonehedge. Will couldn't hear his phone as he sat on his mower, and Mitch knew better than to call his partner while he was working. Most bosses weren't real lenient when they saw their employees yakking on the phone when they had work to do. Will's boss had reminded the grounds crew on more than one occasion to take or make calls on their breaks, not while they were working. Besides the lost time, it could pose a safety hazard. Running high-powered machinery took all of the operator's concentration. One little slip at the wrong moment could be disastrous. As a reminder, there was a picture hanging in the maintenance building of two golfers with bloody faces. Apparently one of the grounds crew at a different course was zipping along trying to get finished before his shift was over, and he ran over an area with some loose rocks. His mower shot them out right into a couple of golfers that were standing close enough for the rocks to still have enough speed to be harmful.

"I'm out here doing my part to line up gigs, and I think I've got something for you. I say you, because I don't see how I could be part of this one, unless you want to give me a bird-dog fee."

"Whatcha got?" asked Will. It never ceased to amaze him how creative Mitch could be when it came to sniffing out opportunities. The act at the poker game in Lansing was Mitch's idea, and except for a couple small surprises, it turned out as expected. The main idea was to walk away with some of the other guy's cash in your pocket. Anything less than that was considered to be a failure, even if Will shot a course record. Of course, if Will shot a course record and they still lost money, somebody screwed up big time on the crafting of the bet. That almost happened at Riverside earlier in the year. Will was one shot off the record, and they ended up walking away with $50. Mitch pocketed the bill for his efforts, citing Will's failure at the onset to put them in a more advantageous position.

"There's this old guy, Julian, at Cedar Creek that I've known for a while. He's unbelievably consistent, shooting around 80 probably eight times out of ten. Anyway, there are these two dudes over at the Battle Creek Country Club that have been hassling him. He's got buddies at the club that invite him over a couple of times a month. When he shows up, these two are usually around, and they get off on giving him a lot of grief. Long story short, it doesn't have big money potential, but you'd be helping Julian out, and it looks like the old guy could use some help."

"Is it worth showing my face over there and having it attached to a sub par score?"

"Good question. I think we both agree that this area has pretty much dried up for money-making ventures on the short grass. Why not risk an enhanced reputation and help out an old timer?"

"All right, man. If you like the scenario, I'm in. I'll talk to grandpa and Eddie. They've played the track before. What are you thinking for a format?"

"I suggested a two-point game with a bonus for birdies, but Julian suggested low total for $300 a hole. You finish four up on them, you walk with $600 each. In addition to the warm feeling you will get by helping out the old guy, my fee is only a steak dinner for Gloria and me. What do you say?"

"Yeah, let's do it. I need new tires on the Camry. I suppose you two will want rib-eyes with all the fixins'?"

"You know it. You should probably invite Ronnie and Eddie and their wives. They'll want to hear all about it. Julian was talking about next Tuesday around two o'clock. Can you get off a couple of hours early?"

"Yeah, my boss is pretty good about that when he knows I'm playing for some cash. I pay him back by helping him with his game. Call me when it's a firm deal."

CHAPTER SIX

-The Battle Creek Country Club

I'm bookin' down the street tryin' to get away from a stinkin' bounty hunter. The dude was a real fat ass, way out of shape. I wasn't even runnin' that fast and I was still pullin' away from him. Then, around the corner steps this private dick, Herman Wakefield, certified badass. What the hell, they're workin' in teams now? I decided to give up right there. I hate going to jail, but it would be even worse if I had to make a stop at the hospital first.

—-Cubby "Shortchange" Eastwood, grifter, petty thief

Herman walked into his office and closed the door. He had just come from a routine surveillance job. Some dude wanted to keep tabs on his wife who appeared to be having an affair. The big man put his feet up on his desk and scrolled through the photos he had taken. She was having an affair, that was certain. The ironic thing was, her little clandestine meetings were with another private dick—one that worked for the city's top political figures. He decided to report his findings, collect his fee, then get the hell away from this guy. A situation like this spelled nothing but trouble. He hated these surveillance jobs anyway. He looked up, surprised to see his secretary standing in front of him.

"Hey, boss," she said as she sat down in one of the client's chairs. "I think I've got something that we might be able to use to help out your friends with the New Yorkers."

"I'm listening, Stell. Tell me I don't have to shoot anybody. It's been a slow week, but I don't need that kind of excitement. Killing mobsters is bad for business and for our health."

"Nope, no one has to get shot. After some diligent research, I've discovered that the New York Trentons have a Hatfield versus McCoy relationship with another crime family. They absolutely hate each other and will do anything to discredit the other family in private or in public. Obviously, in public is better."

"Okay, I'm following you so far," he responded slowly. "What's our angle here?"

"The family they despise is the Karpov family. You know, like the famous chess player from years ago. They're Russian."

"Now I'm not following. They're Russian, and they live in Russia?"

"Yes."

"All right, connect some dots here. How does this feud between them work into our plans? And keep it simple. I'm on straight time here."

"It is simple. Old man Karpov is quite the golfer, and he is grooming his son to play the American Tour. The kid's a real big hitter, and the dad has been bragging him up to the media, or anyone else that will listen, how great he is."

"So?"

"So, you make a deal with the New York family that if your guys play the Russians in a highly publicized match and humiliate them, then they help you with the two crazy family members. A favor for a favor."

"Doll, I know that you are a lot smarter than I am, but this idea is pretty far-fetched. Our guys aren't going to fly half way around the world to a place like Russia to play golf. Hell, if they happen to beat these guys they might never get out of the country. What do Russians care about golf anyway? I'll bet that less than one percent of their population has even seen a course. The same goes for the Russian media. I just don't think this would generate enough interest to achieve the humiliation factor that would impress the Trentons."

Estelle slowly stood and prepared to leave. She loved playing the 'cat and mouse game' with her boss. Most of the time her job wasn't all that exciting, so she seized every opportunity to inject some intrigue or excitement into her duties.

"Well, I thought it was pretty slick. The Russians get embarrassed in front of a huge crowd and the media. The dad appears to be one obnoxious jerk and quite the braggart. This is a scenario where no one gets hurt, and your guys look like heroes to the Trentons."

"Let me think about it, Stell. I know you've done a lot of research on this, and I appreciate your input."

His secretary went back to her desk and sat down behind her computer. Herman leaned back and closed his eyes. Fly to Russia to play a mob boss and his kid? There's got to be a better way to get the Trentons on his side. How could he ingratiate Ronnie and Eddie enough for the Trentons to take action on the two crazy family members?

"Hey, boss," said Estelle from the outer office.

"Yeah?"

"I forgot to mention that the Karpovs are coming to Las Vegas next month. The dad wants the kid to play some American courses to prepare him for the Tour. He's been talking about it to the Russian press for a couple of weeks. He says his kid will tear them up. That and he probably wants to do some gambling and everything else that goes on out there, if you know what I mean."

Herman jumped up from his chair. Now she was on to something! Build up the match to the Las Vegas media, and maybe even the Los Angeles TV stations and newspapers. If the dad was this big blowhard, he could set himself up to lose face in front of a lot of people. The

Trentons would love that, and maybe that would be enough for them to call off their two loose canons.

"Doll, you might be on to something here. If they pull this off, I'm going to take you out for a steak dinner."

"Dinner would be nice, but you know I'm a vegetarian. How about concert tickets or a big fat bonus?"

"I suppose you want front row seats?"

"Any seat in the first twenty rows would be acceptable."

* * *

"Books" Wilson answered the phone at a well-known billiard establishment in Detroit. His real name was Thadius. His parents attempt to buck the white establishment by giving him a non-traditional moniker didn't set well with him. His friends called him "Tha" with a long 'a'. A simple Chuck or Bill would have been fine with him. His penchant for numbers and his extraordinary memory skills changed that one afternoon while playing a simple card game with his eighth grade buddies. It was pouring rain outside so they sat at his kitchen table playing three-handed "War".

The boys were discussing their favorite baseball players when current averages, RBI's, and home run totals came up. Tha was quoting figures like he actually knew what he was talking about. It was only when one of them grabbed the previous day's paper to verify his stats that he gained their respect. From then on he was known as "The Book" or "Books" for short. When a sports statistic or a date in question came up, they would always check with Books. He was seldom wrong.

Books was now pushing eighty, but he still worked at the pool hall desk. He loved mixing it up with the clientele as he studied the racing form. He was a light skinned black man with a white goatee that rested below the never-ending grin on his face. Now that he was a widower, the pool hall, the racetrack, and his six grandchildren took up all of his time. He had kicked around the idea of writing a book about all the characters that he had come in contact with over the years. That thought was running through his mind when the phone rang. One of those characters was on the other end.

"Python Lee's," said Books. Python Lee Jackson, the owner, showed up once or twice a month to check on things. He was one of those guys that the Lynard Skynard song was written about. A genuine, 'don't ask me about my business and I won't tell you no lies' sort of guy.

"Hey, Books," said the voice at the other end. "I heard that Python's latest male enhancement operation didn't take, and now it's down to a whole two inches."

"I'd be careful talkin' like that, if I were you. There's only a few guys that can get away with that kind of talk, and you don't sound like one of them to me."

"What are you sayin'? You don't recognize my voice after all these years?"

"It's startin' to come back to me, but it ain't possible on account of you're supposed to be dead. At least that's the rumor floating around this place."

"Man, I'm getting tired of those rumors," said Eddie. "Listen, I'm lookin' for Doc. Have you seen him around?"

"Yeah, Street, I've seen him around—like every day. In fact, I'm lookin' at him right now."

"What, Python's got him back on the payroll?"

"Nope. Doc did him a few favors a while back, but things are slow here. You know how much the city has dried up compared to the old days. It just ain't the same. Hell, we haven't had a decent money game or a fight in here in months. Python had to let Doc go to save some money. He felt bad about it, but times are tough."

"So what's he doing there?" asked Eddie. "Just hangin' out?"

"Nope. He's gettin' out of his car across the street. That's where he's been livin' for the past couple of months. He even had to pawn his gear."

"No shit. Man, I didn't know it was that bad. How are you doin'?"

"OK. Stayin' even at the track or close to it. You?"

"Same old, same old. Holdin' my own and a little bit of the other guy's. Listen, what will it take to get three and a half out of the safe and into Doc's hands?"

"For you, Python would want four large in a week. That's preferred borrower's rates. It's more expensive than Wells Fargo, but he don't ask as many questions as they do."

"Deal. Will you wave Doc over? I want to talk to him."

Doc entered the building after he saw Books standing out front waving at him and making the phone call gesture. While Books went to the back room to get the money, Eddie asked Doc if $3500 was enough for him to get his gear out of hock. Doc said it was more than enough. Then Eddie gave him directions to the Firekeeper's Casino which was just east of Battle Creek. Doc's calendar was drier than a rain collection barrel in the Atacama Desert. He said he could be there the next afternoon.

* * *

Will was pumped to play the Battle Creek Country Club. Ronnie and Eddie went over everything they could remember about the layout. The total yardage meant little to Will. The two most important points were where to place his tee shots and what the setting was like around and on the greens. When it came to the greens, he needed to know if there were certain areas that he needed to avoid. If he missed his target and was left with a chip shot or a sand shot to a green that sloped drastically away, the situation had bogey written all over it. He was also leery about severe downhill putts, especially the ones where your ball would start picking up speed once it got close to the hole. A competent greenskeeper that knew the game would know better than to place a pin on a spot like that. But, on a weekday, one of his assistants was probably the guy setting the pins.

He picked up Julian at Cedar Creek, and as they rode east on Watkins Lane toward the club, the old guy filled him in on what to expect from the course. There weren't too many spots where a young guy could cut some corners, but there were definitely some birdie holes that he could take advantage of. He assumed Will was a long hitter, even though his physique was on the slender side. Julian seemed a little nervous. It was obvious to Will that this match was not about the money. It was the big 'get even' that Julian had been dreaming about for a long time.

Chaz Worthington and Greg Bengston were exactly as Will had pictured them. They both occupied positions in successful family businesses and oozed arrogance. Chaz stood about 5'

10" with a stocky physique, while Greg was a skinny, weasely type with a Fu Manchu moustache. There didn't appear to be an ounce of humility in either of them, as they started in on Julian even before the opening tee shots were hit. Will hoped their behavior would motivate the old man to play his best. For his part, he needed to flat line his emotions and just play the game—something he had been trained to do.

Julian introduced Chaz and Greg on the first tee. Will was hoping for a two-point game. That way, if he birdied and Julian bogeyed, and their opponents both made par, they would still gain a point with the low ball. But Chaz and Greg weren't buying it. They opted for a simple game of low team total for $200 a hole—a hundred bucks a man. Will sensed that these two were used to being in charge and would hold out until they got their way. It didn't really matter to him. The whole point of this exercise was to beat these guys in their own back yard. Once the word got around to the club members, Julian would get the respect he was looking for, and maybe the jerks would lay off of him. At least that was the plan.

The home team knew they were in trouble when Will carried the left hand fairway trap on number one with a 3-wood and then proceeded to hit his second shot twelve feet left and hole high. The pin was on the far right, so his target was a few feet left of the pin. A miss to the right would have left a tight chip shot, and after all it was the first hole. He was all for aggressive play, but his mentors had schooled him on when to be aggressive and when to err on the side of safety. His birdie putt hit the left edge of the hole and rimmed out.

Chaz two-putted for his par from about thirty feet, and Greg bumped a nice little 8-iron chip shot from the front of the green to two feet. From the front tees, Julian only had about 330 yards to negotiate. He hit a solid drive 200 yards right down the middle. His 7-iron second shot carried all the way to the back of the green. His three-putt bogey cost his team the first hole.

"Damn," whispered Julian as they watched their opponents tee off. "I usually hit my seven about 125. I must be a little juiced up, 'cause I crushed that thing. All I could think of on my first putt was not to putt it off the front of the green."

"Don't worry about it," responded Will. "Once we get into the round you'll calm down. We'll just take them one hole at a time. You'll be fine."

"I know. I just hate to be down even one hole to these bastards."

The second hole had a gentle right-to-left swing. Will surprised the other three by hitting another 3-wood off the tee. Instead of trying to carve his drive to match the fairway, he carried the edge of the left-hand trees. His monster tee shot left him with an easy sand wedge to the hole. He needed the birdie putt to half the hole, because Julian missed the green left and couldn't get up and down for his par.

On the next tee, they stood far enough away from the two members so they could have a quiet conversation. Will could sense that Julian was very up tight, so he attempted to calm the old guy down. It was obvious that Julian wanted this bad. He didn't appear to be choking. He was just super nervous. Bogeys on the first two holes of a round were no big deal for a guy that shoots around eighty. Will told him his swing looked fine, and he should just trust it and quit worrying so much.

"Why didn't you shape your tee shot right-to-left on that last hole?" asked Julian. "I was surprised when you took it over the edge of those trees."

"Well," explained Will, "it would have been my first swing with the driver today, and if I didn't draw it enough and it ran into the right rough, I might have been blocked by the trees over there."

"For a guy that's never played here before, you seem to know a lot about the course."

"Let's just say I've done my homework. Now, how about we get into these guys' wallets?"

On the third, a 520-yard par five, Will pounded his driver out just past the 300-yard mark. Then he followed up with a 4-iron that settled in twenty feet under the hole. His eagle putt came to rest just inches short. They lost the hole when Julian had trouble extricating himself from one of the right greenside bunkers.

"Damn, Will!" exclaimed Chaz. "You're quite the player. I've only seen you play three holes, but I know the game well enough to realize that you're the best golfer I've ever played with. How did you get hooked up with an old has-been like Julian?"

"He's a friend of a friend," answered Will. "And I don't think he's an old has-been. You and I will both be happy to shoot the kind of scores he usually shoots when we're his age."

Will and Julian checked the scorecard before they headed out to the back side. Will was three under, while Julian was even bogey, carding a 45. The old guy appeared to be devastated.

"I'm sorry, Will," said Julian. "I'm way off my game, and you're playing lights out."

"Hang in there partner," said Will, trying to bolster Julian's defeatist attitude. "We're only three holes down. As a team, we're six over and they are five over. They caught a break when they both doubled number seven. They played the hole in four over par, but it only cost them one hole. That's the nature of match play. It's not a round of golf. It's like eighteen little rounds. We'll get them on the back side."

The kid held up his end of the bargain as he continued his brilliant play. He carded two birdies, an eagle, and a bogey on the second nine. The eagle on fifteen was a particular thing of beauty. After a 275-yard cut driver into a slight breeze, he followed up with a 265-yard second shot with the same club. He received fist bumps all the way around when he holed his fifteen-footer for the eagle. However, their opponents continued their solid play adding three more holes to their total on the inward nine.

The winners were very congenial, buying drinks at the bar and complimenting Will's play to anyone that would listen. Will wasn't too crazy about all the publicity, but he was happy about the way the two country clubbers treated Julian. He hoped his appearance and his stellar play would gain some respect for the old guy. The fact that he knew somebody that could show up and beat old man par into the ground should be a feather in his cap. Hopefully now he could come over and play a round with his buddies without getting harassed all the time. If that were the case, it would take some of the sting out of the $600 that they both lost.

* * *

Will felt bad as he sat at the supper table watching his wife put the finishing touches on one of their favorite dishes, chicken enchiladas. She slid the baking pan into the oven, grabbed two wine glasses from the cupboard, then motioned for her husband to follow her into the living room. Will took a bottle of Merlot from the small countertop wine rack and followed her. Once they became engaged, Kathy and Suzanne took Melissa under their collective wings, and despite their age differences, it didn't take the three of them long to become the best of friends. Kathy, the grocery store manager, was obviously the food expert. Suzanne shared her knowledge of wine, entertaining, and of course, legal matters. They both attempted to school their protégé on the subject of men, but in the end, they had to admit that they were just winging it when it came to the opposite sex.

"Okay," said Melissa after they were comfortable on the couch. The evening news was on low volume so they could talk. In the beginning, they made it a practice to watch the news every evening before supper. They would also talk about their day and any other pertinent subjects that would come up. It didn't take them long to turn down all the political bantering that the major networks were hammering the viewers with. The volume was only turned up when the crawl at the bottom of the screen displayed something that they considered newsworthy. It was their time to relax and tell each other what was on their minds.

"Tell me about your match at the Country Club. Did you wow them with your awesome drives or your precisely struck irons to tight pins?"

"Long story short, I lost $600," answered Will, refusing to look at her.

"Ouch. Well, you're not going to win every time you play. So you were a little off your game. Hogan or Nicklaus didn't win every tournament they played in either. Even your grandpa and Eddie have lost money from time to time. What did you do, choke and shoot par?"

"Actually, I shot six under."

"Wait! You're telling me you shot six under and lost money?"

Will gave her a sheepish look as he nodded his head. Melissa sat up and looked her husband in the eye.

"Obviously I wasn't there to witness it, but it sounds like something stinks in Mayberry, Opie."

"You're funny, ya know that?" asked Will as Melissa got up to check on dinner.

"I have my moments," came the reply from the kitchen. "We eat in fifteen minutes."

Will lay on his back with his hands behind his head. Melissa was sleeping quietly beside him. She was lying on her side facing the wall. He found out early on in their marriage that if she slept on her back she would snore something awful. When he brought it up at breakfast, she refused to believe it, saying he was making it up. He would roll her over on her side, but it didn't take long for her to roll back and crank up the chain saw all over again. How could someone so beautiful emit such an irritating sound? He encouraged her to inquire about snoring cures from her nursing instructors. When she refused, he decided that drastic action must be taken. The next time she started in, he grabbed his phone from the nightstand and recorded about a minute of her act.

The next morning, when confronted by the evidence, she started to cry. He stood up and tried to comfort her. The comforting session turned into a five-minute slow dance with some high school reminiscing.

"How was I to know that the object of my high school dreams would turn into a growling she-wolf at night?"

She looked up at him through misty eyes and smiled.

"Well, you better treat me right. You know how mean she-wolves can be if they feel threatened. And, yes, I'll ask my instructors how to reduce the snoring thing. But I'm going to tell them that it's your problem, not mine. I'm embarrassed enough as it is."

"Whatever, just figure out a way to turn that noise off. How can I dream about you when you're lying next to me keeping me awake?"

He couldn't help thinking about what she had said earlier. The match with Julian wasn't a normal gig by any means, but as Melissa said, something did stink. He looked at the bedside clock. It was only 11:00. Maybe Mitch was still up. He decided to call him. He picked up his phone and walked into the bathroom so he wouldn't wake his wife. Mitch sounded a little out of breath when he answered his phone.

"Hey man, what are you doing, working out?"

"Yeah, something like that," came the response. "Why are you calling me at the most romantic time of the evening?"

Will thought he heard a little giggle that sounded like Gloria.

"I never pictured you as the romantic type," continued Will. "You didn't get Gloria drunk again, did you?"

"I'm not drunk, wise guy," said Gloria as she listened in on the call. "I invited myself to a little sleepover. What's the matter, did you strike out tonight?"

"That's none of your business," answered Will. "Mitch, did you see Julian after our match today? Did he come back to Cedar Creek?"

"Actually, he did. I saw him at the bar, and it looked like he had tossed a few back. He told me you guys lost, and he didn't want to talk about it. I figured I would get the story from you tomorrow when we play our usual game."

"It's probably nothing. The old guy did a little choking act. There was a lot on the line for him, and he didn't handle it very well. Anyway, go back to what you were doing. If you can manage."

"You're a funny guy," quipped Gloria. "I'll have you know that my man is ready for action any time, day or night."

"That's more than I need to know," said Will as he killed the call. He went back to bed thinking how devastated Julian must have been after today's loss. Anyway, he had done his part. There was nothing more he could do. Julian was just going to have to live with it.

CHAPTER SEVEN

–Doc

I was a real jerk when I was a kid, picking on guys that were smaller than me. One day this younger kid named Dwayne stood up to me. I kicked his butt, but the way he took it impressed the hell out of me. I don't know what happened to him. He probably went on to make something of himself, working in an honorable profession. The cards have been stacked against me ever since high school. Some guys get all the luck.

—-John Block, career politician

Dwayne Oscar Crewe didn't like either of his first two names, so at the beginning of the third grade he started signing his papers with his initials, DOC. His teacher went along with it, and it didn't take long for the other students to fall in line. His parents were a little surprised when they showed up for a conference and his teacher kept referring to him as Doc. Finally his father interrupted her and asked, "Who the hell is this Doc kid?" When the teacher explained that was what their son wanted to be called, they decided that it was fine with them. The kid had never mentioned it. Not because he was shy. He was busy thinking about other things. Even as an eight year-old, Doc was one serious character.

Doc solidified his reputation in the fifth grade. A big sixth-grader was picking on his older brother Derek, so Doc called the bully out. They walked across the street from the school to a little park that was full of trees. A group of about twenty schoolmates went along to watch the action.

"You need to stop picking on my brother," ordered Doc.

"What are you going to do about it if I don't?" sneered the bully.

Doc put up his fists and waited. The bully's first punch landed square on his jaw sending him to the turf. Derek stepped in and helped his brother up. Then he stood by his side with his fists up. Doc told his brother to step aside as this was his fight. Two of the bully's friends grabbed Derek and dragged him off to the side and held him there so he could watch his brother take a beating. For the first five minutes, Doc was down more than he was up. He did get in one lucky punch right on the bully's nose. It must have hurt, because he retaliated by breaking Doc's nose.

The fifth-grader stood there weaving back and forth on rubbery legs. His right eye was almost swollen shut, and there was blood all over his shirt. Then, just like in the movies, he grinned and spit out a tooth. The bully looked his victim over like he was seeing him for the first time—the blood, the swollen eye, and the hole where the little guy's tooth was. He told Doc that the fight was over. He didn't want to hit him any more. His opponent stood there with his fists up, declaring that it wasn't over. When the bully turned to walk away, Doc hollered, "So that's it, you're done? You're walkin'? Are you going to stop picking on Derek?"

The big kid stopped as if in thought. Then he did the strangest thing. He turned and offered his hand. They shook, and the matter was settled. The crowd quickly dispersed.

As the brothers walked home, Doc explained to Derek that his strategy was to take the bully to a place where he was unwilling to go. Everything went just as he had planned it. Except for the tooth. Halfway home he realized that without the tooth there would be no money under his pillow the next morning.

"Don't worry, bro," said Derek, draping his arm across his kid brother's shoulder. "I'll give you a couple of bucks from my birthday money. You're the bravest guy I know, and I'm proud to have you for a brother."

After high school the brothers went their separate ways. Derek went to college to become a veterinarian, while Doc went where a lot of brave young men go—into the military.

* * *

Doc and Eddie went way back. Python Lee's place was a hotbed of activity twenty years ago. Every week there were big money pool games, dice games, and a couple of poker games in the back where an unlucky sort could drop a couple grand if his cards turned sour or if he was at the wrong table with the wrong people. After a few serious incidents, some of the regulars, including Eddie, went to Python Lee and told him he needed to do something about all the unsavory dudes that were hanging around. There was a lot of money exchanging hands and although the regulars hated losing to an opponent, they didn't want to turn it over to some opportunist looking for some easy money. The owner decided that he needed to bolster his security, so he hired a twenty-four year-old vet who appeared to know how to handle himself. The kid was a third degree black belt in Tae Kwon Do and an avid student of Bruce Lee's particular style of Kung Fu. It didn't take long for Doc to prove that it was money well spent.

* * *

One evening a few years ago Eddie was standing at the counter talking to Books about the Lions' chances of making the playoffs, when Doc strolled in. He was covered with what looked like little scabs, and there was a substantial bruise on his right cheek.

"What the hell happened to you?" asked Eddie.

Doc walked him off to the side as Books went over to answer the phone.

"Keep this under your hat, man, but I had to go on a mission."

"A mission? Where?"

"Don't know. I was in a C-130 for a long time, then a chopper sat me down in a wooded area. I had to walk for about a mile to get to my destination. I had a map and night vision equipment. The house was right where they said it would be. I was about ready to abort, 'cause I'd been waiting a long time, and I was afraid I'd miss my ride out. Then it happened."

"What happened?"

"He came to the window. I got the scratches running back through the woods. When I hit the branch that made this bruise it almost knocked me out. I need to get back into shape. I was puffing like a two-pack-a-day smoker. It was embarrassing."

"Damn, they called you back in to shoot some bad guy?"

"Yeah, I'm pretty sure he was some kind of drug lord. Anyway, since I'm a civilian, if I got caught our military could claim I was some kind of mercenary working for a rival gang, and they had nothing do with it. I don't worry about the politics; I just do what is necessary."

"I hope you got paid well for your efforts," said Eddie.

"Yeah, some cash, and they removed an incident from my record. It all worked out."

Eddie watched as Doc wandered over to two young guys that were playing pool. They were getting a little loud and threatening each other. They both calmed down when Doc wandered into their area and sat on one of the high-backed stools. The guys knew his rep, and they knew enough not to cross him.

* * *

"Okay, here's the game," offered Will. "I'll alternate draws and fades with every shot, and you get two a side for the usual $10 a stroke."

"Does that include putts?" asked Mitch.

The guys were standing on the first tee at GLV's East course. It was around 6:00 p.m., which meant if they played fast they could probably get eighteen in. There was a six-pack in the cart, and the weather was picture perfect.

"Uh, no." answered Will. "I'm a golfer not a stinkin' magician."

"How about this, I'll take my two a side, but you have to tee off with a 7-iron?"

"Even on the par threes?"

"Yup. On every tee."

"Done."

The two friends looked forward to these weekly matches. In addition to the three beers each, they would hook up one of their phones to a small speaker so they could listen to some tunes as the round progressed. This was also the perfect environment to come up with future gigs. Ideas, no matter how ridiculous, were thrown out for the other's consideration. A few weeks earlier they were getting into their cart at Stonehedge, ready to head under the tunnel to the North course, when the head pro walked out of the shop and waved them over.

"Will, can I talk to you for a minute?"

"Sure, pro. What's up?"

"Listen, one of my old college teammates is coming over on Friday. He was always about a stroke better than me, and he's never let me forget it, even to this day. He played some Web.com events after graduation and didn't do too bad. But, after a couple of years he gave it up for the corporate life. It helped to have a father-in-law who was vice-president of the company. Anyway, he's bringing some hotshot client to play, and he wants a game. The client actually played number one for Central Michigan, so he's no slouch. Anyway, would you like to help me get some of my college losses back? The stakes will be smaller than you're used to, but it's more of a personal thing for me."

"Sure. It sounds like fun. Just let me know when."

"Thanks, man. I guarantee you, it will be fun. I'm sure he's still just as competitive as he was back in school, so I'm really looking forward to taking him down."

A new starter named Dave was standing nearby listening to the pro's exchange with Will.

"Hey, pro, that young kid is that good?"

The pro shook his head in the affirmative.

"He's that good and then some."

"But over at Stonehedge the other day I saw him hit a weak slice off the first tee on the South course."

"It's all part of the plan, Dave. Do me a favor and don't mention what I just told you. If you're lucky, maybe some day you'll get a chance to play with him. I wouldn't play him for more than a little beer money though. You're retired, and I assume you don't want to go back into the work force."

After shooting two under on the front side, Will gave Mitch the option of changing the bet. After some thought, Mitch laid it out.

"You are getting ridiculous, dude. No one breaks par hitting their tee shots with a 7-iron. Let's try something different. Now you have to alternate a 4-iron and an 8-iron until you get to the green. And if I shoot par or better, my payoff is doubled on the back side."

"What, I'm now running some kind of charity for soon to be college grads?" asked Will.

"C'mon, man, you're $50 up on me. At this rate, I'll be working tomorrow for nothing."

"Alright, alright," responded Will. "Quit your whining."

"That ain't whining," countered Mitch. "It's just making an observation."

As they walked off eighteen green, Mitch waved his $10 profit in Will's face. He was three holes up, and he shot one under, turning his $30 win into $60 for the back nine, which netted him a cool ten-spot.

"It was a pleasure doing business with you, Mr. Hustler," laughed Mitch as he folded the bill in his money clip.

Will gave his partner a sorrowful look. All it took was two subtle mishits to give Mitch the victory. There was no way he was going to consistently take money off his best friend and faithful business partner.

* * *

Eddie looked up from his poker game at the Firekeeper's Casino on the east side of Battle Creek. A familiar face was staring at him from out on the casino floor. When they made eye contact, the man turned and walked away. A short time later, Eddie excused himself and walked across the gaming floor to the bar. He took a stool next to the new arrival. He ordered a beer and waited until the bartender sat it down. Doc didn't acknowledge his old friend, as he didn't know what the situation was. Maybe some disagreeable dudes were watching Eddie—guys looking to recoup their poker losses as soon as Street hit the parking lot.

"Books tells me you've run into some hard luck," said Eddie, looking straight ahead.

"Yeah, guys with my skills are in short demand. I tried working in a factory a while back. Lasted six months. It was awful."

"Well, I've got a job for someone with your particular set of skills. Did you get your gear?"

"Yeah, it's in the car. Hey, Street, thanks for thinking of me, and thanks for the advance."

"You're the only guy I'd trust for a job like this. C'mon, let's go get some supper, and I'll lay it out for you."

Suzanne looked down at her phone when it started to vibrate. She excused herself from a low-level meeting and walked back to her office. Eddie's message said, *Call me when you get a chance.*

"Hey, doll," greeted Eddie when he saw it was his wife calling.

"What's up?" asked Suzanne.

"Ronnie and I are on our way to Chicago for a business deal. I'll probably be back late tomorrow or the next day."

"Business deal? Meaning you're going there to play golf, right?"

"Well, yeah. That's the business we're in. Listen, I'm a little concerned about what's been going on lately with those two Mafia clowns, so I hired some security for you."

"I thought you said those two were harmless," countered Suzanne.

"I'm pretty sure they are, but I want to play it safe. The guy I hired is cruising around town to get an idea of where things are. He'll stop by tonight and introduce himself. I have complete faith in him. If I didn't, I wouldn't leave town like this. Will you make sure the spare bedroom is shipshape?"

"Okay, if you're sure about this," said Suzanne. "What about Kathy? Does she have someone watching her?"

"Yeah, it's one of Herman's guys named Buck. He's good, but our guy is better."

Ronnie looked over at Eddie and rolled his eyes. Buck was a Hollywood stunt man that did occasional jobs for Herman. He was instrumental in getting the guys out of Chicago with a boatload of cash a few years ago.

"So Doc knows his stuff?" asked Ronnie after his partner finished his call.

"Wait until you meet him. He's definitely one of a kind. Your son would have been proud to know him."

"I feel better that the girls are covered," continued Ronnie. "When Herman called and explained his theory on how to get us out from under our current situation with Greer and Donaldson, I wasn't so sure it would work. Now that I've had time to think about it, I think it might be doable."

"It's certainly worth a try," added Eddie. "And if it doesn't get them off of our backs, maybe we can turn a profit. We haven't played anybody for serious money in quite a while. I'll admit I'm getting a little antsy for some decent action. This Chicago gig you came up with is a good idea. Now tell me again who we're playing and for how much…"

CHAPTER EIGHT

–Revenge Match

I never played a money match with Troy Feltner, and anyone that says I did is a damn liar!

—-Trip Fratello, barely audible through the silver spoon in his mouth

Some smart guy once said that, "Living well is the best revenge". Eddie and Ronnie totally agreed with this statement. Revenge can be risky and quite often downright dangerous. When it comes to the 'big get even', one needs to seriously weigh the pros and cons. There are several questions to be answered: 1. Was the initial offense worth getting in deeper with the offender? 2. Will the action taken achieve the desired result? 3. What are the chances of repercussions? 4. Is it worth starting a war where there could possibly be no winner? If the rational answer is "yes" to the above, or if you just can't let it go, then it's good to have a guy or two with skills that you can count on.

Suzanne sat in a booth at a Battle Creek sports bar with three female friends catching up on all the gossip. The booth was shaped in a semi-circle around the table. Suzanne was at the nine o'clock position as the waiter faced the table. He had just taken their drink orders when a striking woman with red hair came and stood by their table. She was holding a mixed drink in her right hand, and by the looks of her clothes and jewelry, she was well versed in current fashion.

"Ladies," said the woman addressing the group. "I'm kind of in a spot here. There's a guy over at the bar that's been trying to buy me a drink for the last half hour, and he won't take no for an answer. Do you mind if I sit with you for a few minutes? I told him I was supposed to meet someone here, and maybe he'll get the hint and give up. He's kind of creepy."

Suzanne scooted over and made room for the new arrival. The lady said her name was Gwen, and when she looked over her shoulder in the vicinity of the bar, Suzanne's friends gave her some strange looks. She shrugged her shoulders as if asking, 'what are we supposed to do'? Gwen's few minutes turned into an hour. Every so often she would look back toward the bar.

Suzanne and her friends didn't mind the intrusion after their second drink, and besides, Gwen was a fascinating conversationalist. She was funny and appeared to have done a lot of traveling.

The lawyer admitted to one of her friends during a visit to the restroom that initially she thought Gwen might have been a prostitute, but after talking to her they discovered that she was very intelligent and had worked several different jobs. When the friends said good-bye, Gwen rose and left with them. They decided that the guy at the crowded bar that was harassing her must have been a real creep like she said.

Suzanne went left with Gwen when they exited the building. She hesitated before crossing the parking lot. With all that was going on with her husband and Ronnie, should she walk across a dark lot with someone she had just met? She looked over at the redhead.

"So, Gwen, where are you parked?" she asked. Gwen reached into her purse and took out her keys. She hit the unlock button, and the car two spots from Suzanne's came to life, chirping and flashing its lights.

"Sorry," said Suzanne. "A girl can't be too cautious these days. C'mon, let's go. Hopefully your creepy guy isn't out here."

Gwen smiled in agreement and stepped off the curb. The girls were halfway to their cars when not one creepy guy, but two, exited quickly from their car and placed themselves directly in front of them. The women looked at each other wondering what was going on. They both were in high heels, which was going to make it difficult if they decided to run back to the bar. Suzanne reached down into her purse searching for her pepper spray. Gwen just stood there with a concerned look on her face.

"Hello, ladies," said one of the men. They were both a shade over two hundred pounds with an ominous look about them. "I'll bet you're Suzanne. You look just like your picture. Listen, we're not here to hurt anyone. We're just messengers. And the message is…"

"We don't care what your message is!" shrieked Gwen. "Leave us alone!"

"Calm down, bitch," said creep number, two grabbing her by the arm. "I'll knock you out right here if you holler like that again."

Gwen's response was totally unexpected. She stomped down on the guy's foot with her high heel while simultaneously striking him on the nose with a quick back fist, momentarily flattening it across his face. He went down on one knee holding his broken nose. Suzanne and the other man both froze when Gwen went into action. Recovering quickly, the second man stepped back and stuck his hand inside his sport coat. Gwen stepped in and grabbed his wrist before he could bring it back out while launching three quick punches to his face. The third one dropped him to the pavement. She reached into his coat as he lie on his back and came out with a pistol. Gwen grabbed Suzanne gently by the arm and moved her away from the two strangers keeping the gun pointed at them.

"Now you boys get out of here," she ordered. "Don't give us any messages, just leave."

They staggered across the parking lot toward their car. The girls watched as they got in and drove off. Hearing the commotion, two more men walked between the cars and asked if everything was all right. Gwen put the gun behind her back and responded that they were both okay, and thanked them for their concern. When they turned to walk away, she stuck out her hand. Suzanne gave it a confused look.

In a deeper voice he said, "Name's Doc, Eddie sent for me."

* * *

"Doggone it, Liss," remarked Will. "How are we going to start a family if we don't have any money? Maybe I could get a job with some corporation doing public relations. You know, play golf with clients and help them with their games. There has to be some local companies who need that kind of service."

"Maybe, but what would you do in the winter?"

"Good point. They would probably want some sort of degree other than just being a sub par golfer. Hey, I hear your old boyfriend, Troy-boy, landed a job with IBM. Maybe I should call him to see if there might be any opportunities with them. He's a different guy now that he's out of school, and the dude owes me for a little favor I did a couple of years ago."

"I'm sure he is, and why does he owe you?"

"Well, I never told you this, because it's not something that I'm all that proud of. I was young and stupid."

"How long ago was this?'

"Uh, like three years ago when Troy was a senior in college."

"And three years ago you were young and stupid, but now you're older and wiser?"

"You got half of it right—I'm older. Anyway, Troy called me and said he needed a little help with one of the preppie golfers that was on the Western team with him. Troy was playing the number four spot, and this guy was playing number one. He said this guy's dad was a big businessman from Grand Rapids, and the family was filthy rich. They had just played a big rival, and Troy's score cost them the match. The guy started razzing Troy, and it got pretty nasty. So Troy wanted to set up a little grudge match and… "

* * *

"So how's your game, Will?" asked Troy as Will pulled into a parking spot in the spacious lot of a course near Grand Rapids. He got out and shook hands with Troy, then he retrieved his clubs from the trunk. Before he shut it, he saw his old ratty bag way in the back—the one with the broken zippers and no shoulder strap.

"Never better," answered Will. "So this guy is a real jerk, huh?"

"Yeah, he's a real ass. He's a pretty good golfer, but not in your league. If you ask him, he's God's gift to golf, women, and any other subject that comes up. He's like me when we were back in high school—times ten. His name is Doug Fratello, but he wants everyone to call him Trip, because he's a third generation Doug. His partner is Brian Walk. He's not a bad guy. I don't know what he sees in Trip, but it's his problem. They're over on the practice green waiting for us."

"So, it's obvious you want to take some money off of him. We could have a little fun while we're at it. What do you say?"

Troy grinned. "I'm in, man. What do I have to do?"

"Just keep a straight face. You didn't tell them my name, did you?"

"Nope, just said you were an old high school classmate that liked to play golf for a few dollars once in a while."

"Good. In that case, call me Wayne. Why don't you go on up to the practice green. I'll be there in a minute. Remember, no laughing or this won't work."

"Done. Thanks, man. I appreciate this."

Will pulled out the ratty bag and transferred his clubs and other equipment. He took his utility tool out and pulled out the knife blade. He made a couple of holes in his shirt. He wasn't crazy about doing this, as it was one of his favorite shirts. Next, he found one of Mitch's old Styrofoam coffee cups on the floor of the back seat. It still had the lid on it. At the bottom of the cup he found what he was looking for—just enough black liquid to make a few stains. He trickled some of the remaining fluid down the front of his shirt. Checking himself in the mirror, he felt something was lacking. His shirt was stained with holes in it. His bag was one that he had pulled out of a large trashcan years ago. He messed his hair up and pulled his hat down hard on his head.

The finishing touch was in place as he walked up to the putting green, carrying his bag by the handle. He had shoved four sticks of gum in his mouth, and after they softened up, he moved them with his tongue down between his teeth and lower lip, giving the impression that he had a big chew in there.

"Hey, Troy, are these the dudes that want to make a donation to the Wayne Wilson party fund?" asked Will with his hand extended. Troy kept his part of the bargain by not laughing at Will's appearance. The guy couldn't look any more like a dork if he had fallen into a mud puddle or spilled spaghetti sauce down the front of his shirt. Trip was not amused and refused to shake hands.

"Shit, Feltner, this is your high school buddy that likes to play for cash?" asked Trip. "This is a joke, right? Like he's carrying enough to make this interesting."

"Hey, man, I ain't no joke," replied Will, pulling out a small wad of bills from his front pocket. "Troy said you boys like to cuff it around for some real cash. Well, I'm in. Where's our cart?"

"We're walking, Wayne," said Troy. "I paid your green fee so we're good to go. What do you say, guys, a little low ball/low total for fifty dollars a point? If that's too stiff, Trip, we can cut it in half. We don't want to break you. We're just looking for some action."

Trip looked at his partner for his take on the situation. Troy had thrown a real curve at them, and he wasn't sure what to make of it. This nut job couldn't be for real. He looked at Wayne's bag and saw that his clubs didn't even match. Half of Wayne's irons were forged, while the other half were cast. What he didn't know was that although the clubs had different style heads, they had the same shafts and the swing weights and the total weights were perfectly matched. Will had used this set of clubs successfully on several occasions.

"Are you telling me that we have to walk?" protested Will. "My bag strap is broke. How am I going to carry this heavy bag without a strap?"

"You're on, Feltner," said Trip after hearing Wayne's whining. There was no way that a guy who looked like a complete doofus could be good enough to take him and Brian for any decent amount of money. Even if the guy was putting on an act, which was pretty convincing, he still had to play some unbelievable golf to handle their game.

Before they headed for the first tee, the three of them watched as Wayne took off his belt and attached it to his bag as a makeshift strap. Then he ripped a narrow strip off of his towel and used it to replace his belt. The rest of his towel was used to wrap around his belt to soften its feel on his shoulder. He grinned at them and gestured toward the tee.

Wayne's act was just getting started as he teed up a dirty ball and proceeded to play a big slice down the first fairway. Trip and Brian were all smiles as they took one point for low total on the first hole. On number two, Wayne hit his slice about fifteen yards behind the other three tee shots. From there he hit a sweet 8-iron about six feet underneath the hole. His subsequent birdie netted his team two points. He and Troy proceeded to totally demolish their opponents for the rest of the front nine. Wayne made four birdies, and Troy had one of his own. At the turn they were six points up. Trip and Brian were now down $300 each.

"Uh, look Troy," said Trip. "I just got a call from my dad, and he wants me to come home. Something about a problem with the house and he needs my help. I don't have $300 on me, but I'm good for it. How much do you have, Brian?"

"I've got like $150," answered Brian looking through his wallet. "Take this, Wayne. I'll have to owe you the rest."

Troy and Will stood dumfounded as they watched their opponents walk across the parking lot and make a quick getaway in Trip's car.

"You know, I wasn't too crazy about it when my dad refused to pay up after our match back in high school," explained Troy. "That's why I decided to make good on my loss, even though it took me a while. Now that I see it from the other side, I see how much it really stinks. Those guys are total losers. I guess this proves that money can't buy class, huh Will?"

"Nope, according to Eddie, having money only gives you more options in life. A fat bank account doesn't make you any smarter or better lookin' than the next guy."

"Your grandpa and Eddie are a couple of cool cats, aren't they?"

"You have no idea, my man. Here's half of our winnings. Let's go get something to eat."

"Only if you'll let me buy," added Troy, slamming his car trunk. "Damn, you look like a hillbilly golfer. What was all that coughing back on the first hole? Was it part of the act?"

"No," laughed Will. "I almost swallowed my gum back there. I was moving it around in my mouth when it got too close to the back of my throat. I was hoping you knew the Heimlich maneuver, but I managed to cough it out of there."

"You're a real piece of work, man. Thanks for coming and playing some awesome golf. We sure put those two in their place."

"No problem. It's what I do."

*   *   *

"Why didn't you ever mention that little match?" asked Melissa.

"I don't know. I guess I figured you would call me something less than complimentary for lookin' like a complete dork. It was actually kind of fun. Maybe we should go out sometime with me in my hillbilly attire."

"I think not. If one of my friends or someone from school saw you, I would never live it down. I'll tell you what I wouldn't mind. How about we dress up and go out for a nice dinner at a classy place? We haven't done that in a long time."

"I'm in," said Will, standing and offering his hand. "Hardees or Subway?"

"Surprise me, big shot," she giggled, taking his hand.

CHAPTER NINE

–Confession

Confessing is for girly men with no backbone. I don't admit nuthin'. If you think I did something, then you better have proof or keep your mouth shut. I say make the accuser put up or shut up. If it can't be proven in a court of law, then it never happened.

—-Bob Furley, ward of the state

Two days later Eddie pulled into his drive around midnight. The short Chicago trip was more profitable than he and Ronnie had expected. On the first day, they took a couple of forty-somethings for eight hundred a piece, which incensed the losers so much that they challenged the two hustlers for a rematch the next morning. When Ronnie said they were planning on leaving that evening, the challengers dangled enough cash in front of them to convince them to change their minds. The format for the rematch was simple. Each team decided what was to be played for nine holes. Their opponents, both long hitters, won the coin toss and chose to play a scramble. Their substantial length enabled them to reach both of the front nine par fives in two, resulting in an eagle and a birdie. At the turn, the Michigan hustlers were two down.

"Nice playing on the front side," complimented Eddie as they stood on the tenth tee. "You two can really pound it out there. For the back side, let's play a little game of fade only. We'll score it like a best ball. The low ball between us is the best ball."

"What's the fade part then?" asked Kyle, the longest hitter of the four.

"If you don't fade your shot, it doesn't count," answered Eddie. "And once you're inside 100 yards, you don't have to fade it. You can hit it any way you want."

"Let me get this straight, so there's no confusion," said Kyle with a disdainful expression. "Outside of 100 yards if we don't fade or slice it, that player is eliminated from the hole?"

"Exactly. If you hit it straight or draw it, you're out of the running for that hole only. It's that simple. If all four of us hit it straight or draw it, we just move on to the next hole."

"This is bullshit," said Kyle's partner.

"It's still just golf, guys. Only you have to approach it a little differently. It's all about hitting the shots. After watching me play the front side, I'm sure you figured out that left-to-right isn't my favorite way to shape a shot. You're still up, so let's get after it."

Kyle, whose normal shot was a draw, teed up and hit a big slice over the white stakes on the right side of the hole. His partner hit it dead straight down the left side of the fairway, making him a spectator for the rest of number ten. Kyle re-teed and hit another big slice, but kept this one in play. He was now lying three. Ronnie stepped up and hit his patented fade down the left side. The four of them watched as his ball bounded down the fairway coming to rest right on the water line. Eddie had to work a little harder to get his ball to turn left-to-right, but his shot looked similar to Ronnie's.

The guys went ahead to stay on number thirteen when Ronnie rolled in a twelve-foot birdie putt. Their opponents were not happy and had no problem voicing their opinions. Their constant bitching fell on deaf ears as the hustlers plied their trade, eventually finishing four holes up. At $250 a hole, they both pocketed $1000. Eddie became concerned as they rode down the eighteenth fairway. Kyle, riding ahead of them, appeared to be having an intense conversation on his cell phone. It was apparent that he was not taking his loss very well.

"Looks like we're going to have to collect and bolt," he said to Ronnie. "That Kyle dude is taking this a little too seriously. I don't know if it's a case of not being able to pay up comfortably, or maybe he's just a sore loser. Regardless, we don't have time to call for backup, so let's play it this way… "

Eddie picked up the cash off the table and put it in his front pocket.

"Where's your partner?" asked Kyle in a surly tone.

"He's putting our sticks away. He'll be right in. He drinks the same as me. We're gonna have two Killian's. What are you guys drinkin'?"

"The same for us," said Kyle's partner as Eddie headed for the bar. He came back carrying four bottles.

"I'm not too crazy about the way you two swindled us out there, Ferguson," said Kyle in a somewhat threatening voice. "Your game was bullshit, and you know it. If we weren't such gentlemen, we'd catch you in the parking lot and kick your sorry asses."

He looked at his partner and got no argument.

"Look, guys. There's more than one way to hit a golf ball, and there's more than one way to score a match. You should chalk this up to the learning process. You're both good golfers. I'm sure you'll make up what you both lost today in no time."

Eddie pulled a cell phone out and checked it for messages. Seeing none, he excused himself, saying he was going to the restroom. Once around the corner, he went out a side door and hopped into the car that was waiting for him. Ronnie stepped on it, and they sped out of the lot. The tri-state tollway was only a few miles away. In a couple of minutes, they were heading south at eighty miles an hour.

"How did it go?" asked Ronnie as he eased the Monte Carlo into the middle lane.

"As planned," answered Eddie. "I left a dead cell phone that I found on a course back home on the table and pretended to go to the can. Leaving that phone there should have bought us enough time to get clear of those dudes. I hate to run out like that, but with their attitudes and what looked like a very serious phone call, I think it was the best strategy."

"You're the brains of this outfit. I also think it was the right play. These younger guys seem to have a serious problem when things don't go their way. Back when we were kids, when a fight was over you shook hands. Now, the loser is likely to ambush you later with a two-by-four, or he'll go get a bunch of his buddies to even the score. It's like they think they're above losing. Hell, losing is just part of a guy's education. Learn from it so it won't happen again."

"I agree. Hey, if I'm the brains of the outfit, what are you?"

"I thought that was obvious. I'm the looks and the talent. I've got two jobs to do to your one. Maybe we should start splitting the profits two for me and one for you. It's only fair."

"Keep dreamin', dude," said Eddie as he leaned back in his seat and pulled his hat down over his eyes. "And keep it on the road. I'll drive when we get to Benton Harbor."

* * *

Doc sat at the table and watched as Suzanne heaped a pile of scrambled eggs on his plate. She was dressed in her normal business attire while he had on shorts, running shoes, and a Led Zeppelin t-shirt.

"I'll have to admit that I thought Eddie was overreacting when he told me you were coming to serve as my protector. Those guys last night were pretty scary."

"I think that's all they were supposed to do," said Doc. "Scare you, I mean. They didn't look like the type that was willing to get real physical. It was obvious that they were both out of shape. Their beer guts were proof of that. Once you're safely at work, I'm going to take a jog around the neighborhood to get the lay of things. You say Eddie will be back tonight?"

"Yeah, he called right after I went to bed and said he was going to play one more day. You two go way back, don't you?"

Doc laid his fork down on his plate, pushed his chair back, and stood up. Suzanne couldn't believe how fast he ate his breakfast. It was like he inhaled it as opposed to chewing and swallowing.

"The Street and I have known each other for about twenty years," explained Doc. "We sort of looked out for each other. He was always the brains and the financial clout. I was the muscle. We actually made a pretty good team. I was in a little altercation outside of Python Lee's once, and when the cops showed up, they wanted to take me in. Eddie talked them out of it. He said lessons were learned and after a short conversation with the other guy, he decided not to press charges. Eddie can be very persuasive when he wants to be."

"Don't I know it," laughed Suzanne. "I'd hate to go up against him in the courtroom. Well, I'm off to work."

"I'll follow you to make sure you get there safely."

"What could happen at eight in the morning in broad daylight?" asked Suzanne.

"You want a worse case scenario?"

"No. I guess I should just let you do your job, huh?"

"Exactly, lawyer lady."

"You know," remarked Suzanne as they headed out the door, "you looked quite stunning in that dress you were wearing last night."

"You should see me in this little black number that I have. It's a killer."

"I'm looking forward to sharing fashion tips with you."

"We can do that tonight while we're waiting for your husband to get home."

* * *

Will and Mitch were on their second beer sitting on the number three tee at Cedar Creek. The weather was a pleasant seventy-five degrees with a slight breeze. It was perfect for just about any outdoor activity or just lying in the hammock taking a nap. There was a single ahead of them taking his time. He was playing two balls and studying every shot like he had big dollars on it.

"If I didn't know any better," commented Mitch as he motioned with his can of beer, "I'd say that was Julian out there ahead of us. Let's catch up to him and get some answers on the match at the country club. He owes you more than a simple admission that he didn't play very well."

"All right, but don't pressure the old guy too much," said Will. "He seemed to take the loss pretty hard."

Two holes later they drove up as Julian was getting into his cart.

"Hey, Jules," hollered Mitch. "Do you mind if we join you for a couple of holes?"

"I guess that'd be okay," replied the old guy, averting his eyes.

The three of them played the next five holes at a leisurely pace. Will and Mitch challenged each other with golf trivia questions for a buck each and finally got Julian to join in when Will couldn't answer a question about a tour pro getting penalized for giving advice during a round.

"So how did it go again?" asked Will.

Julian explained, "Tom Watson and Lee Trevino were playing an event, and Trevino was a little frustrated with his play. Watson sensed it and wanting to help, he said something like, 'I've never seen you stand so far from the ball, Lee'. The TV mike picked it up and one of the listeners at home called in to say he just saw a rules infraction, and Watson should be penalized for giving advice to an opponent during a match. The rules officials reviewed the tape and agreed, so he was penalized."

"Wow," said Will. "How did Watson take it?"

"Like a true gentleman," responded Julian. "He didn't complain at all. He knew he was at fault, once they explained it to him. The ironic thing was, Watson had authored a simplified rules book with drawings to help explain some of the more complicated rules. Then he gets caught breaking a rule on live television."

"Good for him," added Mitch. "The game has enough sleaze bags. It needs more positive role models like Watson."

When Julian retrieved his ball from the cup on number nine, he just stood there as the other two turned and headed for their cart. Sensing something was wrong, Mitch went back to see what was going on. Maybe the old guy was having some sort of physical issue. As it turned out, it was mental not physical.

"You okay, Jules?" asked Mitch in a concerned voice.

"No, I'm not okay. Let's go inside for a drink. I've got something to get off my chest."

"So that's it?" asked Mitch. "You threw the match because you owed those two preppie types some cash?"

"Yeah, it was a setup from the beginning," explained Julian. "Somehow they knew all about Will and that you two were good friends. I'm sorry, guys. I hate myself for doing it, but it was the only way I could get out from under the situation I was in. Now that I know you better, Will, I realize what a crappy thing it was to do to you. They told me you were a golf cheat, and you preyed on unsuspecting guys that didn't know any better. The truth is, you're the best golfer I've ever seen, and I've watched some of the best in the game play. On top of that, you two are real gentlemen that respect the game. Listen, I'll pay you back every cent."

"Don't worry about it, Julian," consoled Will. "It wasn't that much money, and the fact that I lost a match at the country club might pay dividends down the road."

"Damn, for a young buck you sure seem to have your head on straight. Not many guys your age would have handled it like you're doing."

"I guess I had a couple of great teachers," admitted Will. "You ever heard of Eddie Davis or Ronnie Green?"

"Yeah, I've heard of them," answered Julian. "Green is from Chicago, and Davis is from Detroit. They're supposed to be two of the best. Never saw either of them play. I don't understand why they never tried the Tour. They could have made some serious dough. It's a shame that Davis died the way he did."

Will and Mitch gave each other a surprised look. Mitch's look turned to a questioning one as he nodded toward Julian. Will nodded back, giving his approval.

"Dude, keep this under your hat," said Mitch in a low voice. "Eddie Davis isn't dead. He comes here all the time. And he's with Will's grandpa, Ronnie Green."

"You're shittin' me!" exclaimed Julian. "Green is your grandfather, and he plays here sometimes?"

"Yeah," said Will. "They like the practice range here cause' nobody bothers them. They don't play the course all that often, but they get out once in a while. Bert knows them, but he keeps it on the down low."

"Nobody bothers them 'cept me," added Mitch. "I first met Eddie a few years back when I asked him to look at my swing. I had no idea who I was talking to."

"So, I suppose you two play golf with them all the time?" asked Julian.

"Of course," answered Will. "Mitch and I even get into their pockets from time to time."

"Man, I would love to play a round with them. I bet they have tons of stories to tell. Hey, I didn't mean it to sound like I'm askin' for a favor. I'm the last guy who should be asking anything from you two."

"No worries, Jules," said Mitch. "Will or I will mention it to them. As long as you keep quiet about it, I'm sure they wouldn't mind playing a round with an old duffer like you."

Julian sat quietly for a minute, trying to get his emotions under control. He scams these two, and they don't even get mad. Then they offer to introduce him to two golf legends. What a strange turn of events! They stood and shook hands. Julian watched the two youngsters walk out the door. The corners of his mouth slowly and almost imperceptibly turned up. His dirty little deed for Worthington and Bengston at the country club had resulted in an unbelievable perk for him. There was something about Will that intrigued him. He wasn't lying when he said Will was the best golfer he had ever seen.

After stashing their clubs in the trunk, Will and Mitch stood in front of their cars by the practice green that was used for chipping and sand shots. They were in an intense conversation about whether they should have seen Julian's scam coming and what they should look for in the future. This was one incident that Will hadn't shared with Ronnie or Eddie. He was too embarrassed to mention it. The hustler was about to bring the subject he and Melissa had been discussing, when out of nowhere a fist slammed into the side of his jaw. The force of the blow caused him to fall into Mitch. The caddy instinctly caught his friend and steadied him. He had seen the guy walk up assuming he was just going to get into the car that they were standing by. Before either could react, Mitch was grabbed from behind. A third guy stepped in front of him and delivered two quick punches to his face.

"You mess with one Easy X-er, you mess with us all," whispered the guy that sucker punched Will. "See you later, assholes," said the third guy as they scrambled into their car and sped off.

Stunned, the two of them walked over and sat down by the practice green. Will felt the side of his face and quickly withdrew his hand. He looked over at Mitch, who was doing the same thing.

"Damn, son, who were those guys?" asked Will.

"I got no idea," responded Mitch, lying back on the grass.

"I'm gonna have a shiner for sure," said Will, still probing his face with his fingers. "Man, Melissa is going to be pissed. What the hell did we do to those guys? Do you think it was a case of mistaken identity?"

"I don't think so. You play any college guys lately?"

"Yeah, I took these two guys over at the Hedge for like a hundred bucks a couple of weeks ago. The strange thing was after they paid up, one of them said I had played his older brother a couple of years ago. When Troy was still in college, he and I took like six hundred off of two of his college buddies, but we only saw a fraction of the money. Little brother was a better golfer, so I figured he was trying to get some revenge. Like I said, I only won a hundred bucks. I had to give them everything they wanted, but I played my ass off for that money. You think this little sneak attack was related to that match?"

"Could be. You know what an Easy X-er is?"

"I got no idea."

"It's a fraternity. It's what Sigma Chi dudes sometimes call themselves."

Will stood up and offered his hand. Mitch grabbed it and pulled himself up slowly. Will had no idea that his punch was coming so he was relaxed, not offering any resistance. Mitch saw his two blows coming, and as a result, he had tensed up. It would have been better if he had just went with the flow. He hoped his jaw wasn't broken.

"You okay, partner?" asked Will.

"Yeah, I think so. Man, this golf business is getting more dangerous all the time. Stinkin' losers. What happened to this being a game for gentlemen?"

They walked over and leaned their backs against Will's Camry.

"This pretty much makes my decision for me," said Will. "Next week is the John Deere Classic in the Quad Cities. It's only about a five-hour drive. I think I'll go down, enter the Monday qualifying round, and try to get into the tournament. It could be a stepping-stone to the U. S.

Open. If I don't qualify for the big one there, I can attempt it next year by playing the local and then the sectional qualifier. I need a caddy next week, buddy. Can you make it?"

"I wouldn't miss it for anything. I'll have to skip a couple of classes, but I'm acing the course anyway. The professor is a golfer, so I'm sure he'll understand. He also appreciates the fact that I'm in my sixth year of college, attempting to pay my way as I go. It's been tough getting classes that don't interfere with my work schedule. If he balks, can I promise him a round with you as a bargaining chip?"

"Yeah, go ahead if you have to. But we're not playing for any money. I'm a little leery of college people these days. Present company excluded. All right, let's head home and face the music. I know I'll be getting an earful."

"You and me both. Hey, we're getting married in a couple of months. You want to be my best man?"

"Sure, if I don't have anything else going on, like a movie or a dinner to go to."

"I'm only asking, because once you win the JDC, you'll be able to buy us a huge gift."

"Seriously, partner, I'd be glad to be your best man. But, you're getting the usual silverware and ice bucket."

"What's the going rate for a tour caddy anyway?"

"Ten times more than what you'll be getting."

"Damn, what a tightwad. What a guy won't do for friendship."

They each presented a fist, then got into their respective vehicles. Their usual smile and a kiss would not be waiting for them when they got home. Even though Mitch wasn't a married man yet, Gloria gave it to him just as bad as Melissa chastised Will.

CHAPTER TEN

—Political Correctness

There's this lady lawyer that works in the same building that I work in. I hear she's really smart on top of being unbelievably gorgeous. One day I saw this guy pick her up after work in a '57 Chevy. He had a really dark tan that he probably got from one of those tanning booths. Why she would want to associate with a guy who was that vain is beyond me. I'm willing to bet that he's a boring accountant or a dude that sits in front of a computer all day. It doesn't seem fair that the geeky types like him get all the smart, good-looking women.

—-Jason Billingsworth, insurance adjuster

There are a large number of people today that are afraid to tell it like it is. If a dude is overweight, then he's overweight. If he's short, he's not marginally tall, he's just short. In an effort to save peoples' feelings, these people are trying to turn us into a nation of excuse makers. 'It's not your fault' seems to be their mantra. Guess what? Most of the time it is your fault. Deal with it. If it really isn't your fault, you will still have to deal with it. Telling someone it isn't their fault, when in reality, it is, doesn't do that person any favors. It's giving them a ready-made excuse to do nothing to solve their problems, hoping someone or something will come along and solve it for them. Psychologists call this 'learned helplessness'.

A teacher once told his class that the one thing he would like to give them was mental toughness. The next day he told them he had made a mistake. If he 'gave' them mental toughness, then it wouldn't have the same value as something they had actually earned on their own. Sweat equity is a beautiful thing and can be a very effective teacher.

Mental toughness gives one a proper perspective on events. Small problems appear to be small problems to the mentally tough. Bigger problems require bigger thinking, but the majority of them are not unsolvable. A high school class instructing students on how to become mentally tough might be of value. It's bound to have more value than a class on how not to offend others by looking at them too long or by not being totally sympathetic to their self-imposed anxieties.

Eddie, Suzanne, and Doc sat around the dinner table finishing a meal that Eddie had prepared. Pork chops with a pineapple glaze, garlic mashed potatoes, and green beans with almond slivers constituted the main course. Dessert was a huge piece of apple pie a-la-mode for the guys, while Suzanne only had a small slice. Later, Eddie and his wife would each do a half hour on their elliptical machine. Doc had already run his usual five miles along with other various exercises. In his line of work, being in top physical shape was of prime importance.

"So, Doc?" asked Eddie. "You get into any trouble today while Suzanne was at work?"

Suzanne gave Eddie the old arched eyebrows look that seemed to be asking for an explanation.

"You see," explained Eddie, pointing at Doc with his dessert fork, "Doc is the kind of guy that hates to see the bad guys get away with anything. It's just his nature. He's like a miniature Jack Reacher."

"Never met this Reacher dude, but he sounds like my kind of guy," said Doc. "Now that you mention it, I did have a discussion with one of the neighborhood bullies. It was no big deal."

Eddie and his wife looked at their houseguest waiting for him to continue.

"Okay, like I said, it wasn't that big a thing. I was out running and...."

* * *

The Detroit native jogged up and down the streets of Eddie's neighborhood getting an idea on how everything was set up. There was a cemetery a few blocks to the west and further across the road was a small airport. Once he had an idea as to how things were laid out, he picked up the pace to about eight minute miles. He turned right off of Territorial Avenue when it ran into the airport and ran north to Goguac Street, where he turned back east. He had only passed a few houses when he saw this big guy standing in his driveway looking down on a much smaller man. The little guy had his hands up in a defensive position because the bigger guy had just slapped him alongside the head. Doc stopped at the end of the drive and put his hands on his knees feigning as if he was trying to catch his breath. Out of the corner of his eye, he watched the proceedings. What the hell was going on here? When the big guy faked like he was going to hit the little guy again, Doc strolled up the driveway. He went right up to the smaller man and extended his hand.

"Name's Doc. I specialize in situations that call for something more than expert negotiating skills."

"I'm Dean," said the confused man, shaking Doc's hand.

"What's going on here, Dean?" asked Doc as he looked at the bigger man.

"I'll tell you what's going on, little man," said the bigger guy. "This little shit keeps dropping his car off of his drive and onto my property. I just showed him what's going to happen to him every time he can't keep his car on the pavement."

"His property runs that close to the side of your driveway?" asked Doc.

"It's pretty close," explained Dean. "The problem is my wife isn't all that good at backing up the car, and as you can see, the drive is really narrow. She'll drop a tire off once in a while. And Boomer here seems to think it's a major deal."

"Hey, Doc," interjected Boomer, "If you know what's good for you, you'll keep your nose out of other people's business. Get back to jogging or whatever you were doing while me and the neighbor settle this."

"That's been one of my problems for most of my life," said Doc, sliding his right foot back behind his left to form a 'T' stance. Boomer didn't appear to be sharp enough to see what was coming. "I can't seem to keep my nose out of other people's business. Dean, do you have a dollar?"

"Uh, yeah," said Dean, pulling out his wallet. "Why, do you need some coffee money?"

"Nope," answered Doc, staring intently at Boomer. "Just put the bill in my hand."

Doc took Dean's bill and stuffed it into his pocket.

"Now that I've been paid to settle this little dispute," explained Doc, "I'm going to slap you around until you agree that a tire that drops off the drive from time to time is not something to get excited about, and certainly not something that would cause a big guy like you to abuse a much smaller man. You ready Boomer? It's gonna happen real quick."

"You're gonna teach me a lesson? C'mon, boy, let's see what you've got."

Boomer never even saw the first slap. It rocked his head to the left and as it was returning to its normal position, the second one from the other direction caught him flush and knocked him off balance. He tried to retaliate, but the jogger was way out of his league. It was like he was swinging at air. It only took half a dozen additional blows for the big guy to admit defeat. The sides of his face were red and starting to swell.

"All right, all right," he bellowed, stepping backward. "I'll leave the little shit alone. Jesus, mister, where'd you learn to hit like that?"

Dean wasn't sure what to make of Doc's actions. He just stepped back, hoping the new guy wouldn't get hurt. After the third slap, he figured the chances of that were pretty slim. Doc turned to him and started to say something when Boomer rushed him. Dean was shocked by Doc's next move. He simply waited for his antagonist to close on him, then he grabbed Boomer by the shirt with both hands and let his momentum knock him backward. On his way to the ground, Doc brought both of his feet up in front of Boomer's hips. When he hit the ground, he extended his legs throwing the big guy over him. It was a perfect judo throw called a tomanagi. The throw is rarely used in competition, but effective when being bull-rushed. Boomer landed on the grass with a thud and a big grunt. Doc completed the throw by doing a backward somersault, placing him on Boomer's chest, where he immediately put the dazed attacker into a frontal chokehold.

"Here's the deal," whispered Doc as he leaned in close to the man underneath him. "I'm going to give Dean my number. If he ever calls me to say you are being a problem, verbal or physical, I will come back here, and trust me, you will wish to God that I hadn't. Call some friends if you want. I can bring a dozen guys that can fight or shoot almost as good as I can."

"Get off me, bitch, before I call the cops," hollered Boomer as soon as Doc relaxed his chokehold.

Doc hopped off quickly. They both watched as the shaken bully got up and staggered back across his front lawn.

Once Boomer was close to his front door, he hollered over his shoulder, "I'll think about your proposition, little man. But it probably ain't gonna happen. My brother-in-law is a cop. Maybe I'll give him a call."

Reaching into his back pocket, Doc slowly brought out one of his favorite weapons. He seldom went anywhere without it. He looked around the driveway for something he could use. When he found what he was looking for, he picked it up and turned his attention back to Boomer. He couldn't believe his good fortune when the bully bent over to pick up the morning paper. In one swift motion, Doc put the small rock in his slingshot and let it fly straight at Boomer's right butt cheek. When the projectile made contact, Boomer let out a yelp, then scurried inside holding his aching backside.

"That was unbelievable!" exclaimed Dean. "Who are you?"

"Just a guy that doesn't like to see the bullies of this world win all the time. I'm gonna run back to the house and get one of my cards. I'll just drop it off in your mailbox. If he ever bothers you again, just give me a call. I'm serious. Make the call, and I'll show up again. Hey, did I earn my fee?"

"Best dollar I ever spent," grinned Dean, holding out a fist for Doc to bump.

Later that day, before Dean went into work, he walked out to his mailbox. Underneath the bills and the junk mail was a business card that simply said, "Doc", with a phone number underneath the name. He put it in his wallet for safekeeping.

* * *

Doc left out the part about firing the rock at the fat guy. He figured it wouldn't be a good idea to tell a lawyer that he used a weapon on someone who no longer posed a threat.

"Never a dull moment, hey Doc?" asked Eddie as Suzanne cleared off the dishes.

"Ain't that the truth."

"So, Doc," asked Suzanne coming back into the room, "how long have you been into women's fashion?" She had been curious as to why their visitor had several dresses, pants suits, wigs, and various other female accessories. She had also noticed some fake beards and moustaches laid out on a table in the spare bedroom that their guest had moved into.

"Before I went into the service, I helped out the police back in Detroit. They thought it might be too dangerous for their female officers, and they wanted someone who looked real young. I was only nineteen at the time. It was a combo hooker/drug sting operation. It was dangerous, but I've always been an action junkie. We put a lot of bad guys away in the six months I worked with them. Then I went into the service."

"The military seems like a perfect fit for you," observed Suzanne. "Why didn't you make it a career?"

"No offense, counselor, but once the lawyers got involved, I figured it was time for me to look elsewhere."

"Lawyers?"

"Yeah. Before we could fire on what we felt were obvious bad guys we had to get permission from the JAG officer. We obviously could return fire, but if there was any gray area it had to go through channels. It was a stinkin' bureaucratic nightmare."

"So a lot of insurgents got away while you were waiting for the legal side to give their opinion on whether it was okay to engage?" asked Eddie.

Doc gave them both a serious look.

"Not only did they get away, a lot of our guys died as a result of our political correctness. Those SOB's fire from Mosques and use children as shields. And we're supposed to worry about accidentally damaging a building or hurting somebody that shouldn't be there in the first place. It's a war over there even though a lot of politicians choose to call it something else. It ain't right, but I guess it's the way the world runs today. Anyway, I was sick of it, so I got out."

With all three of them pitching in, the rest of the cleanup only took a couple of minutes. They went into the living room where Suzanne took her usual spot at the end of the sofa. She had several papers to go over, so Eddie turned on the Tiger game with the sound down low. After two innings of lackluster action, Eddie announced that he was going to Big Daddy's for a couple of hours if Doc didn't have any plans. Doc told him to go ahead. Not one to sit around, he asked Suzanne if he could use the elliptical machine in one of the spare bedrooms.

"As long as you don't break it," answered Suzanne. "I thought you already went for a run today."

"That was my morning workout. I need something a little tougher than just running on a flat surface."

"After your workout, why don't you hit Eddie's super tub in the master bath? You'll like it. You can even watch the rest of the game in there."

"What a cushy job," remarked Doc as he jumped up and left the room. "So far I've only had to smack three guys around and no one has done any hospital time."

Suzanne wasn't sure if he was serious or not about the hospital part. Regardless, she knew she was lucky to have him around. He obviously was more than capable. Eddie sure knew some interesting characters.

Eddie came through the door about an hour and a half later. His wife was still in her spot looking over her paperwork.

"No action tonight, Street?" she asked.

"None. B. D.'s was pretty quiet. There were three guys in the back room throwing dice and a low budget poker game with some clown trying to cheat the other card players."

"How was he cheating, and why didn't someone put a stop to it?" asked Suzanne.

"The cheater was dealing 'seconds', and I'm pretty sure that the other guys didn't know what was going on. They should have because it was definitely amateur hour. Like I said, it was a low budget affair. There couldn't have been more than 200 bucks on the table between the six players."

"What are seconds?"

"Instead of dealing off the bottom of the deck, like the movies portray, the dealer will slide the top card back a little and deal the second card to everyone. He's holding the top card back and will deal it to himself or a buddy when the pot is built up. Obviously he knows what the top card is, and it's usually a face card that will help the recipient."

"Now you have piqued my interest," said the lawyer. "If you saw this guy cheating, and were only there for a short time, why didn't the other guys see it?"

"You don't see a mechanic deal seconds, you hear it. The dealer wraps his or her hands around the deck, making it impossible to see what's going on. You catch the cheater by hearing the second card when it's dealt. You have to hold the deck fairly tight, and when the number two card slips out, it makes a little noise. It sounds like 'ffft'. It's very subtle. It helps if the room is noisy, and if there are other distractions."

"What kind of distractions?"

"Like a couple of huge boobs hanging over the table. The mechanic was a large breasted woman with a low cut shirt on. Those guys wouldn't have noticed if she had fire coming out of her ears. Those huge puppies were definitely the main attraction."

"So what did you do?"

"I told Germaine on my way out, and he said he'd take care of it. B. D. doesn't like cheaters working his place. It gives him a bad name, and it would be bad for business if word got around that card cheats were frequenting the back room."

Eddie didn't tell her everything that occurred with Big Daddy's greeter and general keeper of the peace. Years of keeping things to himself made it hard to totally open up to his new wife. In time, he might be more forthright about his business, but he was used to guarding his cards, and that was a hard habit to break…

* * *

"Later, Germaine," said Eddie as he headed toward the door.

"Leaving so soon, Street?" asked the big man, sitting in his usual spot by the door.

"Yeah, not much action tonight. Listen, I'm holding a substantial wad. Would you mind walking with me to my car?"

Eddie's request was not unusual, as Germaine had provided this service before. Big Daddy's was located in a buffer zone that separated several reputable businesses and a few establishments that attracted a lower class of clientele. The area wasn't prone to a lot of crime, but all it took was one opportunist to sully the immediate area's reputation. Eddie could only recall one fight outside of the club, and that was between two drunks that could barely stand. Germaine and his fellow peace keepers were the main reason that Big Daddy's was known as a safe place to party. They walked out together and down the street to Eddie's vehicle. When they got there, Eddie motioned for Germaine to stay a minute.

"I wanted to give you a heads up on the woman playing in the card game," informed Eddie, leaning back on the front fender of his Monte Carlo.

"The one with the huge jugs?" asked Germaine.

"Yeah. She's dealing seconds and obviously working with one or two others. If any of the guys in that game figure it out, there could be trouble. I'm sure B. D. wouldn't appreciate a team like that working his joint."

"You're right, man. I'll take care of it. Hey, thanks."

"One more thing," added Eddie addressing, the real reason he had come tonight. "How's that little girl of yours doing?"

"She's out of the hospital now. If she takes her meds, the doctors think she'll be fine. It's been hard on her and on me and her mom. She's a tough little kid that's for sure. I had no idea what was involved when she was admitted. Hell, when me and the wife took her in it was the first time I ever set foot in a hospital. It was kind of creepy, but it was where she needed to be. Them doctors sure know their stuff."

"They went through a lot of training to get where they're at," agreed Eddie. "Listen, I want to help out."

Eddie reached into his front pocket and pulled out a wad of bills with a rubber band around it. He kept his hand around it, hiding it from view, and handed it to Germaine. If a cop saw the gesture he might have thought a drug deal was going down instead of a guy helping out someone in need. Germaine looked down at Eddie's offering but didn't immediately take it.

"I appreciate it, Street, but we'll get by."

"Listen, man. There have been situations in my life when I was younger and a friend offered to help me out. I felt the same way you do now. I wasn't sure I should accept what he was offering, but I took it and made a vow to myself that I would return the favor to someone else down the road. That's all my friend expected of me. So take this cash. I hope it will take some of the financial pressure off you and your wife. Kids are expensive. I know. I raised two daughters."

Germaine took the bills and stuffed them in his front pocket. His eyes watered up and he stuck out a fist for Eddie to bump.

"Thanks, Street. It hasn't been easy. I hope I will be in a position someday to help someone out like you're doing now."

"I know you will, man. For now, take care of that little girl."

Eddie walked around and got in and started the Monte. He gave Germaine a wave and drove away. When Germaine got home after his stint at B. D.'s, he took the wad of bills out of his front pocket and took the rubber band off. He sat at the kitchen table and counted out the one hundred dollar bills. There were fifty of them. He couldn't believe it! Eddie Davis had given him five thousand dollars. Now he knew what Buggy Whip Johnson was talking about when he called Eddie Davis a legend. He sat back and grinned. Tomorrow was going to be a beautiful day. With this money he could put a stop to all the annoying phone calls asking when he was going to put some money on his outstanding debt. Like Eddie said, hopefully he would be in a position someday to do something similar. It must be a truly awesome feeling to be able to do that.

On the short drive home, Eddie's thoughts went back to the time he pocketed two grand that belonged to another player after a poker game broke up at the club where he was working. He was only seventeen, but he knew his age was no excuse. When the guy died later that night he held onto the money. The guy was rich, so his widow didn't need the dough. He also knew that was faulty reasoning. As he advanced in years, he did what he could to help those in dire circumstances. Even when adjusted for inflation, the two thousand he stole was just a drop in the bucket compared to the cash he had subsequently given to others. He wasn't proud of what he had initially done, but he used his youthful indiscretion to guide him on a more prudent path.

He wouldn't tell Suzanne about what had just transpired with Germaine. Like a lot of things in his life, he would keep it to himself. Close to the vest was the only way he knew how to play the game.

* * *

"Where's Doc?" asked Eddie.

"He's in your tub. I just got out. He's not as big as you, so there's a lot more room to maneuver if you know what I mean."

Eddie moved in on her and grabbed both her hands. Holding them above her head, he leaned in and sniffed her neck. He followed that with a big kiss.

"If I screamed for my bodyguard, he'd be out here in two seconds, and he would kick your ass," she threatened.

"You don't smell like you just got out of the tub. There are still traces of the perfume that you put on this morning. And he's on my payroll. You still gonna scream for assistance?" asked Eddie as he went in for another kiss.

"I guess not," she said with a seductive smile. "Did you know that he carries a slingshot? I saw it peeking out of his back pocket. It reminded me of the Dennis the Menace comics I used to read when I was a kid."

Eddie sat down next to her and drew her in close.

"Yeah, and he's deadly with it. He usually carries a handful of these little steel ball bearings in his pocket. He's not afraid to use them if the situation is serious enough. The guy is definitely one of a kind. He's the perfect person for this job. I have complete trust in him. I talked to Ronnie a few minutes ago, and it looks like our Vegas match is on for next week. If we pull this off, there won't be any more need for personal security."

"What's Doc going to do when this is over? Go back to living in his car when his money runs out?"

"I've got an idea on that little problem. We're going to introduce him to Herman. Maybe there's a spot in his business for someone with Doc's skills. It's worth a shot."

She looked up with an appreciative eye. They were locked in a serious kiss when Doc walked into the room. As usual, he didn't make a noise when he moved about.

"Hey, listen you two. I can go out for coffee or something if you want to be alone."

"No need," said Eddie getting up. "I'm going to hit the machine for about a half hour. Here, Doc, take my place. She's all warmed up."

Suzanne whipped a pillow at him as he left the room.

* * *

Melissa sat across the table from Will, scowling at him. He was holding a bag of frozen peas wrapped in a towel against his right eye.

"I can't believe you're so mad about this," said Will. "I was defending your honor. There were four of them, and this was all I came away with. You should be covering me with kisses and adulation."

"If I called Mitch would he give me the exact same story?" asked Melissa, pulling out her phone.

"I would have never guessed that the trust would have gone out of this relationship after only a few short years," he whined.

Melissa's phone rang. She looked down and saw that it was Gloria calling.

"You've only got a couple of seconds to change your story," she said, holding her phone up for him to see the source of the incoming call.

After listening to Mitch's fiancé rattle on for five minutes about the dangers of playing golf for money, Melissa told her she would talk to Will about being more careful in the future. She terminated the call and looked back at her husband.

"A little sympathy would be nice," he moaned. "This hurts pretty bad."

"I'm sorry for being angry with you," she said, coming around the table. "It just scared me seeing your face like that. So you were jumped by a couple of frat boys, huh?"

"Yeah, we never even saw it coming. Stupid jerks."

She offered her hand, and they went into the living room. Once they were comfortable on the sofa, he went over the whole incident. When he was done, he told her that some sort of sympathetic gesture was in order. She relented and gave him a soft kiss.

"I do have some good news," he announced. "Next week my caddy and I are going to enter, I hope, a legitimate competition. We're going down to Silvis, Illinois, to try and qualify for the U. S. Open. And if we qualify, no one will be wanting to take a swing at either of us. You don't mind if I go, do you?"

"Not if it will keep you from getting beat up again."

"I didn't get beat up. Some dude just sucker punched me. There's a big difference. Hey, let's do a fantasy thing. You can pretend you're making it with a hard core barroom brawler named Gypsy Dan."

"Gypsy Dan?"

"Yeah. I travel around a lot on my chopper and like to get into fights. You can be my hot girlfriend, Gypsy Dawn."

"You're starting to get delirious," she said, rising from the sofa. "Tomorrow we're going to get that eye x-rayed. Let's go watch some TV from the bedroom."

"Gypsy Dan don't need no x-ray. He just needs some good lovin'. What do you say, Gypsy Dawn?"

"I say, doctor, tomorrow morning. Let's go to bed. Bring your peas with you."

CHAPTER ELEVEN

Horse Dreams

Instead of learning how to handicap the races effectively, my buddies and I came up with a foolproof plan. We would stand behind Ronnie Green when he was making a bet and then listen in. He countered our strategy by whispering his bets to the cashier. When that didn't work, he just wrote down the numbers on a little piece of paper and slid them across the counter. I guess he was afraid of other bettors driving down the odds on his picks. That's a selfish move if you ask me. Then one of the boys came up with another plan. That one really sucked and some of us paid a serious price due to our lapse in judgment. We should have figured out a way to make the first one work.

—-Davie "The Weasel" Kaehler, currently doing five-to-seven for race fixing

America has its share of sports nuts, no doubt about it. Not everyone goes crazy over March Madness, the Masters, the World Series, or the Super Bowl. But there are enough followers willing to spend their hard-earned money to keep the players in luxury cars and homes that the average person could not even dream of. Next to your personal fitness and health, is there anything better to be a hard-core fanatic about? Rooting for your team is a great way to forget about all the problems that people are asked to deal with at work and in their personal lives.

Walk into any bar in a strange city and spot your favorite team's jersey on a stranger, and you've just made a friend. You will be welcomed into the group like a long lost high school buddy. They might even buy you a beer if you have an interesting story about one of the team's stars.

Drive through any neighborhood in the summer and you're bound to see moms and dads in the yard playing catch with sons and daughters or kicking a ball around. If there's a basketball hoop at the local park, there's bound to be enough players to get a game up. Yup, if you're going to go overboard on anything in your leisure time, it's hard to beat sports, whether you're a fan or an active participant. Go Cubs!

Herman drove east through southwest Michigan on I-94. He turned off the interstate when he got to the Sprinkle Road exit in Kalamazoo. He was always glad to get out of the city into an environment that was a little more relaxed. The Battle Creek/Kalamazoo area had its share of bad guys, but it was nothing like the big city. People just seemed a little friendlier here. They certainly weren't as obnoxious as the people that he was used to dealing with. Then again, the seedy element in the big city is where he got most of his business. If it weren't for cheaters, scammers, and other devious types, he'd probably be working some dull security job for a big corporation. That's one of the things he liked about doing jobs for the two Michigan hustlers. No matter what the situation was, it always proved to be interesting and exciting at the same time.

The regulars at the Gull Lake View Golf Course bar and grill were used to seeing Herman stride into the room. He usually stopped in the doorway, and after checking out everyone in the room, made his way to Ronnie and Eddie's table. There were varied opinions on what their business was. Some thought he was making payments on a loan to the two golfers. It was impossible to keep their operation under wraps for the several years they had been using the GLV complex as their home base. They weren't crazy about how many people knew their business, but there was nothing they could do about it. Their true colors were bound to come out sooner or later. The other prevailing opinion was that Herman was some sort of government undercover operative reporting to his handlers.

Herman's firm had done business in the past with the Chicago Police Department and the State Police, but he always steered clear of the feds. Politics, hidden agendas, and ambiguous goals were enough to make him turn down the hefty fees they had offered for his services. He had enough challenges to solve without taking on something that could possibly spin way out of his control. That was one thing he admired about his two golf clients. They were usually in full control of their situation. When it got to the point where they weren't in control, they called him.

The private detective sat down at the table where Ronnie, Eddie, Doc, and Buck were having some sort of animated sports discussion. Buck was there to look after Kathy. Like Doc, once she was safely at work, he had most of the day to himself. Doc stood and shook Herman's hand when they were introduced. Herman had heard of him through Ronnie, but this was the first time they had actually seen each other.

"Good to see you, Herman," said Ronnie. "Have a seat. Eddie's buying, so don't hold back."

Herman ordered a club sandwich and ice tea. He wanted to add fries and a burger, but he was struggling to stay around 250. For him, anything over 250 would hamper his ability to do his job. Once the dishes were cleared, Herman got down to business.

"Here's your Vegas itinerary. You fly there on Monday, arriving around noon. The rest of the day is up to you. On Tuesday you play a practice round at the Las Vegas National Golf Club. Your match with the Karpovs will take place on Wednesday, Thursday, and Friday. The format and all the other particulars are up to you. The old man wants to play for $125k a piece. I wouldn't try to smuggle that much cash on a domestic flight, so I suggest you mail it to your buddy, Hot. He can hold it for you until you get there."

Hot Mernan was a Vegas legend in his own right. He was part time gambler, part time gigolo, and part time casino employee. If you asked the Vegas crowd, he was a younger version of the guy who did the "Most Interesting Man in the World" commercials. He was instrumental when the guys went out to Vegas to marry Suzanne and Kathy a few years ago.

"There's one other thing that we had to agree to," continued Herman, "and I hope this isn't going to be a problem. Since you're playing in the U. S. on your home turf, Alexei, the dad, wants to choose the referee for the match. You could have one of your own refs too, but we all know that it would probably lead to more trouble than it would be worth. The guy's name is Viktor. He's Russian, but has been living in the states for a number of years. Owns an import/export business and does quite well. He loves golf and plays to a five handicap. We checked into his business history, and it looks pretty clean. He doesn't have much debt, so he's not into anybody for big dollars."

"It looks like Estelle has done her homework, as usual," commented Ronnie.

"Yeah, she's a marvel when it comes to cyber investigating. She's the one who actually came up with the whole match idea. She's also going to contact several newspapers to play up the human-interest side of the story. You know, a father and son from pretty much a non-golfing country coming to a country filled with golf courses and challenging a couple of experienced players. Remember, the whole point of this exercise is to have the Russians shoot off their mouths about how good Andrei is and how they're going to take down two cocky Americans at their own game. If the media does their thing, and you beat them, it should be a real embarrassment to the Russians. Here are your plane tickets. The rest of the gig is up to you. One more thing: I checked the weather, and it's supposed to be dry and hot. I'm sure I don't need to tell you to start drinkin' early and keep it up throughout the match."

"Damn," said Buck. "This reminds me of a *Mission Impossible* scenario. I was on the stunt team for two of those movies. I wish I could be there to watch it all come together."

"It's going to be a team effort, as usual," added Herman as he stood and wiped his eyebrow with two fingers. It was the hustlers' signal that the hook was set and things looked promising. "We've all got our jobs to do. Good luck, guys. I hope you don't need it."

Eddie stood quickly and followed Herman out. He stopped him at the door and talked quietly for a few minutes. He was smiling when he rejoined the others at the table. When this was over, Doc had an opportunity in Chicago if he chose to head west.

Later that day, Will and Mitch were standing on the range at Cedar Creek. They caught a lot of flak about their appearance. Both of them had nasty looking shiners that looked painful to the touch. On the bright side, Will's x-rays showed no damage to his facial structure. The soft tissue damage would take a while to heal, but other than that, there shouldn't be any lasting complications. Mitch looked a little worse, but his x-rays showed the same result.

Will hit shots with every iron under Mitch's watchful eye. Mitch wasn't the coach that Eddie and Ronnie were, but he knew Will's swing almost as well as they did. The range was empty except for an old man with a close-cropped beard sitting in a lawn chair at the opposite end.

About twenty balls and a few clubs were on the ground in front of him. He appeared to be taking a break, reading a golf magazine—looking for game-improvement tips, no doubt.

"Am I done, Coach?" asked Will after he pounded two picture perfect drives out onto the range.

"No way," responded Mitch. "We've got situation shots that we're going to run into out on the tournament course. I don't know anything about where the qualifier is played, but I will by tomorrow morning."

"C'mon, man," insisted Will. "You know I don't like practicing for more than a half hour at a time. My swing is as good as it's going to get. Let's go play."

"That's what I'm talking about. If you're going to play the Tour, you need to take more of a working man's attitude toward the game."

"You're taking all the fun out of it," said Will.

"All right," explained Mitch. "We'll compromise. If you can hit the next five shots exactly as I describe them, then we'll go play a few holes."

Will hit a high draw with his driver followed by a low cut. Then he flushed his 3-iron out to about 235 yards. His fourth shot was a knockdown sand wedge to the practice green about ninety yards out and to their right. He looked at Mitch waiting for him to describe the fifth and final shot of the challenge.

"Okay, number five," said Mitch, "and if you don't execute this one we hit balls for another half hour and you buy lunch."

"Do you want me to drop my pants while I play the shot?"

"No, wise guy. Just take out your 4-iron and hit it to the middle of the practice green straight out ahead of us."

Will eyed the green that Mitch was referring to. It was about 160 yards out. He choked down a little on his club and played the ball back toward his right foot. With an abbreviated swing, he made contact right on the club's sweet spot. They both watched as the low flying ball hit about ten yards in front of the small green, bounced twice, then trickled onto the front edge.

"You hack!" exclaimed Mitch. "I said the middle of the green, not the front edge."

Will just stood there grinning. His shot was a thing of beauty, and Mitch knew it.

"All right, let's go slap a few around," said Mitch. "But I'm going to make it tough on you. If you're going to go up against the big boys, you're going to have to act like you know what you're doing. I don't want to be embarrassed out there."

"What about you?" asked Will. "How much do you know about caddying in a Tour event?"

"Like the Lynard Skynard song says," replied Mitch. Then he sang, "*I know a little about love, baby I can guess the rest.*"

"Once we get there, maybe I can find some fifth-grader looking for work," lamented Will.

"Whatever, hotshot. I'll go get my clubs. Go get us a cart and meet me over at my car."

"Got it, boss."

Mitch was mumbling to himself as he walked by the old guy who was still reading his magazine. As usual he was in awe of Will's ability to hit a golf ball. The guy could do anything with that little white sphere. Even more impressive, was that if a gun would have been fired over by number nine green in the middle of Will's backswing, he would have still executed the shot perfectly. His power of concentration was truly remarkable. He remembered once when Will was practicing chip shots over at GLV. Mitch had pulled up in a cart to within ten feet directly behind Will. He had three more balls to go, so Mitch just sat there watching. When Will holed the last one, Mitch asked if he was ready to go. Will was startled when he heard Mitch talk to him. He was concentrating so hard that he didn't hear the cart pull up.

The caddy grabbed his clubs from the trunk, and when he slammed the lid a familiar face was standing there. It was one of the frat boys from the other day.

"Hey, nice shiner," he said. "We were informed that we only gave you a $100 beating the other day."

"Yeah," smirked the second guy who had come up behind Mitch. "I guess there was a communication problem. We were supposed to give you a $200 beating. Our bad. Imagine our luck finding you here at the very same spot where you got your first ass whuppin'."

Mitch was grabbed from behind and held by two incredibly strong arms. He braced himself for another punch to the face. When it didn't happen, he opened his eyes to see the taller guy on the ground holding his right side and moaning. Looking to his left he saw the old man running toward them putting something in his back pocket. The guy behind Mitch let him go and took up a defensive stance with fists up. The old man made short work of the college boy. He palmed his feeble punches aside and delivered only two of his own—one to the body and one to the face. That was enough for the young man to ask for mercy.

"Help your friend up, and get out of here," ordered the man. "For the rest of your lives, you and your buddies are to avoid these two at all costs. Trust me, you don't ever want to see me again."

Will pulled up in a cart and watched as the two frat boys walked slowly to their car. He turned back to Mitch and the old man for an explanation. The man stuck out his hand.

"Name's Doc. Street sent me."

"Damn, Doc," said Mitch. "What brought the first guy down? He was laying there holding his side like he was kicked by a horse, and you were still several feet away."

Doc pulled his slingshot out of his back pocket. Then he retrieved a small steel ball bearing from the ground and pocketed it.

"These little guys will kill a small animal, but they just hurt like hell when they hit a human body. I never aim at a guy's face unless someone's life is in danger."

"You ever hit a guy in the face?" asked Will.

"Yeah, once."

"What happened?"

"Like I said, a guy's life was in danger. Hey, when did this game of golf get so dangerous? I thought it was supposed to be a gentleman's game."

"Apparently there are a lot of guys that didn't get the memo on the gentleman part," said Will. "Listen, we're going to grab a sandwich and then head out to play a few holes. You want to play along?"

"Sure, but I'm not in your league."

"No worries," said Will. "By the way, Mitch is buying, so order whatever you want."

"I don't care if he goes in the pro shop and orders a new set of clubs," said Mitch. "It would be worth it. And I'm not just talking about the beating. After that, I would have to go home and face Gloria again. Man was she pissed after the last time. And a lot of it was directed toward you, Will."

"Me? Maybe we should head to Silvis a few days early. This place is getting too dangerous for a couple of law abiding, honest American citizens. By the way, Doc, do you have any cash on you? I'll give you six a side for fifty bucks?"

* * *

Greer and Donaldson's people had not bothered anyone since the parking lot incident with Suzanne and Doc. The entire group, including wives and bodyguards, sat on Ronnie's back patio waiting for their steaks and chicken to come off the grill. The girls and Doc opted for chicken while the others waited patiently for their rib eyes. Ronnie and Kathy both prided themselves on their ability to put a first class meal on the table for their guests. In addition to the meat, there were baked sweet potatoes with cranberries and raisins. Green beans with bacon bits and a simple salad of lettuce, celery, green pepper, and tomatoes, topped with Gorgonzola cheese completed the menu.

"Man, Grip, you sure can throw a feast," said Eddie. "Kathy, did you have any idea that this guy could cook like this when you first met him?"

"Nope," she giggled.

Ronnie, standing by the grill, arched an eyebrow at his wife. The only time she giggled was when she was drinking wine, and it usually took more than one glass. He looked over at Suzanne and saw that she also had a ridiculous grin on her face. Suzanne had driven to Richland straight from work to help with the meal. Ronnie met Eddie's gaze with a 'how much have these women had' sort of look. Eddie just shrugged his shoulders. He knew that his wife was working on an extremely difficult case, so a night of wine and good food certainly wouldn't hurt. And, maybe there would be some of his favorite extra-curricular activities when they got home.

When the meal had disappeared and the dishes cleaned away, Ronnie and Eddie lit up cigars. Gloria was surprised when Mitch accepted a smoke from Eddie and lit it up with the two older guys. She was somewhat aware of Ronnie and Eddie's reputations, but she had no idea what was coming.

"Let's make sure everyone is on the same page here," started Eddie. "Ronnie and I fly out of O'Hare for Las Vegas on Monday. Mitch, when do you and Will leave for the Quad Cities?"

"Early Sunday morning," answered Mitch. "We're going to play a practice round at the qualifier course, then look for some place cheap to stay. The next day, Will qualifies for the tournament."

"Sounds like a plan," said Ronnie. "Except for the cheap place to stay part."

Ronnie pulled out his money clip and peeled off three one hundred dollar bills.

"You can't play first class golf staying at second rate motels. Find a nice place where there won't be any wild parties going on in the next room. You both will need to be well rested."

Eddie followed suit and handed over three hundred of his own.

"And be real careful where and what you eat," he added. "No spicy or greasy food. You don't want to be more concerned about where the next port-o-potty is than the shot you are about to hit."

"Thanks, guys," said Will as he handed Eddie's offering over to Mitch.

"Mitch," said Eddie changing the topic. "What are you going to do with your business degree after you graduate?"

"Well," said Mitch, a little surprised at the question. "Since it's taken me almost six years to get through college, I've had time to think about it. Ideally, I would like to buy a franchise restaurant or a small business with a good location as a starter. An entrepreneur isn't just a guy that starts his own business. He might also take over an existing business that he thinks he can improve. Interest rates are still pretty low, so I'd have to put the pencil to the paper to make sure it was doable. The problem is, I'd have to come up with a substantial amount before a bank would even talk to me. So, I'll obviously have to set my sights a little lower."

"How much cash would you have to come up with to walk into a bank with your proposal?" asked Eddie.

"About 200k," answered Mitch.

Eddie looked over at his partner and got the affirmative nod he was looking for. Mitch's situation was something they had been discussing lately, and they came to the conclusion that if he needed some business start-up money they were willing to take a chance. Mitch was a smart, hard-working young man. Because of this, they both felt that investing in his future would be a noble, and possibly profitable, thing to do.

"Tell you what, Mitch," continued Eddie, pointing his cigar at him. "Ronnie and I will front you the 200k at the least possible interest rate to make sure it doesn't look like a gift to the feds. Maybe later on, we'll turn it into a share of your business empire. We'll let you decide on that."

"That's a lot of money, guys," said Mitch as he mulled over their offer. The proposition was a complete shock, so he needed a little time to process what was going on. He showed his maturity by not coming back with the usual 'are you sure' question. Eddie and Ronnie were both successful men that he respected immensely. He wasn't going to insult them by asking if they were 'sure' about their offer. "And it's bound to be somewhat risky," he added.

"Everything in life is a risk, Mitch," assured Ronnie. "Think about it. You don't have to give us an answer tonight. Go ahead and put the pencil to the paper and see what you come up with."

"Thanks, I'll do that," said Mitch, looking at his fiancé to see what her reaction was.

Gloria couldn't believe what she was hearing.

"You two aren't kidding, right?" she asked. "You would really loan Mitch the money to start up his own business. I mean, 100k each is a lot of money. I don't mean to be impudent, but I guess I didn't realize you were that financially well off. I'm sorry, I probably shouldn't meddle."

"It's all right, Gloria," interjected Suzanne. "You'll get used to these two the more you're around them. By the way, Street, my birthday is coming up. Since you're so loaded and willing to make huge loans, what are you thinking about getting me?"

Eddie looked at her with a glint in his eye. He liked her when she had a couple glasses of wine in her. Her inhibitions dropped quickly after that second glass.

"I was thinking about getting you a '62 red Impala that I've been looking at."

"Is it a stick or an automatic?" she asked.

Her little comment reminded Ronnie when a few years ago he saw the two of them in Eddie's tub together. She had asked to borrow his 'Vette, and Ronnie told her it was a manual transmission. That was when Eddie made his comment about her excellent stick handling abilities.

He was in the middle of sipping on his drink when Suzanne asked her question this time. The sip turned into a surprised gulp and he started coughing. The group gave him a questioning look. Suzanne figured out what his problem was and gave him a devious wink. He immediately looked over at his wife to see if she had caught the gesture. Kathy was still staring at him.

"That would be a very cool gift, Eddie," said Kathy. "I hope my very generous husband doesn't try to outdo you when my birthday rolls around."

"I was thinking about a new set of pots and pans, but maybe they will have to wait until next year," said Ronnie. "The ponies have not been good to me lately."

"I just love his practical side," said Kathy. "He's a better cook than I am, so he would be the one using them anyway."

"Busted, Grandpa," said Will. "Hey, tell us a racing story. How about one where you made a big killing."

"Okay, here's one that I don't think I've ever told anyone. Back when Maywood and Balmoral still had harness racing, I was at Maywood looking for an angle that would hopefully turn into a big profit. To make a long story short, I saw that this one driver was working the first three races at Balmoral, then he showed up on the Maywood program for the sixth race. It's probably about an hour between the two tracks depending on the traffic, so why was he driving three races at one, then driving across town for just the sixth race at Maywood? Then I saw that he was scheduled to drive the tenth race back at Balmoral. That was a lot of traveling for just one race. Why did the trainer or the owner of the horse insist that this guy drive for that particular race? He was the horse's regular driver, but something just didn't add up."

"I assume it was not a misprint?" asked Mitch.

"I decided to wait and see," continued Ronnie. "I had my own rating system for the drivers, and this guy was a solid 'B' in my book. He wasn't one of the top drivers, but he was good enough to bring home a horse that had what it took on any given night. He knew how to keep his horse out of trouble and could be counted on to get him into a position where he would at least finish in the money. When the horses came out, sure enough, he was in the sulky."

"What's a sulky?" asked Gloria.

"The little cart that the horse pulls," answered Mitch.

"Anyway," continued Ronnie, "I'm watching the tote board. The horse started out at 8 to 1, drifted down to 5 to 1, then back up to 7 to 1 just before post time. The so-called "smart" money usually comes in at the end but not always. I assumed that a small bundle that was placed early on him to win dropped his odds by those three figures. Intrigued, I paired him with six other horses in the exacta and put a hundred on him to win. When he won, I made 480 on the exotic bet and 700 on the straight win bet. That's about how much I take off of Eddie each time we play, but that usually takes a couple of hours. This little investment only took about two minutes."

"Since the straight bet paid more, why didn't you just bet more on that one?" asked Gloria, who was about to graduate with a math degree.

"Good question. For two reasons: one, his straight bet odds would have probably dropped if I would have bet, say three or four hundred on him, and two, if one of the other long shots would have come in second, the payoff would have been over a thousand for the exacta. As it was, the second place horse went off at 3 to 1. The third place horse was a 14 to 1 long shot. If that horse would have finished second, the payoff would have been huge."

"Wow, there certainly is a lot of calculating in horse racing," remarked Gloria.

"Yup, and after all the figuring, and over a grand in profits, I still screwed up my betting. Can any of you figure out where I went wrong?"

They all looked at each other, trying to ascertain where a guy who made over a thousand dollars on a race had messed it up. Eddie just sat there with a huge grin on his face. He raised his hand as if he were back in the classroom. Ronnie looked them all over, then called on Eddie.

"This is purely hindsight," explained Eddie. "I liked the way you spread your money out. Depending on how big the pool was, like you said, if you would have bet, say 300 on him to win, his odds might have dropped to 4 to 1 or even worse. You would still have made more, but you would also have risked a lot more. As it was, your total bet was 112 bucks. Would it have been wise to make at least two exact bets on your six horses? It would have only cost you twelve more dollars."

"You got it," said Ronnie. "I should have done that, and I should have made six more exacta bets putting him in second place. It would have only cost me a total of twenty-four more dollars, but I would have gotten the best return on my investment. Damn, Street, you figured that out pretty quick. Why are you wasting your time playing poker?"

"Maybe I should go into the horse racing business," mused Will.

"I think you should stick to golf," said Melissa. "I worry enough about that as it is. Besides, Grandpa Ron says there are a lot of devious types hanging around the race track."

"Why do the women here have the traditional jobs while the guys have the fun, exciting jobs?" asked Gloria. "I mean, we've got body guards and gamblers here tonight. They should make a movie about you guys."

After a short discussion on the pros and cons of an exciting nontraditional job, the women went inside to get the desserts. The guys paired off and made small talk. Doc and Buck were comparing notes on their security jobs. Mitch and Will talked quietly about their upcoming trip to the John Deere Classic. Eddie leaned over and whispered to Ronnie, "Dude, this is great, but we have to eat dessert and run. It's hooker night, and I don't want to mess it up."

Ronnie's eyes went wide. "What do you mean, hooker night?"

"What, you don't role play with Kathy? We've got like hooker night, Hadji, the cabana boy, and Omar, the tentmaker. Just to name a few."

"You're makin' that up," whispered Ronnie in disbelief. "There's no way Suzanne would go for something like that."

"Oh yeah, I forgot Mr. Sakamoto, the Japanese masseuse. I'm just telling you why we have to leave pretty soon. You believe what you want."

Suzanne, looking through the kitchen window, was watching her husband and his partner in an intense conversation. She was pretty good at reading lips, and she thought she recognized the names Omar and Hadji.

As they finished their apple pie, Ronnie leaned over and whispered to his wife. She giggled and shook her head in amazement.

"Don't believe everything you hear, Ronnie," offered Suzanne. "Eddie likes to make things up from time to time just to get a rise out of people. You should know that by now. Sometimes his imagination gets him in trouble."

"I thought so," said Kathy.

They all thanked Ronnie and Kathy for their hospitality and said their goodbyes. The two hosts walked everyone over to their vehicles. Ronnie was standing close to Eddie when he heard Suzanne's comment.

"You lead, Omar, and I'll follow."

He turned to Kathy. "Did you hear that? She just called him Omar!"

"Calm down, Ronnie," cautioned his wife. "I'm sure you're hearing things. Eddie, I don't know what you told him, but you can see it's got him all worked up. C'mon into the house. You and Buck can watch the end of the Cubs game while I clean up the kitchen."

When Kathy turned around, Suzanne suggestively raised her eyebrows at Ronnie and opened her car door.

* * *

Mitch sat up straight in bed and took a couple of deep breaths. Gloria stirred and propped herself up on an elbow.

"What's the matter, hon? Did you have a bad dream?"

"Sort of," he answered in a low, wispy voice. "It's not a nightmare. It's just weird, that's all. And it's not the first time I've had it. I'm gonna go down and get a glass of orange juice. Do you want anything?"

She shook her head and lay back down. When her fiancé didn't return after ten minutes, she slipped out from underneath the covers and went looking for him. Stepping quietly into the kitchen, she saw him sitting at the table staring out the window. Gloria walked softly up behind her future husband and lightly placed her hands on his shoulders. She kneaded his trapezius muscles, hoping it would relax him.

"You want to tell me about it?" she asked in a gentle voice.

"It's kinda stupid, I guess," he answered. "Okay, we're supposed to share everything, right? So, here goes. You know how much I'm into sports, especially huge dramatic moments—like something that happens maybe once in a career or in a lifetime."

Sensing that this was going to be a long-winded explanation, she came around and sat across from him and motioned for him to continue.

"Of all the things I've read about and of all the old video clips I've seen, this one scene from a movie keeps showing up in my dreams. It's unbelievably dramatic, like when Willis Reed came walking out onto the floor in the NBA Championship when no one thought he would be able to play."

She gave him a sympathetic look that said she had no idea what he was talking about.

"You see, Reed was hurt and his appearance was an unbelievable inspiration to his teammates and to the fans. Anyway, Willie Mays' over-the-shoulder catch, off Vic Wertz, in the 1954 World Series was another one. Those two events were one-of-a-kind moments. But that's not like my dream. Remember a couple of weeks ago when I told you about my horse dream? The one where I was standing out in a field watching horses run around like they were playing some kind of game? And there was this one beautiful stallion that was apparently the leader. He was like one in a million or one in a hundred million. I just had a different dream, and now I think I know who that horse romping around in the field is. It's Secretariat, the famous thoroughbred, but in my new dream he's walking down the tunnel before the Belmont Stakes, the last race of the Triple Crown. It was a scene from a movie that I saw a couple of months ago, but it stuck in my mind as an incredibly powerful moment in sports. I have no interest in horse racing, but I see that unbelievable horse walking through the tunnel being led by this guy with a hat on—huge muscles in his legs and steam coming out of his nostrils. He is an amazing physical specimen, I mean, for a horse. Anyway, the guy's face is partially obscured because his hat is pulled down over his eyes.

"So you think you are the guy leading this horse?"

Mitch looked up at her and stared intently into her eyes.

"No. I'm the jockey waiting at the end of the tunnel. I'm my normal size, not small like jockeys are. I don't think it would have mattered how big the jockey was in that race. He won the Belmont by thirty-one lengths! Can you believe it?"

"That's unbelievable," said Gloria, reaching over and taking his hands in hers. "Well, since we're both up, why don't we go back to bed, and you can show me your own personal riding style. It'll help us both go back to sleep."

Mitch got up and followed his fiancé. Her shapely rear in her pajama pants preceded him up the stairs. He was about to have sex with a beautiful woman, but he couldn't get that damn horse out of his mind.

Mitch rolled over on his back and waited for his breathing to return to normal. He and his soon-to-be wife both had satisfied expressions.

"If I didn't know any better, I'd say you were the only stud in this room tonight. I'll take a real stud over a dream one anytime."

Mitch reached over and took her hand in his. He stared at the dimly lit ceiling and tried to make sense of his nocturnal brain activity.

"There's one more thing that I didn't tell you. I think the horse, Secretariat, is a symbol for something else. I know I'm supposed to figure this all out, but the clues are somewhat ambiguous, like a murder mystery, only without the murder."

"A symbol? A symbol for what?"

"Not for what, for who," said Mitch as he rolled half way over to look at the shadowy figure lying next to him. "I think the horse is supposed to be Will. How's that for ironic weirdness? Are you sure you want to marry a guy with stuff like that running through his head?"

"Absolutely. Now I've got a question. If this famous horse in your dream is supposed to be Will, do you think you're getting your hopes up a little too high? You've said before that you two are a couple of small fish in a really big ocean looking for crumbs that the big fish are leaving behind. I mean, you two are such good friends, is there a chance that you are seeing him as you would like him to be and not who he really is?"

Mitch rolled over to his other side and fluffed up his pillow. "Fifty-eight, darling," he whispered. "Fifty-eight. You were there. You saw it. Good night. I'm going back to the field to watch the horses play. Maybe they'll let me join them this time."

CHAPTER TWELVE

–Margarita Round

There's a lot more to my fiancé than meets the eye. On the surface, he looks and acts like a sweet, motivated guy that wants to start his own business once he graduates college. Then you meet his best friend and the other men they hang around with. They're somewhat secretive about their business, and I'm not sure what they do for a living. Hopefully, they aren't into anything illegal. I get the feeling that our life together will be anything but ordinary.

—-Gloria Lockhart, Mitch's fiancé

Eddie zipped up his travel bag and slung it over his shoulder. A few days earlier, he and Ronnie had shipped their clubs to Ronnie's friend, Hot, in Las Vegas. They also sent a package containing $250,000 in one hundred dollar bills via certified mail to him. Ronnie assured his partner that Hot would know what to do with it. He was totally trustworthy.

He checked his watch. It was time to pick up Ronnie in Richland, and then they were off to Chicago. The plan was to leave their car at Herman's place. He, or one of his people, would drop them off and pick them up at O'Hare when they returned. Last night, after seeing Will and Mitch off, they discussed the need for security while they played the Karpovs. They decided to get Herman's take on that issue when they saw him in the Windy City.

* * *

Mitch was at the wheel of Will's trusty Camry rolling west on Interstate 80. The air conditioning was acting up so the windows were down making it hard to carry on a conversation. Will looked over at his caddy as the traffic slowed down to a crawl. Apparently there was some sort of problem ahead. Two minutes later they came to a complete stop.

"You do realize that part of a caddy's job is waiting on me hand and foot like a butler?" asked Will. "I'll need foot rubs, back rubs, and lots of refreshments. I also require a soothing story at bedtime—nothing too scary or too violent."

"Not gonna happen, superstar," returned Mitch. "And I want your word that you will not change after we win this thing. We'll go back to Michigan with fatter wallets and a little bit of notoriety, but other than that, we'll be the same humble, lovable guys that we've always been."

"Of course. I'll be back on my mower Monday morning, like always."

"Heaven forbid, and I don't think this is going to happen, but if we don't win, but do fairly well, would you consider playing a few more Tour events? There should be some that we wouldn't have to travel very far to get to."

"I don't know, man, maybe I should change my attitude about Tour golf. After doing all the talk shows and maybe a few commercials for all the products I'll be asked to endorse, I'll have to cut my ties to the past. I have to think of my image, and I can't let anything or anyone drag me down."

"Geeze, you're gettin' the big head before you've even teed it up."

"Mitch, you know how I feel about all the traveling and all the hype that goes with professional sports today. It's a circus that I'd rather not be a part of. All those company logos on their shirts and hats. They look like walking billboards. I'd be surprised if they actually used the products that they're promoting. I guess I inherited that line of thinking from my grandpa. Can you see me doing an interview without laughing? 'Uh, Will, how did you feel when you hit that wedge two feet from the hole on number one?' or 'Will, did you ever think you could really win a tour event?' I'd be surprised if they didn't ask me what I had for breakfast or my shoe size. Let's just get in there, win some cash, and get out. Oh yeah, and hopefully qualify for the Open. How high do I have to finish to get in to next year's Open?"

"I'm not sure," answered Mitch. "I'll have to check on that."

"Dude, for a Tour caddy, you're getting off to a slow start."

"I'll be back in form once we hit the short green stuff."

"One other thing you forgot to check on."

"What's that?"

"Due to the fact that I have no credentials, I can't just waltz into the qualifying course, plunk down my entry fee, then tee it up. There's a pre-qualifier for guys like me."

"What?" hollered Mitch, squeezing the steering wheel. "You better be kidding!"

"Nope. There's a pre-qualifier for all the nobodies. The actual qualifier will have Tour players in it, and I guess they don't want a bunch of hacks throwing a wrench into their game."

"If they won't let you in, why are we making this trip?"

"Because I went down to the Pinnacle Country Club the day before we got our shiners and played in the pre-qualifier."

Mitch looked in disbelief over at his partner. Will's grin took up his whole face.

"Why didn't you ask me to go? What did you do for a caddy?"

"Some kid was hanging around the pro shop. He said he was a member, so I asked him if he wanted to make fifty bucks. He wasn't you, but he did okay. He kept my clubs clean, and he was pretty good with the yardages."

Will could tell that Mitch wasn't too happy with him for keeping his little trip a secret.

"Look, buddy," explained Will, "I knew you were busy trying to get ahead in the class you're taking so you could take a couple of days off for the real tournament. You told me yourself that the professor wasn't real happy about you missing your two classes this week."

"That's true, but you should have mentioned it. It was only for one day. I could have made it work. Do I need to ask how you did?"

"We're heading back there, aren't we? Okay, that was a little too cocky. I played pretty decent. Birdied the last hole to get to three under and squeaked in. Never made a putt over ten feet."

"With me on the bag it would have probably been six under," said Mitch as the traffic finally started to move.

Ten minutes later they both looked out the passenger window to see what the cause was for the big slowdown. There were two semis off on the shoulder and three guys were transferring the load from the one that was apparently broken down to the other one.

"Are you kidding me?" asked Mitch. "We sat for a half hour because three guys were working on the side of the road. Bunch of stinkin' gawkers."

"Is this a great country or what?" asked Will as he pulled his hat back down over his face and leaned back in his seat.

*　*　*

Herman's secretary dropped the two hustlers and her boss off at O'Hare. Herman decided he needed to accompany them as an extra precaution. He didn't feel comfortable with the guys walking into a possible hostile environment with no backup. He also called Tina to see if she was available. The muscular stuntwoman readily agreed when she heard that Ronnie and Eddie were involved. She lived in Los Angeles, which is about 275 miles from Vegas. The plan was for her to drive up the following morning, giving her and Herman ample time to go over the basic security plan.

They checked with Hot, and he said he could put everybody up, but Tina declined. She said she would stay with a friend in the area. The guys got a kick out of Tina's mysterious lifestyle. She was definitely one of a kind and one tough ally when things got interesting.

"You ever been to Vegas, Herman?" asked Eddie, once the plane leveled off somewhere over Iowa.

"Yeah, I've been there a few times. It was always for a job though. Vegas is the kind of city that preys on guys like me. Gambling ain't my thing. I'll leave that to the guys that know what they're doing. I actually do know a lot about blackjack. A private dick that I know from Reno hired me a few years ago. He put together a team to try and catch a card counting group from New Jersey. Apparently the Vegas casinos don't like skilled card players, so when they catch them, they ban them from the casinos. At least, that's what happens to the lucky ones, if you know what I mean."

"Impress us with your knowledge of blackjack," challenged Ronnie.

"A card counter cruises along with minimum bets until he sees a deck or a shoe that is rich in face cards. More tens means more blackjacks and, the big advantage is, if you have a bad hand, twelve through sixteen, you don't have to hit it while the dealer still does. And there are more double down opportunities when there is a disproportionate number of tens left in the deck. So, when the deck is lean, the counter raises his bet. Of course this might draw the attention of the dealer, the pit boss, and the camera guys upstairs. From what I saw, the casino employees acted like the winners were taking the cash out of their own pockets. It was like they hated to see anybody win. To me, anytime someone wins big, it should be chalked up to good publicity. And that should bring more customers in. It's like a built in marketing plan."

"Makes sense to me," agreed Eddie. "One of the poker regulars back in B. C. told me he tried counting cards for a while. He was up a couple of hundred at a Vegas table when he saw this guy walk from the bar over to his table. The guy played two hands for twenty, then he threw a hundred dollar bill down on the table. He said the dealer was only about half way through the shoe, but he decided to shuffle up anyway. The guy acted like he was pissed and picked up his hundred and left. The pit boss walked over and the dealer told him he just spotted a counter, and when he shuffled up the counter took off."

"Sounds like a high roller on his way to catch his flight out of town and back to the real world," observed Herman.

"That's what this guy said," continued Eddie. "He was the actual counter and the dealer didn't even know it. Unless there was a team working the tables, there's no way a guy could get enough information from two hands that would warrant such a huge increase in his bet. Just like you said, Herm, he was probably on his way to the airport and wanted to end his trip with a big win."

"All right, we're impressed," said Ronnie. "I had no idea you were that knowledgeable. So the casinos don't like guys that can keep track of the cards?"

"Nope, they contend it's a game of luck and not skill, which doesn't make much sense to me," continued Herman. "They admitted to our investigative group that eighty to ninety percent of the counters that think they can count aren't very good at it. So I'm thinking why not open the doors and let the counters have at it? The home team still has the one big advantage—they play last. The dealer could bust and still win six out of the seven hands being played at his table."

When Ronnie gave him a quizzical look, Herman continued, "The players had to play first and all but one busted their hands. By the way, do you know how many players can actually play at a standard blackjack table?"

"Like you said, seven," answered Ronnie.

"Nope. Theoretically twenty-one people can play at one table."

"Where would they sit? There's no room."

"Two people can stand behind the person sitting at the table, and they can place their bets in his circle. The person sitting is the only one that can actually play the hand. And, there are certain conditions. The total bet from all the players at one spot cannot exceed the table limit, and the bet must be stacked so it looks like one bet. That's for the convenience of the dealer if he has to pay off the bet. The players need to take care of dispensing their winnings amongst themselves."

"I can see how it can get somewhat confusing," observed Ronnie. "Especially when you throw alcohol into the mix, which is a given. Why would a guy want to get in on somebody else's action, letting him call the shots?"

"I can think of two reasons," continued Herman. "One, is the obvious—there are no open spots, so betting on someone else's hand is your only option if you want to play. The second one would be that you don't know much about the game, but your buddy does, so you just lay your money on top of his and let him play for you. By the way, did you know that casino employees call the little round discs checks instead of chips?"

"I thought they were poker chips?"

"They are, but they call them checks."

"Did you know that, Eddie?" asked Ronnie.

"Yup," answered Eddie. "Except in the poker rooms. The experienced players call them checks, but the tourists call them chips."

"One more thing about the number of players at a blackjack table," added Herman. "There had better be an experienced dealer and pit boss for it to happen. You know, real take-charge kind of guys, so there isn't a lot of time wasted explaining something simple to a bunch of yuppie types. Their job is to keep the game moving. More hands equals more profit for the house."

"Damn, Herm," said Ronnie. "Since you know so much about the game, are you going to try your luck at the tables?"

"Ha, I've never played the game. Like I said, I got a crash course so I could be an educated observer. And I didn't have a problem with my assignment. The team that we were trying to bust was breaking the rules. If it were just one guy that was an effective counter, then I probably wouldn't have a problem with it. With others doing the counting for him, he could sit back and wait until he got a signal that the shoe was hot, and that's cheating in my book."

* * *

Will and Mitch sat at a clean, comfortable motel in the small river town of Fulton, Illinois, about 45 minutes north of the Tournament Players Club at Deere Run. They decided that all the action at and around the golf course would be distracting, so they opted for someplace quiet to settle down and plan their strategy. Will's four under earlier in the day at the Pinnacle Country Club qualified him for the big show. Tomorrow, they would play a practice round at Deere Run, and since they weren't involved with the pro-am on Wednesday, they had a day to relax and maybe hit a few balls at a local course.

Whatever happened, the next few days were going to be very exciting and a real eye-opener for the hustler and his caddy. Will rarely played in long pants, and he had never played in front of a big crowd before. He didn't think either would be a problem, but the only way to find out was to get out there and play the game. After hanging up his shirts and pants, he decided to take a little nap. Mitch was over at the convenience store across the parking lot looking for snacks and something to drink. As Will lay on the bed, his thoughts went back to the day he shot a 58 on the East Course at GLV. Mitch and Gloria had walked out of the bar area holding a pitcher of margaritas and three plastic cups....

* * *

"Dude, we're going to have to hustle if we want to get all eighteen in," said Mitch. Then he added in an Australian accent, "Hopefully this Sheila won't slow us down."

"You just worry about yourself," challenged Gloria, heading to the first tee.

Will watched Gloria tee up her ball. She was a shapely blond that Mitch had met in college during their freshman year. He marveled at the fact that he, Ronnie, Eddie, and Mitch were all involved with such good-looking women. Gloria, like Melissa, also possessed an outgoing personality that would often turn feisty. He loved the little arguments that he would get into with Melissa. They never argued in a mean sense. It was more of a courtroom discussion, that more often than not, ended up in a wrestling match. Surprisingly, she was fairly strong, and if he let up at all, he would find himself underneath her. He chuckled to himself, thinking that was not an entirely unpleasant experience.

"Hey, amigo," whispered Mitch, "did you just look at my woman's gorgeous backside when she teed up her ball?"

"I did, man, and I must say that you have an excellent taste in female attractiveness."

Gloria walked back to the cart as the guys prepared to hit their drives. She filled three glasses from the pitcher, and when the guys walked over she handed them each one. Then she held hers up for a toast.

"To a beautiful evening on the golf course," she said, following her speech with a big gulp. Apparently there was a little more alcohol in the drink than she was expecting. She started coughing and spit out what she hadn't initially swallowed. Mitch looked over at Will.

"That attractiveness we were talking about is somewhat diminished by her lack of drinking skills. We'll work on it, and if Melissa is allowed to join us the next time, I promise you her manners will be vastly improved."

"You goof," said Gloria, getting behind the wheel. She drove about thirty yards and stopped at her tee shot. After the first hole, they decided that after five shots, Gloria would pick up and carry her ball to the green, where she would putt out.

On the sixth tee the pitcher was almost empty, and by a unanimous vote, they decided to stop for a refill at the turn. Gloria turned to them after another disastrous tee shot and innocently asked, "Do you guys think I could hit the ball better if I had breast reduction surgery?"

"Are you crazy?" wailed Mitch. "Why would you want to mess with one of nature's most beautiful creations? Those little puppies are perfect."

"You should know better than anyone that they're not so little," she said. "Besides, I was talking to Will."

"Uh, no," stammered Will, searching for a way to extract himself from the conversation.

"So it wouldn't bother you at all if you had two balloons strapped to your chest? You could still hit all those beautiful shots?"

"Help me out, partner," pleaded Will. "Your woman is getting out of control here."

Mitch took Gloria gently by the elbow and walked her a few feet away. He gave her a big kiss and looked into her eyes.

"Sweetheart, your boobs aren't the problem with your golf swing," he explained. "There are plenty of ladies on the tour with huge knockers, and they seem to do all right. Have I ever told you how beautiful you are when you get your feisty on?"

"Yes, but that's probably because we were both drinking at the time," she answered. "I'm sorry if I embarrassed you or Will. I thought we were just having fun."

"We are having fun, doll, but it's starting to turn somewhat serious, and I'm afraid the subject of your beautiful chest will have an undue effect on what's going on."

"I don't understand. What's going on? We're just playing golf and drinking margaritas. You two aren't gambling, are you?"

"A little. We always have something on the game. What I'm talking about is that Will has birdied the first five holes. This could get very interesting if he keeps it up."

"And you think that talking about my boobs is distracting him? Is that it?"

"Actually, no. Nothing distracts him on the golf course when he is focused."

"You sure know a lot about him and his golf game, don't you?"

"Yeah, it's my job. What I'm really worried about with all this sexy talk is that I might lose my focus and start choppin' it all over the place and that might throw off his rhythm. It's unbelievable how the Tour guys can play so well in the pro-ams when there's a ton of distractions."

"It's just golf, Mitch. It's not like he's a famous heart surgeon or anything."

"Do you know who his grandpa is?" asked Mitch in a serious tone. "Or who his dad was?"

"No, should I?"

"Let's just say that you won't find them in the ranks of the dull and the ordinary. They are very special people, and Will has the talent to be right up there with them. He is also very special even though he doesn't act like it."

"All right," she said. "I'll do my best to not bother Mr. Awesome."

"Thanks, doll," said Mitch, slapping her affectionately on the rear as she walked back to the cart.

Will was sitting in his cart sipping on his drink thinking about his grandpa and Eddie. He knew they were being hassled by some big city tough guys. Hopefully, they could solve their problems without calling in the big guns. Whenever Herman got involved the tension factor immediately went up. His grandpa had once told him that if the situation became serious, Herman and his late father could be very dangerous people.

"Hey, superstar," said Gloria, releasing him from his thoughts. "I have just been informed that I can't talk anymore about my gorgeous physique. I believe you are up. Let's pick up the pace, guys. I'm thirsty, and I have to pee."

Will almost fell out of the cart when he saw Mitch's expression. He stood and pulled a club from his bag. His tee shot on the short par four sixth was positioned perfectly.

Golfer and caddy sat in Will's cart and looked at the front nine scorecard. They didn't know what the front nine record was, but it was safe to say that a 29 would be right up there. Gloria, on Mitch's orders, came out of the building carrying three ice tees. She also had two emergency beers stuffed in her back pockets. They figured they had about one hour before it would be too dark to see the ball. Gloria offered to just ride along and enjoy the scenery for the back nine.

Will kept up his stellar play by making birdies on the first three holes. On the thirteenth tee, while Mitch was preparing to hit, he walked over and stood by Gloria's cart. He reached into the open compartment and pulled out the beer that she was hiding. He took a big swig and handed it back to her. She raised her open hand for him to slap.

Mitch started the car and looked over at his fiancé. Her eyes were drooping, which meant it was an even money bet that she would be asleep before they got back to B. C. He leaned over and kissed her. She smiled and snuggled into her seat trying to get comfortable.

"I liked playing with you guys more than I thought I would," she admitted. "Let's do it again real soon. So, how did Will do? Did you win any money from him?"

"Not exactly. The jerk shot 58. It was probably the course record, but we need to keep it under our hats."

"So why is he a jerk if he's so good?"

"I meant that affectionately. And he's a jerk because he could be making big bucks out on the Tour, and instead he's hanging around with us slamming margaritas and sneaking beers."

"You weren't supposed to see that. Oh, well. Take me home and show me how special you are."

"Now we're talkin' my area of expertise," said Mitch as he put the car in gear.

* * *

Will opened his eyes when Mitch entered the room with a soda in each hand. He sat Will's on the bed stand.

"I asked around, and there's a whole bunch of restaurants across the river in Clinton, Iowa," said Mitch. "Let's just kick back here for a while and then go exploring. Remember what Ronnie and Eddie said about eating food that wouldn't upset our stomachs."

"I remember," said Will, taking a sip of his drink. "Let's find something to eat and maybe a golf course with a practice area. I actually feel like hitting a few balls. Maybe I'll work on a few trick shots to wow the fans."

"You better be kidding," said Mitch. "We didn't come here to put on a side show. We came here to win this thing and make some real money."

"I like your optimism, partner. I hope you still have it as we walk up the 72nd hole."

"See," said Mitch. "You're already assuming that we will make the cut. It looks like we're on the same page here."

* * *

"Jeeze, it's hot," said Ronnie

"Yeah, but it's a different kind of hot than we're used to," said Eddie, standing on the fifth tee at the Las Vegas National Golf Club. "I'm going to put some small towels in my bag tomorrow, so we can soak them with cold water and put them on the back of our necks."

"Good thinking," added Ronnie. "What's our plan of attack? Remember, you're the brains of the outfit."

"Well, if our opponents win the coin toss or guess odd or even on the tees that the referee is holding, they will choose the first round format. That's fine with me. I want to get a look at their games before we choose."

"And if we win?"

"Simple. We defer our choice, letting them choose first. I can't believe the ref wouldn't let us do that. Even though he's Russian, he's lived in the U. S. for a long time, and I'd wager that he has watched a lot of football games. The winner of the coin toss in football usually defers to the second half. It would also be his first decision on how the match is to be played. If he is going to be biased toward his fellow countrymen, this wouldn't be the time. He would wait until it actually had a bearing on the outcome of the match. Which format we play first shouldn't be as important to them as it is to us. They know what kind of game we will bring to the table. We won't know theirs until we see it. I assume the kid is extremely long, which means he hits a lot of short irons into the fours and can probably reach most of the fives in two. As far as his father's game, your guess is as good as mine. He obviously can play, but is he counting on the kid to carry the team? If he is, we can take advantage of that by making it more of a team game."

"Like an alternate shot?" asked Ronnie.

"Yup. That would force the dad to hit half of their shots from the tee or the fairway. Like I said, I want to see their game before we decide."

"One way or another, this is going to be exciting," observed Ronnie. "Sort of like the good old days, but for a whole lot more money. I hope it comes down to the team that plays the best golf and not some other unpredictable event."

"That's Herman's and Tina's department," said Eddie, looking over at the female side of their security team. She waved from her cart. "I hope this heat won't be a factor as far as security is concerned. Where is the other half of the team anyway?"

"He's back sitting in the air conditioned bar," laughed Ronnie. "One of the perks of being the boss. Don't worry, he's the one we want here if things get ugly."

CHAPTER THIRTEEN

All The Way, Win or Tie

Last week I watched this guy work the crowd for bets at a golf course across the river. It was a long drive contest where they took your three longest drives out of five attempts. There was something about the way he did it. He seemed so confident. That was enough for me to want to get in on the action. Easiest hundred I ever made.

—-Duke Stevenson, golf course manager

Doc and Buck sat in Kathy's kitchen drinking coffee and comparing notes. Greer and Donaldson had struck again with the dead cat routine, putting Kathy and Suzanne on edge. The stunt was ridiculous, but it proved to them that these guys were not going to stop until they got what they wanted. At dinner the previous evening, Doc and Buck found out that their interests ran along the same lines. Buck had to stay in shape for his career as a stuntman, and Doc's nature wouldn't let him be in anything but top physical condition.

Since the latest cat episode, they decided to combine forces. Suzanne was now staying at Kathy's house in Richland. The plan today was to hit the YMCA in Portage. Doc wanted to lift weights for about a half hour, then he was going to swim laps in the pool. Buck wasn't much of a swimmer; so he was going to lift for an hour, then take a five-mile run.

Doc showered and dressed after his swim and went looking for Buck. When he couldn't locate him, he went back to the weight room. Two guys wearing judo gis were practicing on some mats over in the corner of the room. They both had black belts tied around their waists. Doc found a seat on one of the nearby weight benches and quietly observed their technique. After watching for five minutes, he decided that the taller guy was a little more accomplished, but they both seemed a little slow and somewhat sloppy. He wondered if their rank was actually earned or if it was a reward for showing up for a long period of time and paying their dues at the dojo. The taller guy looked over at Doc.

"What do you think?" he asked, not expecting a serious answer.

"I know the space is limited here," explained Doc as he rose and walked over. "But if you want a serious observation, neither of you are getting the kuzushi that you need. What you're doing looks like it's taking too much muscle. If you get your opponent off balance and in the position you want to make the throw, it shouldn't take all that much effort to finish it. As you know, it's all about technique."

The shorter man proved that he was a true judoka when he asked Doc to show them what he was talking about. Doc slipped off his shoes and bowed his way onto the mats. He spent the next ten minutes showing the two of them how to be more effective when making their throws. His manner was smooth and his explanations simple. When he turned to leave, ten people had gathered around watching the three of them.

"Thank you, sensei," said the shorter man.

The taller man added, "Can I ask you who your instructor was?"

"He was a sixth degree black belt from South Korea," answered Doc. "He was a very talented and honorable man. He wasn't too crazy about the Japanese, so he taught us all the throws and terms in English. I had to learn the Japanese terms later."

"He was obviously a great teacher," said the taller man.

"That he was," said Doc as he slipped his shoes back on.

Buck was part of the small crowd that was watching the exhibition.

"Damn, Doc," said Buck as he slapped him on the shoulder. "It sure looks like you know your stuff. I'll bet you could make big money teaching martial arts in the city. Have you ever done that?"

"Nope, never have," replied Doc. Right before he left for Vegas, Eddie had told Doc that Herman might have some work for him back in Chicago. Buck's comment started him thinking about maybe opening up his own dojo when he wasn't working for the big guy. He knew a guy that might lend him some cash to get started. The phone call from Eddie had been a Godsend in more ways than one.

* * *

Will and Mitch sat in the Culver's restaurant parking lot, deciding on their next move.

"You know," said Will. "That grilled chicken salad wasn't bad. A steak would have been better, but since you have taken on the job of food nanny, I have to compliment you on your first choice."

"Thanks, and we'll be picking up some bananas and apples to snack on for later. The guy at the counter back there told me there's a golf course only a couple of miles from here, and they have a practice area. If you still want to hit a few, let's go check it out."

"You're running this show," said Will. "Drive on."

Mitch turned left at the sign that said 'Valley Oaks Golf Course'. Another left, then a right, brought them to the course. The parking lot had at least fifty cars in it, which was surprising for a Monday night. He figured there must be some sort of league play going on. He walked around the building to see what the practice range was like. When he rounded the corner, he was surprised to see that the range was packed with golfers. He turned and went into the building.

"What's going on out there?" asked Mitch, motioning toward the range.

"They're warming up for a long drive contest," answered the guy behind the counter. "It starts in ten minutes over at the first tee. You wanna get in? The fee is a hundred bucks, and it's winner take all. You get to hit five drives and we take the longest three that are between the flags."

Mitch looked out the window at the first hole. There was a small creek about forty yards in front of the tee. Small flags were on either side of the fairway starting at about 230 yards from the tee. The flags ran half way up the hill where the first green sat. He grinned and pulled out one of the hundred dollar bills that Eddie had given him.

He told the counter guy, "This is for my buddy that's out in the car. I'll go get him."

"I'll put him at the end so he has time to warm up," said the guy. "He makes number fifteen, so the winner gets fifteen hundred, cash. What's his name, and where's he from?"

"Willy Green, from Hickory Corners, Michigan. He's just a hack, but this will give me an excuse to make fun of him. I just hope he doesn't embarrass us."

"Whatever, man," said the counter guy, handing over a small mesh bag with about fifteen balls in it. "This should be enough to get him warmed up."

Mitch went back to the car where Will was listening to a serious head-banging tune on the radio. His partner opened the driver's door and turned off the key silencing the radio.

"This is going to be a short practice session," observed Will, looking at the less than full bag of balls in Mitch's hand. "I know we're on a tight budget, but don't you think we could afford a full bag?"

"Grab your 7-iron and your driver," instructed the caddy. "We've got an opportunity to make some money here."

On their way across the parking lot, Mitch explained the situation. They walked around the building to the practice area that was now almost empty. The contestants and the rest of the crowd were headed down the cart path toward the first tee. After going through his stretching routine, Will hit the first five balls with his 7-iron. One of the contestants stopped behind him and watched the last two.

"Nice," he observed. "But you're going to have to hit it a little further than that to win this. There are a couple of real brutes over there."

"Hopefully, we won't come in last," said Mitch grinning.

"We? What are you, like his caddy?" asked the guy over his shoulder.

Will just shook his head as he motioned for Mitch to throw him a ball. Mitch had saved the quality balls for the driver. These were nothing like the Pro V's that would be furnished at the tournament practice range. He wiped the ball clean with his wet towel and tossed it to Will. The hustler teed it up and looked down the range. There was a mound with a small pond behind it at the end of the range and what looked like a white pump house. His first drive carried the mound and landed in water. His second attempt sailed right over the top of the pump house.

"Don't hurt yourself," advised Mitch as he wiped down the next ball. "This is going to be small potatoes compared to what we're going to win on Sunday."

Will stroked the next three balls off the middle of the clubface and said he was ready. They walked down the cart path toward the first tee. There was close to a hundred people standing around rooting for their favorite contestant. A guy held up a sign for quiet, and a ball rocketed off the tee down the fairway. It was between the flags, and a few seconds later a two-way radio came to life. Two eighty-two announced the scorer on the tee. He then wrote the number on a big white board. Will stopped a guy that was walking toward them.

"Hey, do the contestants have to furnish their own balls for this?" he asked.

"Yeah, the guy on the tee will inspect them before you're allowed to hit to make sure they're legal," came the answer.

"You get your balls back, right?" asked Will.

"Yup. The guys out there in the carts will put them in a small bag with the contestant number on it," added the guy.

Mitch turned around and headed back to the pro shop. He came out with two sleeves of Titleists. He caught up with Will as he stood at the edge of the crowd. A huge guy was on the tee taking practice swings. He looked to be around 6' 8" tall and close to 300 pounds. Apparently he was a crowd favorite due to all the clapping and screaming he received right after he was introduced. He tipped his cap and proceeded to rip his drive out to about the 300 mark. Will turned and mouthed "wow" to his caddy. Mitch just shrugged his shoulders and handed over the balls.

When it was Will's turn, the whiteboard was almost full of numbers. The big guy was the leader with an accumulative total of 860 yards. His first two totaled him 600, but the next two were hooked out over the flags, so he had taken a little off his last swing just to keep it in play. He managed a mediocre pop of 260 yards. That still put him in the lead by ten yards.

When Will stepped up on the tee, the crowd had thinned out by half. Apparently they didn't think the skinny kid in the fifteenth spot was up to the task, so they headed back to the bar to celebrate the big guy's imminent victory. On the tee, the announcer looked at his sheet and hollered, "All the way from Hickory Hills, Michigan, Willy Green." Then in a lower voice directed at Will, "Hit 'em quick, kid. I'm getting thirsty."

Will stepped up and went through an exaggerated stretching routine. Mitch used the time to get down a few bets. The contestant that had talked to Will on the practice tee was still in the crowd standing next to his girlfriend. His three best efforts barely got by the 270 mark. He watched Mitch as he moved through the crowd, asking for takers on a hundred dollars. Mitch turned and looked at Will. He shook his head slowly, indicating that he was unsuccessful. Will grinned and teed up his first ball. He aimed left and started the ball toward the practice range. The little white sphere flew straight for a hundred and fifty yards, then it made a radical right turn back toward the fairway, landing dead center and stopping at the 250 yard marker. A guy that had refused Mitch a minute earlier tapped him on the shoulder holding up a hundred dollar bill.

"It's two-to-one now," explained Mitch. "He's only got four balls left."

"Deal," said the man.

As soon as he stepped away another guy took his place. About half of the people remaining immediately turned and headed back toward the clubhouse, figuring this last contestant was somewhat of a joke. The guy standing with his girlfriend had been watching Mitch intently. He turned to a buddy standing behind him.

"Hey, Benny, a hundred says this guy wins it all."

"You can't be serious," said Benny. "You're on."

Mitch looked at the guy and winked when he heard the wager. Will teed up his second ball. Just before he walked up on the tee, Mitch had told him that the right side of the fairway looked a little firmer. On their way down to the tee, he had noticed that the balls landing on the left side weren't rolling very far. Will's second drive cracked off the clubface, straight at the flags that lined the right side of the hole. It made a gentle left turn and bounded down the fairway.

"Two ninety," came the result over the radio.

The remaining crowd whooped it up with clapping and whistling. The line of people that was heading back up the cart path to the clubhouse stopped to see what all the commotion was about. A few started back in the direction of the tee. Will teed up his third ball. Mitch, surprising everyone, stepped onto the tee and encouraged the onlookers to make a lot of noise. Responding to his gestures, the crowd hooted and hollered. Will's third drive was a carbon copy of his second one. The crowd quieted down waiting for the result.

"You won't believe it!" hollered the guy over the radio. "That last shot is only about two feet from the one he just hit. Another 290."

The crowd, fueled by the excitement of the situation and by the alcohol they had consumed, erupted. They kept it up as Will quickly teed up his fourth ball. He wasted little time, making a smooth swing and catching the ball on the center of the clubface. This shot traveled dead straight stopping five yards short of his two previous drives.

Hearing the result over the radio, the guy running the competition told Will he didn't need to hit his last drive. His 865 total was the winner by five yards. The crowd went berserk. Mitch, and the other contestant that bet on Will, collected their winnings.

Back inside the clubhouse, Will laid $200 on the bar, then added another $40 for the two bartenders. He told the people in the bar, at least the ones that could hear him, to drink until it was gone. This brought on another cheer. A young boy came up to Will with a small plastic bag containing four balls. The number '15' was written on the bag. He took three balls out and signed them with a felt tipped pen that was lying on the bar. Then he told the boy to put them in his pocket—joking that they might be worth something some day. Then he signed the other one and nodded towards a teenage girl that was sitting at a table with her parents. He recognized her from the front row down at the first tee cheering him on. He told the boy to give the girl the other ball. Before the girl and her parents could thank him, he and Mitch were out the door.

One of the contestants was standing by the bar, and he happened to see Will sign the balls for the young boy. He elbowed the guy standing next to him.

"Did you see that?" he asked. "That Green dude just signed the balls he used in the contest and gave them to that kid. Who does he think he is, a Tour pro? If he's that good, why doesn't he enter the JDC and play against the big boys? Apparently he thinks that winning a long drive contest makes him a celebrity."

"Man, Iowa sure is a friendly state," commented Mitch as they crossed back over the Mississippi River bridge that separated the two states.

"They were nice," agreed Will. "Most of the people back there were probably farmers. Farmers tend to be decent people. They're usually out working the land or tending to their livestock. That means they don't have any coworkers to screw up the works or to be mad at. The only thing that would piss them off would be the weather. Kinda like our business, huh, Mitch?"

"I'm sure they worry about crop prices too," responded the college business major. "You are right about having no one to blame but ourselves if things go wrong."

"Hey, I gotta ask," added Will. "What was with all the hollering while I was hitting back there?"

"I was worried that someone might scream in your backswing," explained Mitch. "Some dude that had money on the leader or just didn't want to see an outsider win. So, if everybody was making noise, I figured you couldn't be bothered. Noises don't usually bother you anyway, but you might have had an involuntary reaction to something really loud when everyone else was being quiet. Why didn't you correct the guy when he said you were from Hickory Hills instead of Hickory Corners?"

"I don't know," mused Will. "I guess it's all about lying low and not trying to draw attention to myself."

"You do realize that there will be television cameras at the tournament?" asked Mitch, not expecting an answer. "Our days of lying low are pretty much over unless you put on one of Doc's disguises."

"Well, that ain't gonna happen. Truthfully, what are our expectations for this week? We don't really expect to win, do we?"

Mitch pulled into the motel parking lot and turned off the engine. He looked over at his partner and best friend.

"You want the truth? I would be surprised if you didn't win and shocked if you didn't finish in the top ten."

"Just like that?"

"Yup, just like that. I truly believe that we are going to shake up the golf world this week."

"I'm glad you are so confident. What if I tank it and shoot 80 or something? It wouldn't hurt our regular hustling business. I'd look like a big choker, and that wouldn't be all bad."

"True, but even if you win this thing, we can still go back to hustling. You would just have to come up with some games where the opponent, knowing that you have won a Tour event, would still feel that he had a chance. It would test our resourcefulness, but it wouldn't be an impossibility."

"Dude," said Will, holding out a fist to bump, "I'm glad you're on my team."

"I'm with you all the way, man—win or tie."

CHAPTER FOURTEEN

Carmine

Hot Mernan? Yeah, I know him. He sleazes around Vegas like a damn snake, taking advantage of rich, lonely women. I don't know what they see in the guy. My wife says a lot of the local women know who he is, and they view him as some sort of sexual legend. I better not catch her talking to him. If he knows what's good for him, he'll stay out of Mandalay Bay. The last time he was in here, he sat at my table. After twenty minutes, he was up a couple a hundred. The pit boss finally stepped in and told him he should take his winnings and move on. He obviously knew Mernan's rep. Serves him right. We don't need his kind around here.

—-Herbie Phillips, blackjack dealer, jealous husband

Doc, Buck, and their two charges walked out of a Kalamazoo restaurant. They decided that, since there had been no incidents lately, a night out was something they all could use. Doc wondered what the other three would say if they knew that only a few weeks ago he was penniless and living out of his car. He decided that was something he would keep to himself. Thanks to Eddie his life had changed, and he was the type that never forgot a favor.

Doc was about to open the passenger side door for Suzanne when a black cargo van screeched to a halt between them and the building. Two guys jumped out brandishing handguns. They were dressed all in black, and their faces were covered with ski masks. There was nothing the two bodyguards could do, as they were in no position to make any sort of defensive move. The two men motioned for the group to get into the van. There were no seats, so they had to sit on the floor with their backs to the van walls. They drove slowly out of the lot and onto Westnedge Avenue.

"Alright, people," said one of the guys with his face covered. "You know what this is all about. Since you wouldn't listen in the parking lot a while back, we had to take some more drastic measures. By the way, who was that psycho bitch you were with? I couldn't believe it when two of our boys came back and said they got their asses kicked by some dame in high heels. Anyway, we've been watching you for a while, and we've got your routines down. Ladies, what the hell are your husbands thinking? Why don't they just play our bosses and get this whole freakin' stupid thing over with? It's a simple request. Just have them play the match and everything is settled."

"They have their reasons," answered Suzanne.

"I'm sure they do, lawyer lady," said the first man. "But is it worth getting someone hurt over a fucking golf match? This little exercise here is your last warning. Where are they anyway? We haven't seen them around."

"They're out of town," offered Doc. "And they won't be back for a while, so you'll just have to tell your bosses to cool it."

"Listen, Doc. Yeah, we know who you are. Word is that you're one bad sumbitch in a fight. Well, I don't know a man yet that can whip a fast-moving bullet. You need to get your golfers back here so a match can be set up. My boys and I hate this place, and we want to get back to the real world."

"The real world?" asked Kathy.

"New York City, Red," explained guy number two in a thick east coast accent. "How in the hell do you people live here out in the middle of nowhere? There's no action."

"You're just going to tell your bosses they'll have to wait for a few days," explained Doc.

"I can't tell them that," said man number one. "They're pissed enough as it is, and I think you know how unstable they are."

"Set up a meet then," directed Doc. "I'll explain the situation to them."

"Sounds good to me," said the first man as he took off his mask. "You have your talk, and if you guys can get something settled, then our asses are out of here. Hey, the cats and the parking lot scene—those were some other jerks following the bosses orders. It's embarrassing enough working for these clowns, but a guy's got to eat, right? Besides this ain't the kinda job where you get to pick and choose your assignments. We meet in two days at the arboretum on the west side of Battle Creek. Seven in the evening. Just drive back in there, and we'll find you. And you better have some good news. If we have to come back here, somebody could get hurt. It ain't our call. It's just the way it is, right tough guy?"

"I guess," answered Doc as the van slowed to a stop. The guy in the front passenger seat jumped out and opened the sliding door.

"Watch your step, ladies," said the guy offering a hand to Kathy. She refused the hand and stepped lightly down onto the pavement.

"I don't think we should bother Eddie or Ronnie with what just happened here," said Doc as they pulled out of the lot.

"I agree," added Buck. "If they are successful out in Vegas, then maybe this whole thing will go away. They need to do their thing with as few distractions as possible. Sorry about letting them get the upper hand ladies."

"It wasn't your fault," conceded Suzanne. "If someone really wanted to, and had a little bit of imagination, they could find a way to do just about anything to someone else."

"Unless you're the president or a super rich dude," added Kathy. "If you lead a somewhat normal life, you're bound to be exposed at some time or another. You two did fine by not taking any action. If you would have, those guns might have gone off. I know they were there to just scare us, but who knows what might have happened if either of you would have forced their hand."

Once the girls had retired for the evening, Doc and Buck sat at the kitchen table talking in low voices.

"You got a plan for this meeting?" asked Buck.

"Yeah, I had time to think about it during the drive home. I have to make a call tomorrow. I don't know where he is or what his number is, but I have to talk to a guy named Dennis. Books, at Python Lee's, will know how to get in touch with him."

"Who is this Dennis guy?"

"He's a vet and a member of a Detroit motorcycle gang. But that's not the reason I need to talk to him."

"What can he do for us?"

"He's a shooter. And he's one of the best there is."

* * *

Anthony Trenton sat across the dinner table from his father. Alfonz Trenton had built up the family "business" from a small flower shop to a maze of companies. Most of them were tax shelters, but a few of them were legitimate and actually turning a profit. This wasn't due to the fact that his companies were more efficient or more productive than the competition. For some reason, anyone in a similar business within a few hundred miles seemed to run into a series of unfortunate events. Delivery trucks with faulty brake systems, along with several unexplained fires, seemed to plague the competition.

"Pop, there's something going on in Las Vegas that might turn out to be a plus for the family. As you know, my two cousins that shall remain nameless, fancy themselves as pro golfers. Well, they want a rematch against these two old guys from Michigan that they actually beat a while back, but they're not having any luck."

The family patriarch had standing orders for anyone in the family, or working for the family, to keep him informed on anyone's activities that might shed a bad light on their business ventures. They got enough bad publicity as it was. He hated the fact that damage control was essential to his operation, but it was a necessity in today's age of fast moving information that could damage his ability to turn a profit. He motioned for Anthony to continue.

"They've tried to intimidate these guys with their usual weird shit, but so far, they've been unsuccessful. Now the two Michigan guys cooked up a scheme to publicly embarrass the Karpovs, thinking they might earn a small favor from you. They are going to play a three-day golf match with Karpov and his kid. There will be a lot of publicity because the dad thinks Andrei's good enough to play the American Tour. It will be Andrei's 'coming out' party, so to speak."

The old man's interest was piqued when the Karpov name came up. The two families were currently at odds with each other over more than one business interest in New York. He sat back pressing his fingertips together. Anthony started to elaborate further, but his father held up a hand for him to stop.

"If they succeed with their plan, and Alexei Karpov looks like the arrogant jerk that he is to thousands of people, I will consider repaying the favor. Thank you for bringing this to my attention. You did good. Keep me posted on these two Michigan men and the golf match."

* * *

Ronnie and Eddie sat at the Las Vegas National Golf Club bar discussing the practice round they had just finished. Ronnie had carded a 73, with Eddie two strokes higher. Neither was happy with their scoring, and their ball striking seemed to be a tad off. To the untrained eye, their play would still appear to be remarkable. Like any other world class golfers, most observers would enjoy watching them play a substandard round.

"The game is different here," observed Ronnie. "It's harder for me to get a feel for how I should play a shot. I noticed that you were having the same problems."

"Yeah, and it brings your confidence down," reflected Eddie. "At the top of your backswing you want to believe in the shot you are trying to hit. Any indecision, even the tiniest bit, will eventually step up and bite you. Now that we've seen the course, I'm positive we'll putt better tomorrow. And after a good night's sleep, we'll be ready to go."

"You think they'll want to play a scramble for the first round?" asked Ronnie.

"You can count on it," answered Eddie. "If they get first choice, they'll want to take advantage of the kid's length. Like we discussed before, if we get first choice, I think we should defer to them. Either way, it will be a scramble. And I'm sticking with our thinking on an alternate shot for round two. We want to play both of them, not just Andrei."

"I agree. It will be interesting to see what the old man brings to the table. His game will be the deciding factor in all of this."

Ronnie's phone chirped at him. He looked down and read the text from Herman. He laughed and showed it to Eddie. *If you don't need us tonight, Tina and I are going to a show.*

"What's so funny?" asked Eddie.

"Don't let this get around," explained Ronnie in a hushed voice, "but I'd lay five-to-one that the show that Herman wants to see is that Bee Gees tribute band."

"Are you telling me that a big, tough ex-Army Ranger likes the Bee Gees?"

"He loves them," said Ronnie, stifling a laugh. "Charise says he even sings their stuff in the shower."

"To each their own, man," said Eddie, pulling out his phone. "I'm going to check and see if there's anything going on that we'd be interested in. Hot's doing his escort thing, so we might as well find something exciting to do on our own."

"Sounds good. He gave me a key to his place and since the bedrooms are at opposite ends of the house, we shouldn't run into each other."

"What, you think he'll bring her back to his place?" asked Eddie.

"The dude runs a full service operation, so I'd say that is a real possibility."

"Damn!" exclaimed Eddie, looking up from his phone. "You won't believe who's in town, Tony Vegas. The blues rocker himself."

"I love that guy," said Ronnie. "It looks like our evening plans have just been made. Do you think he'll remember us?"

"I think so," said Eddie. "We had a pretty good time with him back at Big Daddy's in Battle Creek. That Cuban plays the guitar like he invented it."

Ronnie nodded toward the end of the bar.

"Did you see those three little metal name tags down there?" he asked.

"I did," answered Eddie. "Sinatra, Martin, and Sammy Davis Jr. They were some very cool cats. Way back, when this was the Stardust Country Club, they used to hang out here after a round. An old boy back in the pro shop told me that after a few cocktails, they would sometimes gather around the piano and sing. Can you see any of today's big entertainers doing that?"

"Not many. I think they like to keep their distance from the fans. There are a lot of freaky dudes out there nowadays who are clueless when it comes to respecting another guy's space. I know some celebrities handle it better than others. I don't think I'd be very good at it. It's like you and I are sitting here talking about stuff that doesn't concern anyone else, and some drunk trying to impress his girl comes over and wants an autograph or a picture. If you tell him to quit bothering us, it would probably end up on the front page of some tabloid. I like the way we operate. Very few people know us, and that's fine with me."

"That's just one of the reasons I like you, Costas," said Eddie. "Let's go over to the MGM Grand. We've still got some time before Tony goes on. I want to play a little poker, and you can check out the sports book. We should also keep our eyes open for Hot, so we can let him know what our plans are."

"Good idea," agreed Ronnie. "We don't want to be in the way if he brings a 'customer' home. What a life that guy leads."

"He's a dandy, that's for sure. Remember, he said if we see him we're supposed to call him Carmine."

"Right. I almost forgot. How ironic is that? We use fake names to lay low, and he uses a fake one to impress the ladies."

"You gotta admit that the name, Hot, doesn't give off a classy aura," observed Eddie. "Give the guy credit. He knows his business."

"So one of the reasons you like me is that I like to keep a low profile?" asked Ronnie as they stood and headed for the door. "You got any other reasons?"

Eddie took several steps before he answered.

"Nope, that's the only one I could think of."

* * *

Mitch and Will sat around the indoor pool at their motel discussing their strategy for the tournament. They decided that they would take whatever the course gave them for the first two rounds, and then on the weekend, they would have to reevaluate. It wouldn't make sense for them to go out and play like they owned the course after only seeing it once. It didn't occur to either of them that Will wouldn't make the cut. They also decided that they needed to play their regular game. Obviously there would be huge crowds and challenges that they normally didn't run into during a gig back home, but they had their way of doing things, and they weren't about to change that just to pacify some spoiled Tour pros.

"I'm sure there are a lot of decent guys out on Tour," observed Mitch. "I just hope we don't get paired with some dude that's full of himself, expecting us to get out of his way so he can collect his big check."

"Once we hit that first tee shot, we're all equal," said Will. "The ball and the course have no idea who is swinging the club or who is trying to break par. We'll just do our thing and let them do theirs. If there is any trouble, it's your job to try and straighten it out. My job is to play good golf. Your job is to manage everything else."

"Sounds like a fifty-fifty split to me. I like it."

"We're a team, Mitch," said Will, holding out a fist to bump. "You know I'll take care of you when this is over."

"I ain't worried about it, partner. Hell, whatever you pay me is gravy. I'm just here for the experience and to watch you on the big stage. It's going to be beautiful to see your name up there on the leader board. Your grandpa and Eddie are going to love it. I wonder how it's going out in Vegas."

Will's eyes teared up at Mitch's mention of Ronnie and Eddie. He owed so much to those two. They taught him how to play the game, and they showed him how to conduct himself with class and dignity. Their lessons paid off well in more ways than one. He wasn't sure if he could run with the big dogs out on the course, but he sure as hell came out on top when it came to his choice for a wife. Melissa was an awesome lady, and he knew that his training was no small factor in his winning her heart. Winning this thing would be nice, but the real goal in the back of his mind was to make them all proud of him, even his best buddy Mitch.

CHAPTER FIFTEEN

The Good Old Days

I've seen just about every type of character come through the door at Python Lee's—tough guys, gamblers, pool players, card players, grifters, and fancy boys. I always liked the guys that weren't tryin' to impress everybody by pretending to be someone important. They were just bein' themselves lookin' for a little action and tryin' not to cause any trouble. They made my job easier, and I appreciated it.

—Books Wilson, pool hall manager

Watching your team, or any team, go down in flames isn't a pretty sight. You generally feel sorry for the players who are in the midst of embarrassing themselves, unless you're the hard-core vindictive type. It takes hard work and a great degree of skill to play at the top level of any sport, but sometimes an individual or an entire team just loses it. Somebody misses a layup at the end of a close basketball game or a running back fumbles on the one-yard line when everyone in the stadium expected him to score. There are hundreds of ways to draw the ire of your fans and catcalls from opposing fans. It's all part of the game. Like the Fleetwood Mac song says, sometimes you have to learn to "pick up the pieces and go home".

Losing is a bitter pill to swallow, but it can also be an instrument of instruction. If you accept it and deal with it, the loss can be a motivational tool. Confucius once said, "You have to learn how to lose before you can learn how to win". On second thought, it might have been the Dali Lama. No, wait; it was the guy behind the counter at the 7-11. Whatever, he seemed to know what he was talking about.

Books sat on his stool behind the counter and looked out over Python Lee's Pool Hall. Times had certainly changed in the last couple of decades. Twenty years ago this place would be rockin' every night. Most of the tables would be full, and there would be four or five card games going on in the back. The cops knew there was money changing hands, but they tended to leave well enough alone as long as there wasn't any major trouble. Like an effective classroom teacher, Books and his enforcers took care of their own discipline. Besides, if the cops were to show up on a regular basis, it would be bad for business. He began to reminisce about earlier times…

* * *

The pool hall was more than just a place to knock little colored balls around on a green-felted table. It was all about hangin' out with a bunch of like-minded guys and even a few like-minded women. The place was frequented by people that were in to sports, gambling, music, and just having a good time. If you were anybody in the Detroit social scene, other than the upper crust types, there was a good chance you would frequent Python Lee's, playing cards, rolling dice, or shooting a game of nine-ball. When the two snooker tables went out of fashion, Python had them removed, giving his customers more room to socialize.

Books and Carlos, the other night manager, had a real feel for what their customers wanted. The music started out low and was turned up as the evening wore on. Even the young guys knew not to complain about the selection of tunes. Carlos, with the help of his teenage daughter, had a whole rack full of cassettes behind the counter that eventually evolved into CD's. The two managers mixed in a lot of Motown, along with Mitch Ryder and other local artists. Books was sitting on his stool the night that Mark Farner from Grand Funk Railroad walked in as one of his band's songs was blaring out of the speakers. As soon as he heard it, he stopped and started singing along. The crowd loved it and gave him a huge ovation.

Around midnight, the booze was flowing and the air was filled with quality blues tunes. Books and Carlos knew they were doing something right when guys started showing up with their dates, dancing back in the corner. They were told that they could dance as long as they stayed out of the way of the usual business. Python didn't want the place to turn into a dance hall, but he didn't mind it if a dozen or so couples wanted to strut their stuff away from the main action. Books remembered the one night when he turned around and saw the mayor of Detroit slow dancing in the corner with his wife. When they locked eyes, the mayor gave him a thumbs up. Books grinned and returned the gesture.

Business started to die out when a motorcycle gang decided they wanted to make Python's their new unofficial headquarters. They had been there about a month when Doc showed up for his first night of work. He was standing by the counter talking to Books and getting the lowdown on the bikers who were gathered around the small bar in the back of the room. Like a lot of gangs, most of them were veterans just looking to blow off some steam while they were trying to adjust to civilian life. Doc, working on his own adjustment to the real world, walked over and shouldered his way through until he stood face to face with the guy that appeared to be the leader. He spoke just loud enough to be heard.

"Name's Doc. I'm the new night bouncer. I'm told you fellas like to get a little rowdy from time to time. Well, I'm here to tell you that if anything crazy or violent goes down, or if anyone has a weapon on them, then I'm holding you personally responsible."

Carl, the gang leader, gave Doc a serious look. At first glance, Doc wasn't very impressive. The ex-marine stood four inches taller than Doc and outweighed him by about fifty pounds. He rotated his fist outward to expose the letters U. S. M. C. and an anchor that was tattooed to his forearm. Doc responded by doing the same, only his much smaller arm was blank. His assignments in the military were all covert, so he and his fellow team members were told to have no distinguishing body marks other than what they were given at birth. Carl laughed loudly in Doc's face. This little shit had a lot of nerve telling him what he could and could not do on his newly adopted turf.

"Little man, you better look around you," threatened Carl. "You are in no position to give any orders or threats, so just back off and we'll let you live another day."

Dennis, one of the bikers, was standing close enough to hear the conversation. He turned to the guy next to him.

"Either this dude has a death wish or he can back up what he says. Which one do you think it is? I'm voting he's one bad son-of-a-bitch. Why would management hire someone that small to keep order in a place like this unless he was capable?"

The biker just shrugged his shoulders and took a drink of beer. A little action would be nice, but so far all he saw was talk.

"I see that you're a non-believer," continued Doc. "Tell you what—you come out back with two of your best, and I'll make my point. I'll take them on one at a time or together. It doesn't matter. When there's two, one guy usually gets in the other guy's way and cramps his style. You can be the observer. When it's over, you decide your course of action. When I win, I want your word as a Marine that your gang will behave and not run off any of the other customers. Deal?"

Carl couldn't believe what the little man was saying. He had some set of balls. He decided to call him on his offer. The gang leader motioned for two of the guys to follow him. When the rest of the group tried to follow, he held up his hand and motioned for them to stay. There was some grumbling, but they did as he requested. A few of them pulled out some bills to see if there were any takers on the outcome. Dennis pulled out his wallet and counted the bills. He had $103. He bet it all on the little guy.

Once they were outside, Doc made quick business of the first guy. He dropped down in a deep crouch and swept his left foot at the guy's legs. A foot sweep on a guy that's balanced with his weight somewhat equal on either foot only works on television or in the movies. Doc's sweep was not intended to take the man's legs out. It was a diversion. Right after he made contact, he jumped from his deep crouch and delivered a powerful one-two combo to the guy's face. On his way down, the other combatant stepped into the action, only to feel Doc's side-kick lash out, catching him in his solar plexus. Both men went down; one was holding his broken nose and the other holding his stomach trying to catch his breath.

"Damn, boy!" hollered Carl. "Where did you learn that shit? In less than ten seconds, you put both my guys on the ground. All right, you get your deal. This place is getting a little stale anyway. Help me get these two back inside."

The gang was stunned when the four of them came back through the door. Doc handed off the guy with the broken nose to another and announced that he was buying a round. They looked to Carl, and he nodded his head in agreement. This brought a cheer. While Doc stood around trading war stories, the guy named Dennis appeared at his side. He introduced himself and gently took Doc's elbow. They made their way to the edge of the crowd.

"I was a Marine sniper for four years in Iraq," he explained. "Only had to get close to the enemy once, but I did my bit for God and country. Anyway, if you're interested, I have a small job for someone like you. It's legal and the pay will be decent. Let me know if this is something you might be interested in. I'll be around."

* * *

Books jumped when the phone rang and brought him back to the present. Those good old days, like the muscle cars way back in the 60's and 70's, were gone. Now they were just memories for old timers like him to look back on and smile. What was the saying that Python Lee was quoting all the time? "The one thing that never changes is that things will always change". Truest statement he had ever heard.

* * *

The two hustlers stood on the first tee at the Las Vegas National Golf Club. It was 8:00 a.m. and already hotter than any August day in the Midwest. Both sides agreed to pony up enough cash to block off a half hour of tee times behind them. The pro wasn't too crazy about it, but his attitude changed as the hundred dollar bills gently fell on the counter in front of him making a nice little pile.

There were about twenty spectators milling around waiting for the match to get started. A few of them had pads and a writing utensil, while another carried a small hand held tape recorder. Andrei had his people contact the media as far away as Los Angeles, trying to drum up interest in his son's match. The Russian contingent drove up in their cart along with Viktor, the match's referee. Alexei, wearing a big straw hat for maximum shade, looked to be of average physique. He appeared to be around fifty and sported a dark tan like Eddie's. Andrei was nothing like his dad. He stood at 6'4" with a thick chest and forearms to match. Unlike the Americans, who were both dressed in shorts and white shirts, father and son had on long black pants and red shirts. Eddie looked at Ronnie and smiled.

"You'd think that after all these years dealing with western culture, these dudes would learn how to dress," he whispered. "I remember watching Russian dignitaries in the news back in the sixties, and I'm no fashion expert, but it was obvious that their suits didn't fit them. If a guy like me noticed that sort of stuff, it had to be really bad."

Ronnie kept his response to himself as Viktor called for the teams to come together. They shook hands all the way around. Alexei tried to intimidate them with a crushing grip. The hustlers expected it and held their own. Viktor held out his hand and asked Eddie to guess odd or even. He guessed correctly, and as previously discussed, he told the referee that they would like to defer until the second match. Viktor didn't seem to have a problem with it, but it took some explaining to get the other team to agree. Andrei wasn't the problem. The old man seemed to be the type that was going to question everything.

He looked at his opponents and said, "Nice trick. But it will be your last. We would like to play a traditional scramble. All four tee off. Each team chooses their best shot, then both players hit again from there. We do it this way until the ball is holed out. Agreed?"

"No problem," said Eddie.

"One point of clarification," explained Viktor. Unlike the other two Russians, he was sensibly dressed in shorts and a light blue shirt. A straw hat similar to Alexei's sat atop his head. His most distinguishing feature was a black handlebar mustache that extended out beyond his cheeks. "The players can bump the ball all over the course. No more than six inches and no nearer to the hole. The player hitting second can place his ball under the six-inch rule. Understood?"

All four players nodded in agreement. Viktor stuck out another closed fist and asked Ronnie to make the call. In the interest of fairness, he had asked the Americans to do the guessing both times, making sure there was no hint of collusion between him and his once fellow countrymen. Ronnie guessed correctly and stepped to the tee. He striped his tee shot down the center of the fairway. Eddie followed suit, coming up a few yards short of his partner's ball. The crowd clapped politely after both shots.

Alexei stepped to the tee and took a few practice swings. The Americans had warmed up over on the practice range about fifty yards to the right of the first tee. Apparently the Russians had found another spot to prepare for the match, because they were nowhere to be seen until they drove up to the first tee. The Michigan hustlers watched attentively as the dad prepared to hit. He sat the club down behind the ball with his right hand and looked down the fairway. After slightly adjusting his stance, he placed his left hand on the grip. His swing was very mechanical and a little jerky, producing a drive of about 250 yards down the right side.

"Looks like the guy learned the game from a book," commented Ronnie.

Eddie shook his head in agreement as Andrei prepared to hit. His swing was totally different from his dad's. He took the club back slowly in a wide arc and then exploded into the ball. The result was a 300-yard drive also down the right side of the fairway. The crowd voiced its approval. Eddie looked at his partner and raised his right eyebrow, indicating that he was impressed.

The first hole at the National was a par five, playing around 515 yards. A pond up by the green sat on the right side. The Michigan team respected the hazard and hit safe layups down the left side. Their best shot left them fifteen yards short of the putting surface. Alexei hit a decent ball, ending up ten yards behind Ronnie and Eddie. His shot was of no consequence as his son's mid-iron cleared the right trap, settling in about thirty feet from the cup. There were now only about ten diehard fans following the group, and they screamed their approval.

"So much for being the home team favorites," observed Ronnie.

"Hey, check it out," said Eddie, pointing to his left. "That gives 'undercover' a whole new meaning."

Herman and Tina sat in a cart about ten yards behind them in the rough. Herman also had on a wide brim straw hat. Tina was wearing a pink sleeveless top with pink shorts. Her ponytail stuck through the hole of a white U. S. C. baseball cap. Both were wearing mirrored sunglasses. They waved when Eddie acknowledged them.

Both hustlers hit similar knockdown wedges toward the hole. Ronnie's ended up two feet short of the cup, so they marked that one. The Russians could do no better than two feet right of the hole with their first putts.

"Good, good?" asked Eddie, indicating that they should both concede the opponents' putt. Viktor had to explain this to Alexei as he had never heard of this mutual concession. It was already hot out, and the temperature was expected to rise another ten degrees before they finished. This, and the fact that Eddie didn't want the match to come down to a piddly little putting contest, was the reason for his offer. After some discussion, Viktor turned and informed them that all putts were to be putted out. Ronnie stepped up and drilled his team's putt into the back of the hole. Alexei followed and did the unthinkable. He missed the two-footer. Andrei coolly placed his ball on the green and rolled it in. Like they said, Alexei's play would be the determining factor in this match. Andrei's skills were obvious. Whether he could keep it together for the entire match was still in question. Alexei was definitely the weak link. It took only one hole for the two hustlers to figure out that they had to get the dad to play a more prominent role in the contest. They couldn't let the old man cruise to victory riding the kid's coattails.

CHAPTER SIXTEEN

–Creepy Noises

I have heard stories about the famous Eddie Davis and Ronnie Green. I'm thinking those stories were slightly exaggerated. They're good, but no match for Andrei and me. They should have done more research on my son before getting in way over their heads. Americans tend to think they know more than they really do. This time, it's going to cost them.

—-Alexei Karpov, "businessman"

Doc and Buck stood in an area that was surrounded by higher ground on three sides. There were several trees in the vicinity but not enough of them to block anyone's view. The surrounding terrain was steepest to the southeast. An old building, the Kingman Museum, sat on the road at the crest of the hill. They had arrived at the Battle Creek arboretum a half hour early to set the stage for their meeting. Doc walked over to a nearby tree and tacked up a small white paper rectangle about the size of a magazine cover.

"You think this will make an impression on these guys?" asked Buck.

"Yeah, we're just making a statement here," answered Doc. "It's all for show. If the show's good enough, I think we'll buy some time. We need to prove to these clowns that we're a force to reckon with, and that we can get to them from a distance if it came to that. These New York City types tend to look down on anyone that's not from the big time. Chicago and L. A. get a little respect, but that's as far as it goes. I think they'll be surprised and maybe a little impressed."

A black Crown Victoria wound its way slowly toward them. It slowed down to a crawl, then eventually stopped in the small parking area next to the other vehicle. The two men from the other day got out of the front seat and opened the back doors. Both of them had short sleeve shirts on with visible shoulder holsters. Greer and Donaldson stepped out and walked down to meet Doc and Buck. The two armed guards fanned out, looking over the surrounding area with a suspicious eye. The two golfers were wearing black pants and white golf shirts. Their demeanor showed their displeasure when they discovered that Ronnie and Eddie were not present.

"Where's our golfers?" asked Greer. "We were told they were going to be here."

"They're out of town," explained Doc. "They should be back in a couple of days. Hopefully, by the time they get back, this whole situation can be settled."

"The only thing that can settle this fucking situation is for them to tee it up with us," added Donaldson. "They disrespected us when they threw our first match, and we want satisfaction."

"Like I said," continued Doc in a calm voice, "they're out of town and won't be back for a couple of days. You'll just have to be patient."

"Maybe we should break a couple of bones to show how serious we are," threatened Greer as he looked over at his partner. "I don't think Davis and Green know what we're capable of. Now they send these jokers to stall us off."

"Oh, they know what kind of men you are," said Doc. "Those dead cats have them scared shitless."

Greer made a little motion to his henchmen. They took a threatening step forward, which caused Doc to raise his open hand to his face. Some bark flew off the nearby tree and a hole appeared in the paper.

"Well, look at that!" exclaimed Doc. "A bullet hole just showed up out of nowhere. And it looks like a large caliber. Probably a six or a six point five mm."

Greer and Donaldson's people froze. They looked over at their bosses.

"I wouldn't pull those weapons, guys," advised Doc. "You're outgunned and out- maneuvered. We're holding the high ground here. It's so much more efficient from a distance, wouldn't you agree? It's not as personal, but the results are the same."

He raised his hand to his face again and another hole appeared in the paper. It was only a few inches from the first hole.

"Damn, another one right by the first one! It's like magic, isn't it? You think we're bluffing? Look at your shirts."

Greer looked at the back of Donaldson's shirt. There was a small red dot on it. The rest of them turned around and looked down at their chest region. There was a small red dot on all of them.

"Here's the deal," said Doc. "You sit tight and do nothing until our guys get back. And when I say nothing, I mean it. No cats and no more stupid warnings. Check in with the manager at Cedar Creek for a message in a few days. He'll let you know what the story is. Hey, it's beautiful here. Relax and play some golf. It'll be good for you. I'd say this meeting is over."

"That was great shooting," said Doc, raising his glass to Dennis.

The sniper and three members of his motorcycle "club" sat with Doc and Buck at a small bar on the east end of Battle Creek. Buck couldn't believe it when he saw the toy rifles with lasers taped to them. Doc explained that he had bought them earlier and distributed them to Dennis's guys. They needed something that they could hold steady while they pointed the lasers at their targets.

"The tree with the target on it was perfect," complimented Dennis. "There was nothing but trees behind it, so if I missed no one would have been in any danger. We checked out the area behind it with our glasses, and it was totally empty. Your plan went off as smooth as you said it would. Personally, I would have liked to see you kick the shit out of those two goons. My guys here have never seen you fight."

"It crossed my mind," said Doc. "But those dudes were packin', so I went with the original plan. We never even heard the shots. Those hi-tech suppressors are unbelievable. Listen, I appreciate your good work, guys. Here's some traveling money for your efforts."

Doc slid fifteen one hundred dollar bills across the bar. Dennis looked at the bills but didn't pick them up.

"I know you were just doing me a favor," continued Doc, "but the guys that hired us definitely want you to have it. Believe me, they can afford it."

The vet, turned biker, picked up the bills and stuck out his hand.

"Thanks, Doc," said Dennis, rising from his stool. "These guys will have to wait for another time to see you in action. We'd better get back to the city. You take care, you hear. It was nice meeting you, Buck. If you hang with this guy, you must be a genuine tough guy too."

"He regularly kicks my ass," grinned Doc.

"I ain't believin' that for a minute," said Dennis laughing.

Doc and Buck sat finishing their beers in silence. Their plan had bought them the time they needed for the hustlers to take care of business on their end.

"I really didn't do much, but I'm glad it all worked out," said Buck. "Your boy was unbelievable."

"He was, wasn't he? He told me a while back that he actually knew Carlos Hathcock, one of the best shooters ever."

"Damn, that's some prestigious company."

"He was a cut above, Buck. Just like the guys we're working for. Let's get back to Richland. The women should be able to breathe easier for a few days. By the way, can you loan me a few dollars? I just gave away the rest of my fee to Dennis and his boys."

* * *

The Michigan hustlers knew they were in trouble after only three holes. On hole number two, Andrei blasted another prodigious drive and followed it with a wedge to twelve feet. This time his dad rolled it in, putting them one up. Number three was playing about 180 yards which was a hard 6-iron for Eddie and a smooth 5-iron for Ronnie. Andrei only had to hit an 8-iron. The dad was feeling it. He opted to walk the par three instead of ride. He strutted along jabbering to the people in Russian and in English. The few spectators that were still following along laughed at his attempts to be funny.

"The dude should be doing stand-up at one of the clubs around here," whispered Eddie. "He's riding the kid's game, and there's nothing we can do about it."

"We'll hang tough," said Ronnie. "The first few holes don't make the whole match. Their demeanor could change if something doesn't go their way. I will admit, the kid is more than just a long ball hitter. Let's keep the pressure on and see what kind of staying power he has."

Ronnie's prediction proved to be an accurate one when the kid had a mini meltdown on the back side. On the short par four thirteenth, he tried to reach the green with his tee shot. The result was a wet ball at the bottom of the far pond up by the green. They played the old man's ball about 75 yards back up the fairway and consequently left both their second shots in the right greenside trap. Alexei played a decent explosion to about twelve feet. Andrei's shot was a different story. He caught it thin and blew it completely over the green. This was the first trap they had been in. Andrei's miscue started the guys wondering. Was this the flaw in the kid's game? Is this why he hadn't taken a shot at the Tour Qualifying School?

When Ronnie's par putt dropped on thirteen, the hustlers were only down two holes. They got one more back on sixteen when they both hit low irons into the green. The course superintendent had the tees up, making the hole play approximately 180 yards into a slight breeze. Alexei's tee shot struggled to get to the front of the green. A fortunate forward bounce left it between the traps a few feet short of the putting surface. Andrei tried to muscle a 7-iron at the flag, and he got every bit of it. Before the wind had a chance to be a major factor, his ball was over the back of the green. It landed in the back fringe, and when it came to a stop, it was next to one of the trees behind the green. They chipped Alexei's ball up to two feet and lost the hole when Eddie dropped in a fifteen-foot bird. The good guys were now only one down with two to play.

Eddie lit up a Macanudo as Andrei prepared to hit his pitch shot into seventeen. The hole was actually driveable for the kid, but he opted to hit a 3-metal off the tee. Amazingly, it was against his dad's advice. Alexei wanted him to try and reach the green, but it would have taken a pinpoint drive to get by the right greenside bunker up onto a slightly elevated green. It was a low-percentage shot, and Andrei knew it. Besides, with both of them hitting from thirty yards out, there would be a good chance one of them would snuggle one up to the pin.

The hustler approved of the kid's shot selection back at the tee. Like he and Ronnie had discussed on multiple occasions: If you hit the shot ten times, what would be the probable outcome? And add to that, the match situation and who the competition is. There were a lot of factors to plug into the equation. Golf is a thinking man's game as long as you didn't let too much analysis get in the way of executing the shot at hand.

Andrei took two smooth practice swings barely clipping the grass. He could see Ronnie's ball up on the green sitting less than ten feet past the pin. His dad's shot was almost laughable given the situation. He had buried his club in the turf, leaving it just short of the front edge. Andrei made a precision stroke with his hands well ahead of the clubface at impact. The ball flew low into the green, took two hops, and then hit the brakes two feet right of the pin. To the Russians' surprise, both Eddie and Ronnie clapped, showing an appreciation for a well-struck shot. They halved the hole with birdies.

Number eighteen was made for Andrei's game. He hit a drive and a 4-iron onto the surface. Their thirty-foot eagle putt didn't fall, but it didn't need to. Birdies on both sides gave the Russians the first day match. Alexei never stopped talking all the way to the clubhouse and into the bar. He announced that drinks were on him. Once inside he held court with anyone that would listen about his son's superb talent and, in his opinion, the three-day match was all but over. The Americans had played well, but they were outclassed.

Eddie and Ronnie sat at the end of the bar listening to Alexei's account of how his team hadn't even played that well but still came away with a decisive win.

"You'd think the Cold War was still going on," observed Ronnie. "The press appears to be eating it up. What do you think? We shot several under and still couldn't handle them."

"The kid's good. There's no doubt about that. It's obvious that we can't stay with them in a scramble. Let's go with alternate shot tomorrow as planned. Alexei will have to hit half of their shots, which will minimize his son's contribution. If he chunks a couple like he did back on seventeen, we've got a chance."

Ronnie was about to respond when a handful of reporters walked over to get their take on the day's events. Two of the reporters were Russian. Andrei must have paid their way to the U.S. to get some 'unbiased' coverage back home in the Russian newspapers. The guy was definitely going all out on behalf of his son. The hustlers would have been somewhat, but not totally surprised, to read the Russian version of the match. According to them, the Americans were a couple of hacks that were in way over their heads. The Karpovs showed America what Russia could do when they decide to get serious about a western sport. The only reason Russian golfers were not dominating all the professional tours was their lack of enthusiasm for the game. Golf just wasn't exciting enough. But maybe, with the Karpov's victory, it would generate some more interest in what was considered back in Russia to be a rich man's game.

Herman and Tina joined up with the golfers back at Hot's place. Herman voiced his opinion on what might happen if Ronnie and Eddie pulled ahead in the next day's match. It wouldn't surprise him if the Russians had some sort of plan in place to disrupt the Americans. Alexei struck him as a guy that hated to lose and would do just about anything to come out on top.

After a quick glass of wine, Tina excused herself to go have dinner with her Vegas friends. Herman decided he wanted to go downtown to take in the sights, so he took the rental car. Ronnie and Eddie decided to eat a light supper, then head over to the MGM Grand to check out the action. Hot had a '95 minivan that they were welcome to use. His other car was a new Cadillac. He always took the Caddy when he was "working". They weren't sure what he was up to, but they knew that he often hung around the MGM casino.

Ronnie had just settled into his seat at the MGM Sports Book when he spied Hot walking by with a sixty-something lady on his arm. She was carrying about twenty extra pounds but relatively good looking with tons of jewelry on. Something told Ronnie that the stones in her necklace and bracelets weren't available at the local Wal-Mart. When Hot saw Ronnie, he excused himself and headed to the nearest restroom. A few seconds later, Ronnie rose and followed him.

"Hey, uh, Carmine," said Ronnie. "Is this what you call work? If so, is there a sheet where Eddie and I can sign up?"

"I'm sure your wives would approve," said Hot, looking in the mirror. He pulled out a miniature bottle of cologne and splashed some on. "Then again, they might if they found out what I'm making tonight. Listen, we'll be home late so don't be alarmed. I'm usually quiet like a cat, but I have no idea how much noise we'll make after a few cocktails. I heard you two lost today's match. Where's your partner?"

"He's over playing poker. How did you hear about our match?"

"It's all over the place. Apparently the Russian dude likes the limelight. He was on a local television channel a couple of hours ago talking up his son's expertise on the short grass. He said you two were good but no match for his son's power off the tee and his finesse around the greens. He sounds like an arrogant sort."

"He is," said Ronnie. "But it ain't over yet. We're poised to make a comeback."

"If you win it all, let's all have dinner at Hugo's Cellar," suggested Hot. "It's a classy place below the Four Queens. I promised Shelly we'd go someplace really nice before she has to head home, and I'll score some points by bringing a couple of low-level celebrities like you two."

"Shelly? What's her story?"

"Typical. She's recently divorced from some CEO back east. She found out he was having a couple of affairs and took him to the cleaners. Now she's out here trying to make up for some of the excitement that she had been missing out on being the dutiful wife. That's where I come in. As you know, I'm Mr. Excitement."

"Sounds good. What if we lose tomorrow?"

"I'm still taking her to Hugo's," said Hot over his shoulder on his way to the door. "You two should probably save your money and hit up one of the buffets. I've got some coupons in one of the kitchen drawers. Help yourself."

"You're a prince, you know that?"

"I do my best. Good luck tomorrow."

The two golfers were in bed by 11:00. They were sharing one of the bedrooms at the opposite end of the house from Hot's bedroom. It was decorated with albums in frames from the good old days. It was obvious that Hot was a Bruce Springsteen fan, as the Boss's music was plastered all over the walls. They each had a comfortable single bed that sat against opposite walls of the room. Herman was in the room across the hall. He had a king size bed and a huge flat screen. There was no telling what the house's owner did in this room. All three guests woke around 2:00 a.m., when they heard strange noises coming from the other end of the house.

"What the hell was that?" muttered Eddie.

"I don't know," answered Ronnie. "It sounded like someone was trying to strangle a cat over there. There it goes again."

Herman's shadow appeared in their doorway.

"What the fuck is that noise?" he demanded.

"I think it's Hot with his lady friend," said Ronnie. "He said they might be a little noisy. Damn, what is going on over there?"

"Now that I'm awake, I'm going to get a glass of water," said Eddie, getting out of bed.

"Make it fast," said Ronnie. "You don't want to be standing there if our host and his guest decide to take their activities to another room."

Eddie gave Ronnie a wave of disgust and headed out the door and across the spacious main room toward the kitchen. Herman went back to his room muttering to himself.

Eddie stood in the kitchen sipping at his water and looking out the window. A dark figure appeared behind him. Hot, wearing black silk pajama bottoms and no shirt, walked quietly past and turned on the faucet above the sink. Eddie watched silently as his host washed his face, then turned his head sideways to slurp down some water. He grabbed a towel, and after drying his face, looked over at Eddie.

"Damn, Hot," said Eddie. "What is all that noise? We don't need to call an ambulance, do we?"

"Not hardly," grinned Hot. "Let's just say that her rich former husband knew a lot about making money and very little about pleasing his woman. I happen to be a black belt in that department."

"Care to share your technique? A guy's never too old to add to his repertoire."

"Let me ask you this; in the few days that you have left here, can you teach me to play golf as good as you?"

"Nope."

"Well, there's your answer. Just knowing what to do isn't good enough. You have to be able to execute, and all situations aren't the same. You also have to be able to adapt on the fly. I'd better get back. Don't worry, we'll be sleeping soon. Go get 'em tomorrow."

Eddie shook his head as he watched a different type of legend head back to his bedroom. Give the guy credit; he's got skills. Skills that most men would gladly pay to acquire.

When Eddie slipped back into his room, Ronnie was snoring quietly. *Good*, he thought, *he's gonna need his rest. The Russians were good, but I didn't come all the way out here to drop 125k, and I know Ronnie didn't either. Tomorrow's going to be our day.*

CHAPTER SEVENTEEN

A Gentlemen's Game

The game of golf is all offense and no defense. That's what makes it unique. It's just the golfer versus the course and whatever Mother Nature throws at you. That's why I was excited when I got the job of head golf coach at the school where I teach. I lost some of my enthusiasm for my new position when my golfers caught two of our opponents cheating in our very first match. One of the culprits took two practice swings standing under a tree, smacking the small branches that hung over his head, breaking a couple of them. My player said he had leaves all over him before he played his actual shot. And get this—his coach was sitting in a cart about thirty yards away, and she swore he didn't do it. We were fortunate that a rules committee member also observed the infraction.

Another one of my guys observed an opponent as he discretely dropped a ball in the short rough claiming it was his tee shot. Before he could hit, my golfer pointed out a ball that had settled down into some thicker grass. Upon further examination, they decided it was his original ball. He hacked it out, eventually making double bogey on the hole. Stinking cheaters. They have no respect for themselves or the game.

—Roger Sodaberg, high school golf coach

To excel at the game of golf one needs to be not only skilled but able to establish some sort of rhythm. If something is going on, either externally or internally to disrupt that rhythm, then one needs to get himself back on track as quickly as possible. An accomplished touring pro, in the middle of a round, can quite often fix what is necessary to get his rhythm back. This is a trait that sets the successful ones apart from the also-rans. If a pro is grinning after carding a 73, that means he just salvaged a round that should have been a much higher number. His grin is testimony that his skills and temperament got the most out of what could have been a major disaster.

Will and Mitch walked over to the last spot on the Deere Run practice tee. They got some strange looks from the fans that were milling around. Golfers and caddies with traces of black eyes were an unusual site on the tour. The swelling had gone down on their faces, but there was still some discoloration. If they had to guess, the fans would probably have said that the two of them had gotten into a fight with each other. Whatever happened, they didn't look like the usual entries in a tour event.

It was 6:45 in the morning, and they were scheduled to tee off in forty minutes. Will looked down at the little sign with his name on it. The guy that printed his name had decided that it needed an extra 'e' on the end.

"Check it out," said Will, tapping the sign with his wedge. "I hope this isn't an omen. Do you think I'll be able to cash my check if my name is misspelled on it?"

Ted Charles, a mid-level tour pro just off to their left, looked up when he heard Will's comment.

"I wouldn't worry about cashing a check, newbie. I'd worry more about gagging and puking all over myself once you get out there, if I were you. This is the Tour, boy, not a game of bingo, bango, bongo back at your local muni."

"Hey, thanks for the advice," chirped Mitch. "Up in the hills where we're from, gaggin' and pukin' is part of the game. Gosh, now we know that it's not allowed, we'll do our best to mind our manners."

The tour pro's caddy, Louie Burfine, gave Mitch a nasty stare and made a condescending sound. Will looked at his caddy and shrugged his shoulders. Apparently it was dog-eat-dog out here and not one big fraternity as it was often advertised. It didn't matter to them. Grumpy opponents were something they had run into before. The ones you had to worry about were the sore losers who carried a piece in their bag. It was a safe bet that none of the golfers playing this week were carrying a firearm.

Mitch pulled a sharpie marker out of his back pocket and walked over to Will's range sign. He reached down and made a big 'X' through the final 'e' in Will's last name. Louie let out with a big laugh. This brought a disapproving look from his player. It was time to get down to business, which meant the joking and general chatter needed to stop. Will walked about fifteen more feet to his right to create some more room. He was at the end of the line, and when he looked back to where the spectators were standing, there was one old man leaning on the fence. He gave Will a small wave and a smile. Will smiled back. His caddy tossed him a ball, and he hit his first practice shot in a Tour event. It came off the center of the clubface and went about thirty yards. Will held up the club for Mitch to see where he had made contact. Mitch grinned and tossed him another ball.

"Next on the tee from Hickory Corners, Michigan, Will Green."

Will gave a small tip of his cap to the few early morning spectators and proceeded to hammer his drive up the right side of number one fairway. At the end of its flight, the ball curved a few feet to the left, ending up in the middle of the short grass. Even though it would be one of the better drives off number one for the whole day, he received only a smattering of applause.

"Tough crowd," commented Mitch, sliding the driver back in the bag as they walked off the tee and down the hill that fronted it. "They're saving their applause for the big dogs. They know you're a nobody by the bag I'm carrying. A millionaire tour pro doesn't usually have a bag with legs on it. That, and your shirt isn't plastered with a bunch of shameless advertising."

"It's okay by me," responded Will. "If I had my way, I wouldn't even be playing under my real name. All this publicity can't be good for our operation back home."

"That's why we have to make the most of it this week. Get in, grab some cash, then make our escape."

"You're treating this like some sort of robbery," observed Will as they stopped for Chris Spangler, the third member of the group, to hit his second shot. Spangler was a graduate of the Tour Qualifying School, and so far, had made only one cut for the season. He was a solid enough player, but as the round progressed, they could see a certain lack of resourcefulness in his game. To be successful on the tour, a guy had to have that something extra, and Chris didn't appear to be one of those guys. They decided that he was probably playing the circuit, trying to stay away from a 9 to 5 job at a club back home.

"It is a little like stealing," continued Mitch. "You show up, play four rounds, then if you don't crash and burn, you get a check equal to some poor schmuck's yearly salary and sometimes a whole lot more. Like your grandpa always says, 'is this a great country, or what?'"

"It's the American way dude," said Will as they stopped at his ball. "If you have a skill that very few people have, then people are willing to pay to watch you perform. Most of the people that make big money performing work real hard at their craft."

"True, but you are an exception to that rule. You never practice for more than a half hour at a time, and if someone else is nearby, you end up socializing more than practicing."

"True that," laughed Will, looking over Mitch's shoulder. Burfine was motioning for Will to get on with it. He gave him a small wave, then hit a smooth wedge ten feet below the cup. "Mitch, my boy, this game's just too easy."

"Smart ass," remarked Mitch as he hustled to replace the divot. "I hope you are in the same frame of mind when we walk up the 72nd fairway."

Louie Burfine looked over at the other caddy in the group, Renny Diaz, and made a strange face. Diaz just shrugged his shoulders. Burfine's pro, Ted Charles, had cashed a couple of modest checks, but he was by no means a household name. Charles had more talent than Spangler, but hadn't as of yet, played up to his potential. What both caddies were afraid of was some untested type, like Will, screwing up their rhythm. And from what they saw on this first hole, it looked like Will and Mitch might be a distraction. This was serious golf, and these two apparently weren't aware of that. Louie decided to say something to Mitch if it looked like the two newbies were going to be a problem.

Will and his caddy were disappointed when they didn't make four on number two, a hole they expected to birdie. From the left side of the fairway, Will hit a 3-metal into the right trap. They both thought the ball was on a perfect line, working its way back toward the green, but it caught the edge of the bunker. When they got to the ball they couldn't believe their misfortune. First, the ball hit only two feet inside the left edge of the trap. A couple of feet left, and they would have been putting for a three. Secondly, the ball was half buried in the sand. How does a shot from 260 yards away with a low trajectory hit and bury itself? Will's explosion from the sand was decent enough, but then he lipped out his eight-footer. From then on the rest of the round didn't get much better.

On number three tee, Louie decided that he had seen enough of the boys from the "sticks". When he found out that his guy was paired with a player that had yet to play in a P.G.A. event, he Googled him and got absolutely nothing. The dude never played college golf and apparently had never made any kind of noise in the golf world at all.

"Hey, Mitch," whispered Louie as they watched Will prepare to hit. "This "hicks from the sticks" routine might play at the club back in Hickorytown or wherever, but you guys are on the Tour now. You need to cut the idle chatter and hit 'em quick. If you haven't noticed, you've got two experienced pros in the group that are trying to make a living."

Mitch didn't look at Louie. He just whispered out of the side of his mouth.

"A hundred bucks says my guy beats yours," was all he said.

"We're not supposed to be betting out here, but I'll take it," said Louie. "You two will disappear after two rounds. How in the hell did Will get into this thing, anyway?"

Will was calling on all his resources and training to keep his train on the tracks. Burfine's comment to Mitch back on three tee was upsetting, and he knew he should get over it, but for some reason it had hit a nerve. Who was he to think he could show up at his first Tour event and take it by storm? A guy should be confident in his game, but was his confidence misguided? Admittedly, he had no tournament experience. On the other hand, he had the sort of experience that most of these guys didn't have. How many of them had played for big money out of their own pockets? Maybe not big money by Tour standards, but that was a matter of perspective. It was definitely different when your own funds were at stake.

The majority of the Tour pros were pretty good guys. On occasion, they would even help a competitor out on the practice tee. If the lower half at the end of a tournament had to reach deep into their pockets to pay the upper half, the mutual admiration society might take on a different face. Gamesmanship might rear its ugly head from time to time, especially if you were close to the halfway mark. Winning money was the reason they were here, and it was a sure bet that none of the participants would be willing to part with a portion of their bankroll without a fight.

Will wondered if Louie was trying to get into their heads a little. He decided that it would be a ridiculous move on his part. Why mess with a complete unknown that, in his own words, wouldn't make it to the weekend? Now he was thinking too much and in jeopardy of making a mess of things.

The Winston/Green team hit the back nine in a state of total shock. They carded a one over 36, on the front side, which put them behind a whole bunch of people. Will's ball striking wasn't up to its usual overall excellence, but that was only part of it. On number four he laced his drive right at the tree that stood in the middle of the fairway. His ball slammed into the tree and rebounded into parts unknown. They were pretty sure the ball went left off the tree, because it hit on the left side and didn't rattle around in the branches. There were a few people walking along the left side of the hole by the cart path. They stopped when they heard the ball smack into the tree, but none of them had any idea where the ball ended up. The fans helped to search the thick rough in the low area across the cartpath but to no avail.

After the allotted five minutes, Will announced to his opponents that he was going back to the tee. He took three steps and there, nestled down in the thick grass, was his ball. He stood there for a couple seconds with hands on hips collecting his thoughts. Then he did something that is rarely seen at a PGA Tour event. He reached down and picked it up, under no penalty! He looked over at a young boy that was helping to look and tossed the ball to him. The boy caught it and waved it excitedly at his parents.

"Now there's a trivia question that very few golfers would be able to answer," quipped Mitch as they walked back to the tee.

"What's that?" asked Will.

"When can a golfer pick up his ball when he's not on the green, and when he is not playing lift, clean, and place and not be penalized for it?"

"That's a good one," agreed Will.

As they were walking, a fan fell in step. Normally spectators didn't talk to the pros during a round but this fan got the impression that these two wouldn't mind. He heard the exchange between player and caddy and asked what had just happened and why Will would not be penalized for picking up his ball.

"Once Will declared the ball lost," explained Mitch, "it was no longer in play. A guy can't say he has lost his ball, start back to the tee to hit under stroke and distance penalty, then declare that his ball is now found again. You get five minutes to search for a ball that you can't immediately locate. Once five minutes is up, the ball is lost, even if you find it a few seconds later. It's a good rule, otherwise guys would spend way too much time looking for their ball, especially if it meant winning or losing a match."

"Thanks, guys," said the fan as golfer and caddy walked into the fairway where the fans were not allowed. "I'm a sportswriter, and you just gave me some good stuff."

When Will and Mitch got back to the tee, the group behind them was standing there. They didn't even acknowledge them as Will teed up another ball and ripped it just right of the tree out to the 315 mark. His subsequent wedge ended up eight feet from the hole. The boy and his parents clapped wildly as Will rolled in the putt for a bogey. As the players walked off the green, the dad explained what had just happened to his son. He also explained that Will did a tremendous job handling the unfortunate bounce and the lost ball. He said golf is still a gentlemen's game, and they had just witnessed how a gentleman handles himself on the golf course.

* * *

"So how much do you think Hot made last night for his efforts?" asked Ronnie as they pulled into the Las Vegas National for round two.

"I figure if he got paid twenty-five dollars a squeal, he should be rolling in dough," offered Eddie.

Herman was stretched out in the back seat of the mini-van.

"I ain't gonna tell Charise about what Hot does for a living. He said I can stay at his place anytime I'm in town, and I want to keep that invitation open. If I ever come back, I'll bring my noise canceling headphones and some earplugs."

"Did you get any sleep, partner?" asked Ronnie.

"Yeah, once the caterwauling died down I was out. You won't believe what Hot said to me in the kitchen while he was taking a break. When I questioned him about his business, he said that it was what he did and that it took a long time and a lot of practice to acquire the necessary skills."

"I could use just a couple of tips on how to improve my game," said Herman.

"Ask him," said Ronnie. "Maybe he'll draw you a picture."

Tina walked up as the guys got out of Hot's minivan. They were still chuckling over Ronnie's comment.

"So what were you three grown men talking about to get into such a jovial mood?" she asked.

This brought another chorus of chuckles but no definitive answer to her question.

"Don't tell me it's a guy thing," challenged Tina with a sinister smile. "Well, you'd be surprised what women talk about when we get together. It ain't all flowers and fashion, if you know what I mean."

"Alright, guys, keep yourself alive today," said Herman. "No pun intended. Tina and I will step up our scrutiny of all potentially dangerous people. When you two take the lead in today's match, things might get interesting. If you don't, our job will be at the top of the boredom chart."

Thanks to Alexei's efforts, word had gotten out on the big match. There were now around 100 people milling around the first tee, which included a few more reporters. If the Americans had to guess, they would say that well over half of the fans were of Russian descent.

"Are you diggin' this?" asked Eddie, referring to the huge crowd.

Ronnie looked over at his partner.

"Hotter than blazes, possible hostile fans, playing for big money—hell yes I'm diggin' this. I just hope this comes down to whoever plays the best golf and nothing else."

"Me too, buddy. Let's go make some money."

The Russian team pulled up in their cart with Viktor right behind them. Alexei jumped out from behind the wheel and offered his hand to his opponents. He was exceptionally jubilant, and he had a right to be. His team was one up, and his son had demonstrated that he was the best golfer of the four. Like he told the press in the three interviews that he did after yesterday's match—it was all but over. The Americans couldn't handle Andrei's length off the tee or his accurate short irons. Also, if his putting stroke carried over from the first match, they might put the Americans away early in the round.

Eddie announced that the format for the day would be an alternate shot. One team member would drive off the odd numbered holes while the other would drive off the even numbered holes. From where the tee shots lay, they would alternate shots until the ball was holed out. Each team would use only one ball, and it was not to be moved until it was on the putting surface. Alexei knew this was coming, so there was very little discussion. Viktor again held out a closed fist. Ronnie guessed even and stepped to the tee when Viktor showed two tees in his open hand. His tee shot was well-played, slightly down the left side of the fairway.

The Americans were surprised when the old man stepped up and hit one about fifteen yards short of Ronnie's ball. They got in their carts and drove slowly, giving the walkers time to keep up. The pro suggested that the fans follow the golfers up to three tee, then after watching them hit their tee shots on the par three, they could walk over to seven tee and follow the teams back in when they came around. A refreshment cart would be stationed out there, and it was bound to do a lot of business.

"They're saving Andrei so he can hit their tee shot on eighteen," said Eddie as they rode out to Ronnie's drive. "For that strategy to be effective, we will have to be tied coming up to the last hole, or we won't be playing it. If we're not tied, the shorter hitter will have driven off on two of the par fives, and the long ball will have only hit off of one, number four. I would have had Andrei step up here and crank one. Then the dad could at least get it to the front edge in two."

"I was thinking the same thing," echoed Ronnie. "They know we're going to lay up here, so getting on or real close in two would be a great start for them. Did you see any unsavory types among the crowd?"

"I'm not worrying about that," said Eddie. "I'm just here to dazzle you with my awesome shot making."

"How about you start right here," said Ronnie, looking over at Andrei as he prepared to hit his team's second shot.

The young man's inexperience showed when he tried to stick his 4-iron next to the back pin. The center of the green should have been his target, given that the other team probably couldn't get home in two. His ball hit just past the flag and rolled into the back left bunker. Eddie stepped up and hit a 5-metal fifteen yards short of the green. Ronnie followed Eddie's second with a nice pitch about seven feet to the right of the hole. When the Russians failed to get up and down from the trap, Eddie had the short putt to win the hole. There was a gasp from the crowd when Eddie's putt did a 360, coming to rest a couple of inches in front of the hole.

"I hope that's not an omen," remarked Ronnie.

"Nah, I hit a good putt there. Shit happens out here. You know that. It doesn't help to get excited when you get a bad break. There are enough bad breaks out here for everyone."

* * *

Will stepped up to the eighteenth tee and watched the group ahead hit their second shots into the green. To say he was disappointed would be an understatement. Mitch and he had high hopes at the beginning of the round. This was the kind of course that Will expected to eat up, but the birdies just didn't come. He had just birdied number seventeen, an interesting par five, to get back to even par. The television camera did catch his second shot as it faded into the center of the green. His two-putt birdie was the first time he had ever been on television. The big names were starting to make their appearance, so the majority of the airtime was focused on them. Max Worth was running the Golf Channel control center, and he was not happy when Will's birdie made it to the air.

"No one cares about this nobody," he thundered. "Kid gets lucky and weasels his way into the tournament. Friday evening he will be on his way back home to Hickory Sticks, or wherever, feeling like a world-beater. It'll probably be the highlight of his entire golfing life. His bio says he has never even played in a tournament. It stinks that he's taking up a spot that a real Tour pro, trying to earn a living, could have. I'm sure he's happy just to walk the same course that the real golfers are playing. I wouldn't be surprised if he ends up with a whole pocket full of autographs. Stinkin' amateurs."

"Tell us how you really feel, boss," said Denny Holmes who was perched behind his monitor. "Personally, I think it would be very cool to have a real unknown come out of nowhere and win a title. The JDC has had a lot of first time winners, but I don't think a guy that has never won any type of formal competition has ever won a Tour event. The kid's got an awesome swing if you ask me."

"Well, I ain't askin' you, hotshot," complained Max. "It's tough enough out here with all the foreign players coming over taking up spots that American guys should have. I just don't like it, that's all."

"What if he gets hot and wins the whole thing, or even finishes in the top ten? That would be a huge story."

"How much do you want to bet that he doesn't even make the cut?" asked Max. "Put up or shut up, Denny."

"I think I'll pass. I'm just saying that it could happen."

"Not the way the Tour is structured today, Einstein. This guy sneaking in is a true anomaly. One that will disappear soon enough."

Max grunted his disapproval when Will birdied the eighteenth to finish one under. Denny looked over at the young lady sitting beside him and raised his hand for a high five. She responded without taking her eyes off her screen.

* * *

Eddie and Ronnie held a two-up lead at the turn. They were holding up fairly well under the extreme temperature, but Alexei wasn't looking so good. Eddie had a bunch of clean bar towels stashed in his bag. He pulled four of them out and went over to the refreshment cart for ice. Alexei was looking a little haggard when Eddie walked up and gave him two of the ice-filled towels.

"Put them on the back of your necks, Alexei," he explained.

"Thanks, Eddie. I knew it would be hot here, but this is ridiculous. Back home in Russia it never gets this hot."

"Yeah, the argument, 'but it's a dry heat', doesn't hold up when the temp goes north of a hundred. We can take a short break if you want to. Though I wouldn't advise going inside into the air conditioning. It'll just seem worse when you come back out."

The Americans went three-up on the short par four thirteenth, but gave it right back when Andrei stuck his tee shot on the fourteenth, a foot and a half from the hole. When Ronnie missed his twenty-footer, Eddie picked up the Russians' ball. There was no way he was going to ask Alexei to putt a foot and a half putt after a shot like that. Alexei gave him a strange look and shrugged his shoulders.

The old man never said what happened with his tee shot on the par five fifteenth. Something could have distracted him in his backswing or maybe his grip was too sweaty. Whatever the cause, his ball ended up in the pond off to the right of the tee. The crowd let out with a big gasp as the ball made an awkward flight like a drunk goose trying to get its bearings, finally landing in the middle of the water. With sagging shoulders, he walked slowly back to the cart and sat down.

Now three-up with three to go, all the Americans had to do was tie a hole and the second round was theirs. Eddie's tee shot on sixteen put immense pressure on the Russians. His 4-iron draw settled in about twelve feet from the hole. Andrei's shot was decent, leaving his dad with a twenty-two footer to extend the match. Alexei's putt caught a portion of the cup, but it was moving too fast to fall. Ronnie rolled their birdie putt to six inches. Alexei picked it up and tossed it back to him. It was the first putt he had given to his opponents. The match was now all square.

* * *

Will sat in the passenger seat as Mitch drove back up Highway 84 to their motel. He went over his round in his head hole by hole. He had hit the ball solid enough, but his putting was less than exemplary. Still, that wasn't the reason for his score. His round lacked its usual awesomeness, as Mitch often put it. He didn't approach the course in attack mode. It was like he was just trying not to embarrass himself. It really didn't matter if Charles's caddy and his comment on number three had sat him back on his heels. As he and Mitch had discussed numerous times, you are in control of your own destiny out on the golf course. No complaints and no excuses.

"Sorry about my performance out there today, Will," confessed Mitch. "I didn't know what to make of it when that jerk, Louie, got on our case. I turned into a bag-toting robot instead of a caddy. It won't happen again."

"Dude, you got nothing to apologize for. I was the one swinging the club. Tomorrow will be another day. Did you see the forecast? There's a front coming through, and it's supposed to be real windy. We love the wind."

"True that," agreed Mitch. "Let's go out tomorrow and play our game. To hell with those other guys. I'm going to bet Louie two hundred tomorrow."

"What, you were betting on me? I don't think that's legal."

"What are they going to do, kick you off the Tour? You're not a member of the PGA or the Tournament Players Association. Technically, you're not even a pro. If you want to collect any prize money, you will have to declare yourself a professional when this is over."

"Yeah, I know."

Mitch slowed down to cross some railroad tracks. On the other side they both looked to their right at a guy standing next to a sickly yellowish-orange looking Ford Topaz. The hood was up, and he was looking down at the engine.

"Hey, I've seen that guy before!" exclaimed Mitch. "He's the one that talked to us on number four today when we were on our way back to the tee. He said he was a reporter. I'm gonna stop. It looks like he needs some help."

Mitch hit the brakes and pulled over. He backed up on the shoulder, and they both got out.

"Hey, dude, remember us?" asked Mitch.

The guy's face lit up when he saw someone familiar.

"Yeah, pro golfer and caddy. What are you doing this far north of the course?"

"We wanted someplace to stay that was away from all the action. I'm Mitch, and this is Will. What's up with your machine?"

Luke Slowinski introduced himself. He stood about 6' 2" with short black hair. He had an inquisitive smile and an air about him that showed he was a likable, easy-going sort. At 200 pounds, he looked like he was capable of playing several sports. He explained that he was attending Missouri A&M University and was studying journalism. This summer he was working as an intern for the Dubuque Telegraph Herald. The paper had sent him down to cover the golf tournament. Golf was a challenging assignment for him, as he knew next to nothing about the sport. On the drive down from Dubuque, he passed the motel just up the road and decided that it would be a good place to stay.

"I've got no idea what the problem is with this beast," admitted Luke. "It's got 150 thousand miles on it. I was hoping to get 200 thousand. If ya'll could give me a ride back to the motel, I'd appreciate it. From there, I can ask around about getting it repaired."

"No problem, man, hop in," said Will.

"I couldn't help but notice the slight accent," said Mitch. "Missouri's not that far south."

"I'm from Reston, Texas," said Luke. "It's just north of Fort Worth."

"So let me guess, you were a big athlete back in high school so you decided to go into sports journalism?" asked Mitch.

"Not hardly. I was never a good athlete. My fiancé is though. Her and a couple of her good friends were some of the best female athletes in the whole state of Texas. They're legends back home in the Lone Star State."

"You don't say?" said Mitch. "I'll have you know that you're riding with a future legend."

"Stop it," objected Will.

"Seriously, Luke. This guy here is going to win the first golf tournament that he's ever played in. Now there's a story for you."

"It would be quite the scoop," agreed Luke as they pulled into the parking lot. "I don't want to impose, but could I ride to the course with you two tomorrow? I doubt if they could get my car fixed soon enough for me to drive it."

"No worries," said Mitch. "Tell you what. You find out where you need to take it, and we'll do a 'midnight tow job' to get it there. Real tow trucks are expensive. Just make sure it's local. We don't want to be pushing your ride over the bridge. That's too risky even for us. Meet us in the lobby in a couple of hours. We're heading across the river for sub sandwiches."

"Thanks, guys. You've just turned a potential major disaster into a minor inconvenience."

After supper, golfer, caddy, and fledgling reporter sat around the motel pool sipping drinks. The plan was to go out around midnight and push Luke's Topaz to Mike's Transmissions, which was only about two miles away. Will was playing in the afternoon session with a tee time of 1:15. According to the weather forecast the wind was supposed to come up in the afternoon as the front passed through. The morning guys were definitely going to have the advantage come tomorrow. Following the winds, around 2:00 in the morning, there were supposed to be some strong showers. If the forecast was accurate, the sun would be back out for the Saturday morning tee times. Lift, clean, and place might be the order for the day.

"How much will the wind bother you, Will?" asked Luke.

Mitch jumped in and answered for his guy.

"I guarantee you, he's one of the best wind players at the tournament. It's not necessarily windy where we're from, but my boy is a master at it."

"I'd be careful what you say to this guy," added Will. "If he quotes you, it will make us look like arrogant jerks. The truth is, Luke, I work at a golf course in Michigan. I play for a little money now and then and have been doing fairly well. Mitch and I thought it would be fun to play in a tour event. That's why we're here."

Mitch started to add his two cents when he received a stern look from Will indicating that he should zip it. Luke seemed like a nice guy, but he was a reporter, and sometimes when the press gets a hold of some information or a quote, the printed word takes on an entirely different connotation. Mitch got the hint and said no more. Will's phone buzzed, and he looked down to see if it was the call he was waiting for. His grandfather was on the other end.

CHAPTER EIGHTEEN

–Wind Player

A lot of my fellow countrymen just piss me off. They think by putting a "Support Our Troops" bumper sticker on their car, they're doing their bit for the men and women who risk everything for this great country. I ain't saying the stickers are a bad thing. But, if all you do is put that little sticker on, thinking you're doing us a great service, then I'd rather you do nothing at all. Patriotism that's all for show with no substance is shameful.

—-Ernie Dosland, Gunnery Sergeant, U. S. Army (retired)

The Michigan hustlers sat at the Harrah's Sports Book smoking cigars and watching several ball games on the flat screens plastered all over the wall in front of them. They discussed Will's situation.

"He's up to it," reassured Eddie. "Shooting one under in his first round was quite an accomplishment. I wouldn't worry about him."

"I know. I was just hoping he'd be a few strokes lower. I stand to make some major jing on that boy if he wins."

"You found a place that's taking bets on the JDC?"

"I didn't, but Hot did. I was waiting to surprise you. His name wasn't on the sheet, so he's what's called a 'field' bet. The sheet is full of the name players and a few that I've never even heard of. If your name isn't displayed, you're considered to be the rest of the field. Sometimes a field bet will be twenty, thirty, or even fifty-to-one. I think I got a real good deal. You want half?"

"You know it."

"I haven't told you how much I bet or what his odds were."

"I don't care what you bet or what his odds are. I'll take half of it."

"I bet ten G's at 40 to 1."

Eddie's eyes went wide. At 40 to 1, the payoff on ten large was $400,000.

"Did I ever tell you that I like your style, Mr. Costas?"

"You have, Mr. Ferguson, and the feeling is mutual."

"You know what I'm going to do after we win here? I'm going to fly down to Florida and Texas to visit my daughters and grandkids. After we watch Will play the final round at the JDC, of course."

"You're heading south in the summer?" asked Ronnie.

"Are you serious?" countered Eddie. "Look where we're sitting. How much hotter can it be down there?"

Ronnie lifted his drink for his partner to touch glasses. They agreed that two drinks were going to be their limit until their match was over. They both looked up at the screen directly in front of them to see two Chicago Cubs cross the plate after a monstrous home run. The young players that the Cubs were acquiring had certainly changed the way they approached the game. The north siders went from trying to just put on a good show for the fans to actually winning.

"You're awfully proud of your daughters, aren't you, buddy?" asked Ronnie.

"Yeah, they've both got good heads on their shoulders. Today, with all the political correctness going on, it's tough to raise a decent kid. A lot of parents nowadays try to shelter their kids from anything and everything that's even a little distasteful. And in the mean time, it seems like morals and principles have been taking a back seat to greed and self-centeredness. I can't tell you exactly why that is. It's probably a combination of things. I know you're proud of Will. He has turned out to be an exceptional young man."

"He has, and I know that his dad would be extremely proud of him too. That's huge isn't it? Knowing that your parents are proud of you?"

"It is, my friend. It certainly is."

"Why is it that I'm getting an uneasy vibe from you, Eddie? I know you well enough to sense that something is making you uncomfortable."

"You know me that well?"

"I do."

"Okay," said Eddie, placing his Macanudo in a nearby ashtray. "You know that one of my rules is never to anger people that can do me harm. Well, I don't like having to deal with the type of people we've been dealing with lately. But, that being said, I sense that Alexei Karpov has taken a liking to us in his own strange sort of way."

"I think he saw us in a new light when you offered the cold towels. We're just a couple of smooth operators that like to play golf for money. Maybe the sort of life that he pictures for his kid, or maybe for him if he had grown up in a different environment."

"Maybe," mused Eddie. "I've got an idea on what our play should be if he takes it real hard when he loses. It's a little rough, but I'll have it figured out by the time we tee it up tomorrow. I'll let you in on it then."

"Sounds good to me," said Ronnie, rising from his seat. "There's going to be a lot of action tomorrow—here and back in Illinois."

"Lets hope we're both up to it, partner."

"We will be. By the way, you owe me five large."

"I didn't forget. I'll pay you out of my winnings tomorrow."

"I love your confidence. Man, I hope Hot isn't bringing home another "client" tonight. I didn't think older women could moan that loud. That lady last night must have been part banshee. We need our rest."

"Hot's one of a kind, that's for sure. I'm sure he was paid well for his efforts."

"Any chance he would let us in on some of his secret techniques?" asked Ronnie.

"Probably not. Listen if you're having problems in the bedroom, maybe I can give you a couple of tips."

"Dude, golf and poker tips from you would be the only areas that I would be receptive to."

"Are you sure?" asked Eddie. "Guaranteed to get results."

"Thanks, but I'll pass, Mr. Casanova."

Ronnie propped himself up on one elbow and looked across the dark room at his golf partner. The room was just light enough to reveal Eddie's shadowy figure as he repositioned himself from his back to his side. He was now facing the far wall.

"Okay," whispered Ronnie.

"Okay, what?" responded Eddie barely audible.

"Give me just one tip."

* * *

Will Green and his caddy walked out to the practice range and took their usual spot at the far end. Luke stood behind the ropes until Mitch waved him over. Caddies and players were supposed to be the only ones on the tee, but Mitch noticed a few swing coaches and one of the Golf Channel announcers standing around talking to the players. Luke had a small hand-held tape recorder that he spoke into when he heard or saw anything he considered relevant to his upcoming article.

As predicted, the wind came up around noon, and it spared no one. Gray clouds could be seen out to the west, but the rain was supposed to hold off until the day's action was completed. Players and spectators had their hats pulled down tight on their heads. Even so, a few covers still managed to escape from their owners making a bid for freedom. Will was scheduled to tee off in thirty minutes, which meant they would warm up for fifteen minutes, then putt for ten minutes. The tenth tee, which would be Will's first for the day, was just across the cart path from the practice green, so there would be no problem with their timing. As they walked over to the practice green, a top ten player on the money list walked by with a security guard in tow. He gave them a respectful nod.

"Hey, where's our security guy?" hollered Mitch.

The pro looked back over his shoulder and grinned. He raised his hand and rubbed his fingers together, signaling that you had to be at the top of the money chain to get a guy in uniform. Bottom feeders were expected to fend for themselves. The three of them looked at each other and laughed. Luke asked Will if he would answer some questions as he putted. The hustler told him to fire away.

"You do realize that you're probably the only guy playing in the tournament that would agree to an interview just before he was about to tee off," commented Luke.

Will answered without looking up.

"I have been trained to not only focus on the task at hand but to also multitask. Part of my brain is working on my stroke while another part is doing the interview."

"Can I ask who trained you to do that?"

"That, I will not divulge," answered Will as he made a deft stroke, rolling in a putt from ten feet. "I don't want you to know, and they don't want you to know."

"So it was more than one person. What was it, like a team of coaches?"

"No comment."

Luke turned off his recorder, indicating that there was a pause in the interview.

"Why won't you answer that question? What is it, a matter of national security?"

Mitch broke in and answered before Will had a chance.

"Off the record, the guys Will hangs around with like to keep a low profile. So low that several people who know one of them think he's actually dead."

"That or living the good life down in Florida," chuckled Will. "He still can't figure out why so many of his old acquaintances think that, but it works into his plans."

"It sounds like you two know some very interesting people," said Luke.

"Interesting would be an understatement," said Mitch.

The caddy looked down at his watch and motioned that they had to get going. Their tee time was one minute away. As they crossed the cart path, the young boy that Will had given his "lost" ball to the previous day was standing there holding the ball out. Luke watched as Will did the second thing that most Tour pros wouldn't do right before they teed it up. He stopped and talked to the boy and signed his ball. Spangler and Charles stood on the tenth tee looking more than a little irritated. For one thing, the morning players had dodged a bullet playing before the wind started to blow, and now, Andy Taylor and his deputy, Barney Fife, were walking up to the tee not a second too soon. The starter motioned for Will to step up. He had to increase his volume due to the strong wind.

"Introducing the one fifteen tee time. From Hickory Corners, Michigan, please welcome…"

Wham! Will drilled a low draw down the fairway into the teeth of the wind. It was easily one of the best drives of the afternoon starters. Today they were going to play their game. His two opponents just stared at him open-mouthed. They'd never seen a player hit before his introduction was finished. Will picked up his tee and gave them a subtle wave. Then he jogged all the way up the small hill behind the tee and stood by the boy with the autographed ball. His parents and the fans loved it. Louie Burfine eased over to Mitch as his guy was preparing to hit.

"Jesus, dude," whispered Louie, "don't make any waves today. This wind is going to be tough enough. The morning guys are already back at their motels sipping gin and tonics. We're going to have to claw and scratch for everything we can get out here this afternoon."

"What's that?' asked Mitch, looking straight ahead. "You want to put 200 on today's round? Sounds good to me."

"You're on, Country. Just stay out of our way."

There were only three birdies on number ten in the afternoon session. The strong winds turned what was usually a decent birdie hole into a monster. Will's opening four was one of the three birds. He followed up on the next hole with an iron off the tee. With the wind now behind him, he was afraid of hitting it through the short grass and into the thick rough at the bottom of the sloping fairway. He played his tee shot to the 150-yard marker. From there, he hit a sweet little knockdown 9-iron that came to rest six feet from the hole. He rolled that in to go two under for the day.

After making par on number twelve, Will stepped up to the thirteenth tee and hit a low, screaming wind-busting hook down the right side. His ball stayed under the wind and when it hit, it kicked down the slope to the left curling around the fairway trap. Several of the spectators who were milling around the practice area and number ten tee, decided to follow Will and his group out onto the back nine. Golfer and caddy stood way over on the left side of the hole watching Spangler and Charles extricate themselves from the right fairway trap. The hustler's drive was another twenty-five yards closer to the green, on the left side of the fairway.

There seemed to be a lot of decision-making and general messing around across the fairway, so Mitch decided to stump his guy with a tune he had in the back of his mind.

"No way you will get this one," declared Mitch. He put his lips together and mouthed the opening beat. "Bum ba ba bum ba ba bum bum." He did it three or four times for emphasis.

Will gave him an exasperated look.

"Too easy, dude. It's "Ice Ice Baby" by Vanilla Ice."

"Nope," said Mitch.

"Give it to me again. That has to be it."

Mitch repeated the cadence. When Will said he was going to stick with his original song, a fan standing behind them on the other side of the rope offered "Under Pressure" by David Bowie.

"That's it," said Mitch. "Give that guy a cigar."

Will quickly unzipped a pocket in his bag and handed over a Macanudo to the fan. The crowd laughed and broke into a loud applause. Chris Spangler looked over from the far side of the fairway. He had just stepped into the sand assessing his shot, but apparently he wanted every living creature on the planet to keep still until he was done with his business. Will and Mitch stood like statues until Spangler clipped his ball out of the trap. He slammed his club down when his ball got caught up in the wind leaving him ten yards short of the green. Will walked briskly to his ball and looked over his 105-yard shot. He hit a low sand wedge right at the flagstick.

"Sweet Luretta Martin, be close," hollered Mitch.

"I flushed it, man," said Will grimacing. "It's too much."

"Get back, Luretta!" admonished Mitch.

The fans that could hear the golfers let out with loud laughter, which turned to amazed gasps, when Will's ball hit on the back of the green, hopped into the taller grass, then jumped back onto the green as if there was a string attached to it. Will looked at his caddy.

"I told you I flushed it. That sucker had some nasty spin on it."

The Beatles, "Get Back", came a shout from the crowd.

Mitch reached into the bag and threw another cigar toward the voice. The fans laughed and clapped their appreciation for the little sideshow they had just witnessed. A large number of them hustled back to the fairway crossing to watch him play the next hole.

While the spectators waited on the short par four fourteenth tee, a huge roar went up from the vicinity of thirteen green. Will was now three under, playing in very trying conditions. Spangler and Charles just rolled their eyes.

With the wind behind them on fourteen, all the contestants hit fairway metals. Will's was by far the most effective. He played a draw over the left edge of the tree that sat on the right side of the fairway. During his practice round, he hit a straight driver over the same tree, but when they got to the bottom of the hill they discovered that there was a second tree a tad further down to the right, with his ball sitting directly behind it. There was also a trap there to catch tee shots that didn't carry far enough. Will's tee shot was the best of the three ending up ten feet short of the green. The crowd continued to swell as they sensed something special was happening. Will's opponents both played acceptable pitches to within ten feet of the hole. They both would end up making their putts, but only after Will holed his chip to get to five under. He pulled his ball out of the cup and walked over to the edge of the green. A man in a wheel chair was sitting in front of the crowd with an "Iraq War Veteran" cap on. Will walked over to him and handed him the ball.

"Thanks for everything you did over there," he said quietly. "My dad was a Ranger, and he did more than one tour in Iraq."

The veteran reached out and shook Will's hand. In a gravelly voice, he asked Will what his father's name was.

"Robbie Green," answered Will.

The man's eyes went wide, then immediately began to fill with tears. He just sat there nodding his head up and down knowingly as the tears flowed silently down his cheeks.

"Damn, dude," whispered Mitch as they walked toward fifteen. "That was emotional, even for a guy like me. Do you think the television cameras got that?"

"I hope not," answered Will. "Can you believe that guy actually knew my dad? I guess the old saying, 'it's a small world' isn't just a figure of speech."

As he walked up fifteen fairway, Will veered over to the right so he could have a word with Luke. There was no hurry, as there appeared to be a delay up ahead. One of the players was waiting for a ruling. Fifteen was at the far eastern edge of the course, and there was no easy way to get to the hole. Luke was talking quietly into his recorder when Will motioned him over. The fans parted so Luke could get through.

"Hey, Luke, you're not going to write about what happened back there with the veteran in the wheelchair are you?"

"If I do, I assure you that I will be extremely respectful," answered Luke. "I wouldn't want to cheapen or dishonor a meeting like that."

"You're a good man," said Will as he started back to the fairway. "By the way, you're buying dinner tonight, and it's steak night."

The few people by the rope that could hear the conversation between golfer and reporter crowded around Luke to ask him questions about the kid from Michigan, who was now five under on an afternoon where even par was an excellent score.

CHAPTER NINETEEN

—Legendary Action

Eddie Davis? He's pulled more wins out of his anatomy than any guy I know. There was this one time when I was way ahead in a match with him, and in my mind, already spending my winnings. That turned out to be a huge mistake. Underestimating him can lead to a major loss of capital.

—-Claude Kensington, Texas golf hustler

"Last day, Alexei," said Eddie as they met their opponents on the first tee. "I hope you're enjoying this."

"Yes, I have enjoyed it," said the Russian. "And it's been a good experience for my son. The big crowd will give him an idea what the U. S. Tour is like."

Ronnie held in his smile. Two hundred people was by no means a big crowd by Tour standards. At almost any event, a player could expect thousands of fans lining the fairway from tee to green on crucial holes. Now that would be a crowd.

"I assume we're playing a scramble for the front nine?" asked Eddie.

"Yes," answered Alexei with a laugh. "We figure we will put you out of your misery on the front side. Then we can just cruise the back, thinking about where we'll be spending your money."

"Don't get ahead of yourself," cautioned Eddie. "Overconfidence can have a detrimental effect on one's game."

"Good advice, Eddie. Let's play some golf."

Tina and Herman were on high alert for any strange behavior or out of place characters. The larger crowd might pose a few problems, so they decided to split up. Tina was going to walk along with the crowd while her boss cruised the outer edges in a cart. They both had a small pair of binoculars, pepper spray, and a taser. As it was, there was no reason for any of Alexei's men to take any sort of action. The Russians won three of the first four holes.

Andrei was playing some superb golf, and his father was playing just well enough to not give away any holes. The kid's length was just too much for the hustlers to overcome in a straight scramble. They birdied five and six to get back to one down. Andrei responded by crushing huge drives on seven and nine, which resulted in two more birdies. The crowd was getting more boisterous as the match progressed. On the seventh tee, Ronnie whispered to Eddie that anyone with even a remote tie to Russia that lived within 100 miles must be at the course. Eddie nodded his agreement.

At the turn, the good guys were three holes down, and things were looking pretty grim. Against their better judgment, they decided to take a short break from the heat and go over their strategy for the second nine. The Russian team had no problem with this decision. They were in the driver's seat, and they felt the match was in the bag. Alexei was playing to the crowd and the press, talking up his son and his potential to win on the American Tour. While Alexei entertained the onlookers, Eddie and Ronnie sat inside and discussed their options.

* * *

"I don't want this rookie to get much air time unless he starts to fall apart," bellowed Max Worth inside the Golf Channel trailer. "I don't care if he does have the best round going this afternoon. His bubble will burst when he gets to the front nine. All that's left will be his excuses and his tears. I've seen it a hundred times before. Young kid breaks par a few times at his home course and he's ready to challenge the world. They should have more respect for the game and stay home until they've won something that means anything. And I ain't talking about winning a couple grand in the club Calcutta."

"Hey, boss, the kid just hit a beautiful fade into seventeen, and he's got a twenty-five footer for an eagle," alerted Denny Holmes, looking at one of the screens in front of him.

"All right, show the putt, but break away to a name player as soon as he misses," ordered Max as he stomped around the room. A couple of minutes later, he asked Denny what the results were on Will's putt.

"He left it three inches short, dead center. A choke job if I've ever seen one."

"Yuk it up, wise guy," said Max. "I'm tellin' you right now that this weekend will be a nightmare for him. Once he's paired with a big name, he will melt like an ice cream cone in the desert heat."

Angela Thurmond, sitting beside Denny, chipped in with a comment.

"Chief, did you know there are several very cold deserts on earth? There are places where ice cream cones wouldn't melt."

"Name one outside of Antarctica," challenged Max.

"How about the Namib desert in Africa. It's cold. Or the Gobi in China and Mongolia. I don't think you'd have to worry about getting heat stroke there."

"What are you a geography professor? Just do your job and keep things running smoothly. I'm going out for a smoke."

Max came back inside a few minutes later and asked for an update.

"Great news, boss," said Denny. "Green only made a par on eighteen. He's six under for the day, heading for the front side."

* * *

"Shit, Street, we've got ourselves in a bit of a pickle here," observed Ronnie. "It's bad enough to lose 125k a piece to these guys, but when it's done, we'll still be on the psychos' radar. The way the stinking press has been covering this, a win could definitely put us on the plus side with the Trentons. A loss will just give those New Yorkers a good laugh. I'd wager even money, and you know how much I abhor even money bets, that Anthony has filled in the old man on what's going on out here. If we lose this thing, and I'm still saying "if", Greer and Donaldson will want to play us more than ever. You know, wanting to one-up the Karpovs. I hope you've got a plan. This is a good time for you to come up with some of that legendary action that you're known for."

Eddie sipped his ice tea and gave his partner a look. It was a look that set him apart from the majority of the thousands of talented golfers that roamed the world's courses looking to turn their skills into cash. Ronnie had the look on occasion. Will had acquired it at an early age. The look could mean many things, but mainly it was an expression of extreme clarity—an expression that said, to those who knew how to read it, that the owner was completely in charge of the situation. It offered no guarantees, but the understanding behind it would often be the difference between success and failure.

Eddie leaned back in his chair, savoring the moment. He clasped his hands on top of his head and looked his partner in the eye.

"What has made us so successful in the hustling business all these years? Are we the two best senior golfers in the world?"

"No," answered Ronnie. "There are several seniors that I would consider better at the game than we are. Maybe not better ball strikers, but better golfers as a whole. They travel all over the country, sleep in strange beds, and still perform at the highest level in front of huge crowds. To answer your question, I would say that we are consistent, we know what we're capable of, and we are pretty damn good at hitting the money shot when the situation calls for it. That's why we've been so successful."

"You missed one crucial element," whispered Eddie as he leaned across the table. "We know how to set the stage. Like you said, even money is for suckers. Rarely have we teed it up for big money without covering all the angles. Sure the unexpected comes up from time to time, but most of the time after a couple of holes, we have a real good idea how the match is going to end and how much of our opponent's cash is going to find its way into our pockets."

"I like this kind of talk," said Ronnie.

"It's like we've told the kid dozens of times—deal from a position of strength, not desperation. Do you trust me?"

"Absolutely."

"With a hundred thousand?"

"Yup."

"With your wife?"

"Uh."

"Forget that one," said Street. "Maybe we'll come back to it. Moneywise, where does your comfort zone stop?"

Ronnie paused, thinking about this one. "Anything over a quarter mil."

"Good. All I need you to do is show some negative theatre as we set the back nine format. That and play the best golf you've ever played. If you don't, there's a good chance we won't have to worry about money ever again. We'll probably end up somewhere out in the desert in unmarked graves. I get the feeling you're about as fond of sand as I am."

"Dude, with that kind of talk, I won't be acting. You are kidding about taking a last sandy nap, right?"

"No guarantees, my man," said Eddie, slapping the table and grinning. "Let's get out there and see what these two are made of. C'mon partner, let's step on the fuckin' gas."

Eddie walked through the door and went over to his bag. He pulled out a fresh Macanudo and lit it up, savoring the smoke as he stared in the direction of the tenth tee. The crowd still looked to be around 200. The old man was pulling out all the stops trying to get as much publicity as he could out of their match and the subsequent thrashing of the arrogant Americans. Ronnie walked up with the Karpovs and Viktor right behind him. They were laughing it up, probably discussing where they were going to have dinner after the Americans were humiliated.

"All right, Mr. Davis," said Alexei. "What have you decided? Remember, nothing ridiculous, like playing left-handed or putting backwards through your legs. It has to be legitimate golf."

"Absolutely, Alexei. We don't want to disappoint all your fans with a show that would disrespect the game. But, before we decide the format, we'd like to discuss the money part of this competition."

"I hope you aren't going to tell me that you didn't bring the cash to cover your losses. That would be disrespectful to me and somewhat dangerous on your part."

"No, no," responded Eddie. "That's not what I was getting at. Ronnie and I each have 125 grand in our bags. We would never back out of a bet. That would be a chicken shit way to conduct business, and our reputation would suffer."

"Trust me, Mr. Street, your reputation wouldn't be the only thing to suffer. What are you talking about?"

Eddie took a long drag on his cigar and blew the smoke off to the side. He stepped in closer to the Russians. It was time to turn this thing into something he could control. As he alluded to Ronnie, dealing from a position of strength was a beautiful thing.

"What I'm talking about, sir, is doubling the bet."

"Done," said an excited Andrei before his father had time to process what was being offered.

"Wait a minute, Eddie," protested Ronnie right on cue. "We don't have that much cash with us, and I'm sure the Karpovs didn't bring that kind of dough with them either."

"Not a problem," said Eddie. "The loser will just pay the 125k in cash and wire the rest to the account that the winners provide. No worries, right, Alexei?"

Mr. Karpov, recovering from this strange turn of events, was trying to get a handle on the situation. Why would a man three holes down, playing someone as good as him and especially his son, want to play for more money? What was he up to, and why was his partner acting skeptical? Didn't they discuss Eddie's offer beforehand?

"Let's do it, dad," pleaded Andrei. "They can't beat us even if we were playing with croquet mallets."

"Hold on, I don't want to be too hasty," responded Alexei. "Before we agree on anything, I want to know the format."

"It's simple," said Eddie. "We play low total using only our 4-irons and putters."

Alexei looked at Viktor. "It sounds like a trick. What do you think?"

"I don't think limiting the clubs to two violates the agreement," responded Viktor. "It's still regular golf, just with fewer clubs. You make the call."

"I still don't like it, Eddie," complained Alexei.

"Tell you what," offered the hustler like a python stealthily encircling its prey. "We'll play that way for four holes, and if you don't like it, we'll play a scramble, with a little twist, for the last five."

"This little twist, do we get to use all our clubs in the scramble?"

"Yes."

"And my son and I both get to hit every time?"

"Absolutely."

"Alright, we play for 250 thousand each. I have the cash, but you can wire the rest of your losses to my account in the Caymans."

The crowd around the tee was buzzing about the new arrangement. They didn't know the details, but the word was that the stakes just went up substantially. One old boy in the back just stood there with a knowing smile on his face. Before he became a citizen, he had been to America several times to visit relatives, and it just so happened that they lived in the Detroit area. They were both a lot younger then, but he recognized Eddie as soon as he saw his picture in the paper promoting the match. Whatever the two Americans were up to, he knew that it would be memorable enough to take off of work as a dealer at Treasure Island. He wanted to be there when all the action took place. He also had a week's pay on the two Americans at three-to-two odds.

The Karpovs still had the tee. Alexei hit a decent 4-iron out to about 175 yards. Andrei followed with a 225-yard blast that drew a huge ovation from the crowd. Eddie gave the crowd a sheepish look and proceeded to hit his patented draw out to about 190. Ronnie followed suit, five yards shorter than his partner. The par four tenth was playing about 385, which left Ronnie with a second shot of 200 yards and Eddie with 195 yards. Alexei had no thoughts of getting home in two. He hit a big 4-iron for him, but was still fifteen yards short of the green. The hustlers both knew that Andrei's second shot would decide the hole. He was only about 160 yards out.

The young Russian looked out at the green. Ronnie was lying about ten yards short and Eddie was on the front edge and would probably have no problem getting down in two. This meant that he had to match Eddie's par or he and his dad would lose the first hole on the back side. He choked down on his club and, using a three-quarter swing, tried to guide his ball between the greenside traps. As with a lot of less-than-full shots if they aren't hit aggressively enough, the player's hands don't quite get into position at impact. The ball flew off the center of Andrei's club, but the face was a tad open. Players and spectators saw a puff of sand kick up when Andrei's ball landed in the right trap.

Andrei discovered that extricating oneself from the sand with a 4-iron was harder than it looked. If it was hard sand with no lip, it might have been possible to chip it out like a lot of old-timers like to do. But this was not the case. His trap problems cost his team the hole and put a look of determination on his father's face. It only took one hole for the old man to figure out that playing with these two clubs called for a lot more strategy than his son's usual "pound out a drive, followed by a short iron into the green". They tied the eleventh, thanks to Andrei's thirty-foot putt. When it fell, he turned to the crowd and did a strange dance that a fan might see during an NFL game after a receiver caught a simple slant pass for a first down. His dad gave him a look of disapproval but didn't say anything.

The Russians dropped another hole on the twelfth. All four balls were short of the green on their second shots. Eddie hit the stick with his bump and run. The ball came in a little hot, but it hit the pin dead center, bouncing straight back leaving him a one-foot putt. Ronnie and Alexei hit decent chips and were four foot away on opposite sides of the hole. Alexei followed his son's miss from fifteen feet with a miss of his own. A sportsman would have given Ronnie his putt, since all he had to do was two-putt to win the hole. Alexei said nothing and stood stoically as Ronnie rolled his putt dead center. The Americans were now only one down.

The thirteenth was halved, which meant the visitors could now opt for the change of format. Eddie looked at his partner and pretended to scratch his right eyebrow with two fingers. It was a modified two-finger salute that told Ronnie the real hook was about to be set.

"Nice move, Eddie," said Alexei as they stood on the fourteenth tee. The fourteenth, a par three playing about 190 yards, was a perfect distance for the Americans. It was a little too far for Alexei to get his tee shot to the putting surface and it would call for Andrei to hit another choke-down attempt, that so far, he hadn't shown any real expertise at.

"How about we finish with the scramble you talked about? No more salad forks off the tee, okay?"

"Not a problem, sir. Like I said, we'll just play a scramble with a little twist."

"Agreed. Anything to get away from your stupid 4-iron tricks."

"It wasn't a trick, man. It was a test to see who had control of all their clubs, not just a driver and a wedge. Okay, here's the twist. As you know, a scramble is also called a best shot. A team hits their tee shots, and then they play the best shot for their second."

"Yes, yes, we all know that," responded Alexei as he indicated the crowd that was waiting impatiently for the action to continue. For a large crowd, they were fairly quiet, as they also wanted to know what the next format was going to be. Some of the fans were betting on every hole in addition to the match's final outcome. The Russian immigrant had made back his front nine losses and was now up two grand. He too, thought America was a great country.

"Well," continued Eddie. "We're going to play something we used to play back in the Motor City. It's called a 'second best shot'. We usually played it as a foursome, but it'll work with any number of players. Hell, I've even played it head to head with one other guy. We would both hit two shots, then played the worst one. Anyway, for our match, both players hit off the tee, and then they pick up their best shot and play the other ball. If there is a problem deciding which shot is the best one, their opponents will tell them which one to hit. And we play it that way right into the hole."

"This is stupid," complained Alexei.

"On the contrary, sir," continued Eddie. "It would be stupid for us to give you a fifty-yard advantage off every tee. This way, the team that plays the best golf from here on out will win. Not the team with the longest hitter. Andrei can really smoke it, so let's put the rest of his game to the test. Hell, it'll test all of us."

"So if one of us makes an eight-footer, the other guy still has to putt?"

"Yup. That first putt was the best shot. The second one will have to drop too, or you'll still be putting."

Alexei pulled Viktor off to the side, and they had a short discussion. The people that were close enough to hear the new terms were shouting their opinions. The two Russians came back and agreed to the new deal. The golfers waited for the crowd to place their bets with one another. While they were waiting for the commotion to subside, Eddie looked over at Alexei and gave him a big smile.

"You Americans love to gamble, don't you, Eddie?" asked the Russian.

"We love a lot of things," answered Ronnie. "We're rather partial to gambling, cool cars, rock & roll, good whiskey, and obviously, our freedoms."

"Let's not talk ideology while we're playing golf," cautioned Alexei. "By the way, what is the Motor City?"

"Detroit!" came the answer from about twenty of the fans.

With the new format, there would now be a totally different kind of pressure. If your partner stuck his approach shot in tight ahead of you, then it was obvious whose shot the team was going to play for their next one. There is a saying in golf that "you're only as good as your bad shots", and this was a game that would put that saying to the test. Unlike in a normal best shot, the cost of a poor shot was now at a premium. The Karpovs came to realize this on the very next hole.

Eddie hit first, carving a nice little 4-iron draw to about eighteen feet right of the pin. Ronnie followed with the same club, two feet inside of Eddie's shot. He received a little fist bump of appreciation from his partner.

The senior Karpov hit first and left it on the right fringe, leaving a 35-foot slightly downhill chip or maybe a putt if he decided to use the flat stick from there. Andrei hit a sweet 7-iron five feet behind the hole. It was a beautiful shot that drew a huge applause. Ronnie gave his partner a quizzical look.

"Don't they know that the Ruskies will have to pick that one up?"

"I think they're betting on every shot," answered Eddie. "This is my kind of crowd."

Alexei's subsequent chip shot was going too fast as it neared the vicinity of the cup— too fast unless it hit the pin dead center, which is exactly what it did. When it disappeared into the hole, he pointed at the Americans in celebration. The Michigan contingent gave him a wave of admiration. Once the bills exchanged hands and the crowd settled down, Andrei stepped up and bumped his 7-iron toward the flag. It wasn't going quite as fast as his dad's, but it was still way too aggressive. He only missed the pin by a couple of inches, but those few inches were crucial. The Russians and their backers in the crowd watched in horror as the balled slowly trickled all the way down to the opposite fringe and stopped up against the longer cut of grass. They were still 30-feet away, and they hadn't lost their turn.

The Karpov's decided to let Andrei putt first. His feel for the speed was a little tentative. He watched in dismay as his ball stopped eight feet short of the cup. Alexei scowled as he watched his son mark his ball. He stepped up and swatted his ball with little preparation. His putt rolled two feet inside Andrei's mark, which was all he was trying to do. As soon as the anemic first putt stopped, Alexei knew that was the ball they'd be playing. Subsequently, they both still had to make the eight-footer remaining. Alexei stomped off when his son left his putt on the front edge.

The younger Karpov showed a great deal of maturity as he stood there motioning for the Americans to putt out. Eddie gingerly tapped his ball and watched as it trickled down stopping a foot from the hole. Ronnie followed suit and hit the exact same putt. Andrei picked up Ronnie's ball and tossed it to him. The match was now even as they headed to the fifteenth.

It was obvious that the new format didn't agree with Alexei. The roles of father and son, teacher and student, now seemed to be reversed. Andrei tried to calm his father down as they prepared to hit their tee shots on the fifteenth, a long par five. The older man was having none of it. Very few golfers play better when they are mad or frustrated, and Alexei was not one of those few.

CHAPTER TWENTY

"I Only Beg For Two Things"

Begging is beneath most men and it's unbelievably pathetic. Besides, it rarely gets you anywhere.

—-Chris Mortenson, poor bastard on an 0 for 20 streak

Mitch, Will, and Luke sat on a bench looking out at the Mississippi River. They all seemed to be lost in their thoughts as they watched the brown water glide by. Will's 61 was by far the low score of the day, and the fact that he played under conditions that were not conducive to low scoring made it all the more remarkable. He was taken by surprise when a young woman with a microphone asked him a few questions when he exited the scorer's tent. Since this was the first pro tournament that he had ever played in, and consequently the first event where he found himself only one stroke off of the lead, he decided to plead ignorance the following day when he would inevitably be asked why he didn't show up for a few questions in the press tent.

Chris Spangler and Ted Charles had a quiet little conversation of their own in the players' locker room after the round. At first, they were in agreement that someone should say something to a tournament official about Will and Mitch's conduct out on the course. It wasn't any one major thing; it was just their whole demeanor. They interacted constantly with the crowd and played little music games with each other. Mitch almost got into it with a fan because of his New York Yankee cap. They halted for a few seconds, giving Will time to hit his shot, then the insults started in again. The crowd went wild when the two shook hands and traded caps—Yankees for Tigers. That sort of thing just wasn't supposed to happen out on the Tour.

The bitching session came around to Will's game and his unbelievable score. Charles finally calmed Spangler down, pointing out that if they were household names, then their concerns might carry some weight. As it was, their scores of 73 and 74 would arouse some suspicion with the officials. Will had bested them both by more than ten strokes! They decided to wait until tomorrow and let the big names deal with the whole mess. Besides, they had both made the cut by one stroke, so they would both be on the receiving end of a check. As they followed each other out of the locker room, Charles muttered to himself, "Best round of golf I have ever seen."

"Why does this water look so dirty?" asked Luke.

"There's a lot of current whipping around down there stirring up the mud," answered Will. "Back home in Michigan on a calm day you can read a book in ten feet of water."

Luke looked at Mitch to see if Will was spoofing him. Mitch shook his head in agreement.

"There are a lot of lakes where we live, Luke. Kids that grow up on them learn to walk and swim about the same time. I once went to pick up my date to the Homecoming Dance and she was out water-skiing. When she saw me waving at her from shore she motioned for the boat driver that she wanted to go in. He raced by the little beach that came right up to her back yard, and she let go of the rope at the perfect time. She literally stepped out of her ski and onto the sand. She had spent a lot of money on her hair, so when I asked her what she would have done if she had fallen into the water, she he gave me a strange look and said the last time she fell off her skis she was about ten years old. She also hadn't skied on more than one ski for that same period of time."

"Sounds like a talented girl," said Will.

"She is," said Mitch. "She's at Michigan State studying to be a doctor. Didn't you say your fiancé was an athlete, Luke?"

"Yup. A whole bunch of us from Reston are at Missouri A. & M. The girls are all on athletic scholarships, and I even got a partial one for journalism. My advisor told me that mine was the first scholarship of its kind ever awarded at the university. The strange thing is, I never even applied for it. It just showed up one day in the mail."

"Free school—you can't beat that," added Mitch. "I'll be paying on my loans for quite a while, or as soon as Will wins this tournament. I'm hoping for the latter."

"Hey, what do you say that we all get drunk to celebrate me making the cut?" asked Will, showing youthful excitement.

"How about this for an alternative plan?" offered Mitch. "We have two beers each and hit the rack around eleven. You're twenty-one, aren't you, Luke?"

"I'm legal, and I'll even buy if I can continue my interview with Will for the article that I'm going to write on him. My boss at the paper left my assignment wide open. He's going to be in for a shock when he finds out I hung out all week with the tournament winner and his awesome caddy."

"Did you know that the word 'awesome' is considered one of the most overused words in the English language?" asked Mitch, rising from the bench. "But in this case, it is entirely appropriate. Hey, when will your car be done?"

"Tomorrow afternoon," responded Luke. "They had to order the parts. I can't believe they didn't have Topaz parts in stock. That machine is a classic."

* * *

The fifteenth at Las Vegas National is the longest hole on the course. It was the hole where, on the previous day, Alexei had squirreled his tee shot into the pond just off the tee. After hitting matching drives, Eddie and Ronnie went over and stood by the drink cart. The crowd parted to let the players through. One man stood his ground in front of Eddie.

"You win this, and you might not live to spend the money," he whispered. "You decide what's more important, a handful of cash or the ability to breathe."

Herman had traded with Tina and was now on foot. He didn't hear the exchange, but he could tell that some serious words had just been spoken. He grabbed the man by the arm and pulled him away from Eddie. He then steered him off to the side of the crowd.

"Listen, little man," threatened the big guy. "I don't want you talking to the golfers. Let them play. They don't need any distractions."

"Do you know who I am?" asked the man in an indignant tone.

"Well, you're not Reese Witherspoon," responded Herman. "You've got a lotta nerve stealing her line."

Having no clue what Herman was talking about, the man tore himself free of the bigger man's grasp and stalked off. Herman looked over at Tina and pointed toward his eyes and then toward the man. She acknowledged his gesture.

The two teams halved number fifteen with impressive pars. The Americans had a tap-in, but the Russians had to work a little harder for their five. Alexei rolled in a six-footer on their first putt. Andrei stepped up with little fanfare and duplicated his father's stroke. If he would have missed the putt, his team would have went from three-up at the turn to one-down with three to play. The old man slapped his son on the back. Parental pride was a commonality even in families with less than stellar reputations.

Sixteen was a medium length par three with greenside traps right and left. Ronnie and Eddie made smooth swings putting both of their shots on the putting surface. The tension was starting to show on the head of the Karpov family. He had to give the Americans credit—they had put the responsibility of winning squarely on his shoulders. He had agreed to the match assuming that his son's game would dominate the fifty-something Americans. Andrei proved that he was up to the task, which meant that he, Alexei, was the determining factor. With all these thoughts running through his head, it was no wonder he didn't quite finish his swing, steering his ball to the right front trap. It was like he was playing the Americans all by himself!

Eddie watched Alexei's face as he walked over to his cart. The man looked utterly defeated. He had seen that look before and it didn't give him a lot of pleasure, but when people were playing for high stakes it was bound to happen. He turned to Ronnie as they rode up to the sixteenth green.

"I think the old man just figured it out that it's him, and only him, against us. I know he thinks we tricked him. We need to do something to lesson the bitterness that's going to result from this match."

"I know you're not talkin' about us dumping this thing," said Ronnie. "We've tried that before with these type of people, and it didn't work."

"No, man, we ain't dumping."

"Then what's your plan?" asked Ronnie.

"We're going to ask him out to dinner."

Herman was standing in the shade of one of the few trees between fifteen green and sixteen tee. Tina was up by the green in her cart. Except for the confrontation with the creepy looking dude, the day was going smoothly. The private detective was glad this thing was about over, and he was doubly glad that his boys were in the driver's seat, poised to collect 250 grand each. Leave it to them to turn what looked like disaster into a profitable venture. He also marveled at Estelle's plan to earn points with the Trentons. All in all, it looked like this was going to be a win/win situation. He was thinking how nice it would be to get back to livable temperatures when everything went black. He didn't even feel himself hit the ground.

The two teams stood on number seventeen looking across the water that crossed the hole in front of the tee. The Americans were one up as they waited for the match's followers to straggle up to the tee. They had to give their fans credit. They had hung in there, walking all the way in the heat. The gamblers who appeared to be on the losing end of the match were still making bets, hoping to take some of the sting out of the final payoff. Eddie and Ronnie again hit matching tee shots about 260 yards out and in the fairway. The heat was taking its toll on them also. Andrei stood up and hit another blast a few steps short of the green. Alexei's drive only went about 225 yards, leaving his team with a 75-yard wedge into a narrow front to back green.

The pin was cut behind the right front trap that covered the whole right side of the green. The hustlers had already decided that they were not going to go for the pin. Even though they had a much shorter pitch than their opponents, a ball left in the trap would be disastrous. The Karpovs, on the other hand, decided that they needed a little magic to not have the match end right here. Alexei wiped his grip with a towel and settled in to make his shot. Right before he pulled the trigger, he stood and walked back to his cart. He wiped his face and his grip one more time. He sensed that this was going to be the money shot of the match. He went back and addressed his ball. After a couple of abbreviated practice swings he went into the ball with a short stabbing swing. The crowd was as quiet as they had been for the last three days. The ball flew toward the pin on the desired trajectory. All eyes were on it as it descended toward the green. When it splashed down in the trap a foot short from clearing the sand, a large moan, along with a few sighs of relief, escaped the fans. Alexei walked over to the hustlers' cart.

"I could almost hear you begging for that shot to fall short," he said addressing Eddie.

"I only beg for two things, Alexei," responded Eddie. "And one of them is morphine."

It only took Alexei a few steps to figure out Eddie's comment. He started chuckling to himself and kept it up all the way into the trap. He waited for his opponents to hit. Their worst shot ended up 25 feet left of the pin. The way they had been putting, there was a very good chance they would get both of their lags within a couple of feet. Alexei shook his head and hit one of the best sand shots of his life. With all the pressure it was quite remarkable. The ball landed ten feet short of the stick and proceeded to roll up to about eighteen inches. He waved to the spectators acknowledging their appreciation for a well-played shot.

Andrei was next to hit. He retrieved his ball from the putting surface and gently placed it on the top of the sand. He wiggled his feet to get comfortable. After confidently looking at the flag, he took the club back and thinned his shot completely over the green into the far bunker. There were a few murmurs from the crowd, but nothing discernible.

The Michigan team watched their opponents walk to the back trap. Their only hope was to hole both shots out for a par. The crowd was coldly silent, waiting for the scene to play out. There was no more betting to be done.

Surprisingly, under the circumstances, both of the Russians hit beautiful shots. They marked the worst, which was three feet away and motioned for their opponents to putt. It was time for the Michigan hustlers to do what they did best. Eddie rolled his putt inches from the hole. When Ronnie's effort stopped a foot away, Alexei swatted it back and stuck out his hand. The crowd cheered, even some that had lost money. This was a different sort of action, and they had been privy to it. Both teams had played fabulous golf and the match came down to the last two holes. They couldn't wait to regale their friends on how two fifty-something Americans took a wad of cash from the two Russians.

Herman looked up through foggy vision at the man in front of him. He was sitting against a tree, but other than that, he wasn't sure where he was. The only thing he did know was that his head hurt like hell. He finally recognized the guy that he had moved away from Eddie a while back. What was going on? The man had a nightstick in his hand. Herman chuckled to himself. A nightstick is also called a blackjack. How ironic. Apparently being hit with a blackjack in Vegas had more than one meaning.

"You think this is funny?" asked the man with a slight accent. Herman hadn't noticed the accent the first time they had talked. "I doubt if you will be laughing when I break both of your kneecaps."

"Who the hell are you?" asked Herman, stalling for time. He tried to bring his hands in front of him, but they were tied with something that felt like twine.

"I'm Edgar Karpov. You might say that I'm the black sheep of the family. As you Americans say, 'no pun intended'. You shouldn't have interfered with my business. Now you are going to have to pay. Say good-bye to your healthy knees and your normal walk. That is all about to change."

Edgar lifted the stick to strike and was taken completely off the ground by a hurtling body. Tina hit Edgar like J. J. Watt sacking a quarterback. After driving the Russian to the ground, she pinned him and immediately ripped the stick out of his hands. She brought it across the Russian's throat and looked over her shoulder at her boss. Herman worked his way up the tree so he could stand. He jerked hard on the twine and it separated. He walked calmly over to the two of them.

"Meet Tina, my assistant. I don't think she likes you. If I don't ask her nicely to get up, she might just kill you."

Tina stood and pulled a knife out of her back pocket and cut the loose hanging bonds from Herman's wrists. After frisking Edgar, the three of them walked over to Tina's cart and rode back to the clubhouse. Herman sat on the far right with a huge arm draped over Edgar's shoulders. His hands were secured with the plastic cuffs that the private detective always carried in his back pocket. There was no way he was going anywhere.

On the ride back, Edgar explained why he attacked Herman. He felt that if in some small way, he could help his dad and his brother win the match, then his father would be grateful. He was pissed at Herman for getting in the way when he threatened Eddie. Edgar was the typical neglected son. Andrei apparently got all the paternal attention because of his golf skills. Herman asked Tina what she thought they should do with their captive. She thought his question was out of character for the guy who was in charge of security.

They pulled up to the clubhouse just as the competitors arrived. Alexei saw his other son with the cuffs around his wrists and stormed over with Ronnie, Eddie, and Andrei right behind. Tina gave him the facts on what happened. Alexei was very gracious. He asked Herman if it would be okay with him if this were handled as a family matter. Herman just nodded and smiled back at him. The golfers agreed to have dinner later at Hugo's Cellar below the 4 Queens casino. All business matters would be concluded after dinner. The private detective still had a stupid grin on his face as Andrei walked away with his two sons and a few Russian followers.

"Tina, we need to get out of here. The Cub game is about to start," said Herman. "Damn, it's hot here."

"I'm taking this one to the hospital," she explained. "He's pretty much out of it, which means possible concussion. That Russian dude must have cracked him pretty good. I'll call you later with an update."

CHAPTER TWENTY-ONE

BNP's and Celebrities

Vegas is a wonderful place. There are all kinds of famous people walking around. The last time I was there, I got an autograph from the guy that played George on Seinfeld. He seemed like a decent guy. Not like some of those other stuck up stars that think they're better than everybody else.

—-Barry Lewis, full time accountant, part time drunk

Golfer, caddy, and reporter stood on the practice tee. Will was in the second-to-last group, only two strokes behind the leaders. There was a huge crowd standing behind the rope that kept the spectators off the tee. They wanted to see the guy that shot the 61 yesterday in the frightful conditions. With only forty-five minutes to go, the kid from Hickory Corners still hadn't hit a shot. He was still soaking up the atmosphere. Mitch finally told him to get on with it. The people wanted to see if he was for real or just a guy that had just played the round of a lifetime.

Will pulled his sand wedge from the bag and took a few practice swings. A couple of BNP's, or Big Name Players, to their left stopped hitting so they could see the guy that the sports channels were raving about. Sensing there were several sets of eyes on him, Will put the wedge back and took out a 5-iron. His first shot went out and took a 90-degree turn to the right, a humongous slice. Then he thinned one that never got above six feet as it flew out over the range. The pros to his left looked at each other and stifled a laugh. His playing partner for the day was several spots away, so he didn't see Will's little show of hackery. A few of the spectators were actually laughing.

"Luke, do you know how many golfers can take one swing, then hit half way up a ball on purpose?" asked Mitch.

"I'm guessing not many," responded Luke.

"Exactly," said Mitch, looking at his player. "Now hit a few decent ones before security gives us the bum's rush."

Will hit three shots with each club, which, for him, was a full practice session. He knew that the big boys hit a lot of balls on the road and when they practiced at home. For some reason, after all the balls he had hit when he was younger, the thrill of pounding balls to make-believe targets had diminished over the years. He also knew that one of the primary reasons for hitting large numbers of balls was to hone a guy's timing. When the time came to hit that last 5-iron to a tough green for a big payoff, there had to be no question in the back of the golfer's mind that he was going to hit the ball in the center of the clubface—not fat, not thin, but dead center. He might pull it left or push it right of the target or misjudge the distance. But that would be the result of something different than a ball departing anywhere except the center of the club. If a Tour pro was having trouble finding the center of the club on the majority of his shots, he was home working on it and watching the tournament on television.

The crowd behind Will was impressed when he started hitting serious shots. He worked quickly through his bag, hitting what looked like bullets out over the range. The two closest pros snuck a few peeks and just shrugged their shoulders. A lot of guys were good at hitting practice balls. The problem for those guys was none of these shots counted. Could he take his impressive swing out on the course and perform in a high-pressure situation?

"How much time do we have?" asked Will.

Mitch looked over at the big clock at the end of the range.

"We've got a half hour," said Mitch.

"Can you believe the old guys won all that dough out in Vegas?" asked Will.

Ronnie had called with the good news right after they had dinner with the Karpovs and Viktor. The one thing he didn't divulge was the surprise that Eddie pulled right after the money exchanged hands.

*   *   *

When the plates were cleared away, Alexei signaled to his man sitting over by the entrance of the dark room. The man got up and brought two small utility bags with drawstrings over. He handed one each to Ronnie and Eddie. Alexei looked at the bags, noticing the Adidas logos on them.

"Fucking Germans," he laughed. "Gentlemen, you aren't even going to look at your winnings?"

"Not necessary," answered Eddie, placing his bag on his lap. "Listen, Alexei, there's something Ronnie and I want to talk to you about."

Alexei sat back in his chair waiting for what he thought would be a request for a favor. After losing a substantial amount of cash to these two, he was not in a receptive mood to do something more for them. However, he was willing to listen. If pressed, he would admit that he actually respected the two gentlemen sitting across the table. They were a couple of slick operators, and they were highly skilled at a game where he hoped his son would make a name for himself.

"My partner and I were talking, and we think Andrei here has what it takes to play the American Tour. He's got everything he needs except a solid sand game. If he were to spend a solid month with a top short game instructor here in the states, we think he has a good chance to be successful out on the pro circuit."

"Do you know such a teacher that would take my son on as a student?" asked Alexei, a little perplexed.

"We do, and if you want we will give him a call. He's very expensive, but he owes us a favor, and I'm sure he'll do it for no charge."

Alexei was still wary of the Americans' intentions. Why were they offering to do this? He decided he needed a little more information.

"What is it that you liked about Andrei's game, my friend?"

Eddie looked over at Ronnie asking him to join in on the conversation.

"Besides he hits the shit out of the ball," offered Ronnie, "we liked his composure. He was not only playing for substantial money; he was playing for his father's money—the man he respects most in this world. And when things weren't going well, he kept his cool and played some of his best shots of the whole match. Attitude means a lot when things go wrong. Quite often it's the difference between success and failure."

"Let's say he improves his sand game enough to give it a shot," continued Alexei. "Do either of you know a way that he could play on the Pro Tour immediately? The Qualifying School is a long way off."

"You'd have to check into the Monday morning qualifiers for each tournament," said Ronnie. "You might also check into sponsors' exemptions. I don't think there are any Russians playing on the Tour, and if a tournament sponsor has even a remote connection to a Russian business, there might be a way to use that as leverage. Maybe he should try the web.com Tour or whatever they are calling it nowadays. It's like the minor leagues of golf. If he's successful there, then he should be ready for the big time."

"I thank you for your advice and the offer of providing a teacher," said the Russian, standing and offering his hand. "I can't say it was a pleasure losing money to you two, but I will say that you have surprised me in more ways than one. I would also like to apologize one more time for the actions of my other son. I don't know what he was thinking. In many ways, he has always been a real challenge, if you know what I mean. Please give my man your phone number, so I can get back to you with our decision on the teacher. Good-bye gentlemen."

The two hustlers climbed up the stairs from the restaurant. Tina was sitting there playing a slot machine. They decided that it would send the wrong signal if she joined them for dinner. They gave her a nod and each offered her an arm. She stepped in between them.

"Who do you know that's a great short game teacher?" asked Ronnie.

"I don't," answered Eddie. "But I figure we could make a top instructor an offer he couldn't refuse, if you know what I mean."

"And why are we doing this?"

"It's called insurance, my man. Remember my policy of never pissing off people that can do you harm? Well, you just saw an example of that policy at work. I think our offer might have changed his thinking toward us. He's not the sort of man that I would want to get on the bad side of. We just took a boatload of cash off him. That's reason enough for him to want us to have some sort of unfortunate accident. Now he thinks we're good guys for wanting to help his son."

"That's why I like you, Street. You're always thinking about my health and my money."

"Is that the only reason you like me?"

Ronnie didn't answer until they walked out the door onto Fremont Street. Loud music was blaring and four people on zip lines flew over their heads screaming. Both men squeezed their bags a little tighter.

"Yup, that's the only reason I can think of. I got one more question. That line about begging for morphine. I thought it was excellent. Did you make that up on the spot?"

"Naw, man. I heard it from a guy when I was playing down in Florida. I figured that was a perfect time to use it. I'll admit, I was a little surprised when the Russian actually got it."

"I trust everything went according to plan?" asked Tina.

"No worries," said Ronnie.

"They're keeping Herman overnight at the hospital," said Tina. "It's just a precaution. Do you want to stop and have a drink to celebrate your victory?"

"Sounds good to us," said Eddie. "But let's do it back at Hot's place after we pay Herman a quick visit. We need to get off the street as soon as we can."

"Why's that?" asked Tina.

"We're carrying half a million dollars in these bags."

* * *

"I don't want to hit anymore practice balls," said Will. "Let's go over and talk to some of these spectators. They look like nice people. Hard-working mid-westerners, just like us."

Luke gave Mitch a questioning look and got an eye roll for a response. They stood back as Will went over to the dividing rope and introduced himself to the people standing there. Several of them held out programs and hats for him to sign. He did his best to accommodate them and in the process received several pen marks on his white shirt. It didn't bother him at all. Like he said, they were nice people.

The Green/Winston team decided to approach Saturday's round with the same attitude as yesterday. They were going to stay relaxed, kidding with each other and with the crowd. For them it was a good way to stay loose. Even though there was a lot of money on the line, it was still, in their minds, the greatest game ever. Beautiful scenery, pleasant weather, and cash on the line—what else could a guy ask for?

Will and his caddy walked onto the first tee to a thunderous applause. For most of the fans it was their first look at the kid that was the main topic of conversation on any television or radio network that covered sports. How could a guy come literally out of nowhere and do what he was doing? It would be some story if he won the whole thing. They walked over and introduced themselves to Carl Cummings and his caddy, Budgie Comstock. Mitch had done his research on today's pairing. After the cut had whittled down the field, the format went from threesomes to twosomes. Cummings was from California and had been on the Tour for five years. He was yet to win, but seemed poised to break through at any time. His caddy, Budgie, got his name from the other caddies for his repeated attempts to cut in line ahead of others. He was also from California—a surfer turned caddy. Both Mitch and Will liked the day's grouping, especially when they heard the first words out of Budgie's mouth.

"Dudes, nice round yesterday. You guys lapped the field with that one. Hit 'em solid today. If you see any good-looking women in the crowd, point 'em out. I'm trying to put together a harem, and there are still a few openings. No gold-diggers. Just babes with a sense of adventure."

The Michigan entry wasn't sure if Budgie was putting them on or not. Regardless, they liked the guy's relaxed demeanor. It would be a totally different experience than the last two days with Spangler and Charles. Those two, due to Friday rounds in the mid-seventies, were way back in the pack. The starter raised his hands to get the crowd's attention, as Will teed up his ball. Like the day before, he smashed his drive when the starter was half way through his introduction. There were a few laughs mixed with a substantial applause as Will picked up his tee and went over to stand by Mitch.

"Not your normal first tee drive, man," whispered Budgie. He ran the first two words together making them sound like one. "That's going to be your Tour name with the caddies, Nacho. What do you think?"

Will stuck out a fist for Budgie to bump. Carl hit his tee shot and received a half-hearted applause. The group headed out across the tee and down into the little valley that fronted it. Mitch looked over at Budgie, who seemed to be humming a song to himself.

"Hey, Budgie, what's my Tour name?" he asked, hoping for something exotic that he could tell Gloria about when he called her later.

"Herd," replied the surfer.

"Herd? How did you come up with that?"

"You two are the only ones in the tournament that no one's ever heard of," replied Budgie. "And since Nacho's already got a name, yours is Herd."

"Can't argue with that logic," laughed Mitch.

Carl and Budgie were a perfect match for Will and Mitch. Carl had a dry sense of humor and wasn't afraid to speak his mind when it came to his fellow pros or their bag toters. He wasn't hurting for money, as his dad owned a ball bearing factory. For him, playing professional golf kept him out of the company's front office working a public relations job that he would have hated. It was also, as his caddy had alluded to earlier, a way to meet women. He was definitely a maverick, which meant the other pros either liked the guy or didn't particularly care for him.

The tone for the day was set early in the round when after a five minute wait on number two to hit his second shot, Carl finally hit a fairway metal up by the green. He looked up the fairway and to his left to see Will and his caddy in what looked like an animated discussion with an elderly couple. The man and his wife were sitting in lawn chairs in the left rough just behind the crowd rope. Carl and his caddy hustled over to see what the problem was.

"I'm telling you young man, I know the name of that song," said the elderly man. "It was way before your time."

Carl and Budgie walked up with questioning looks on their faces.

"Hey, Carl," said Will. "See if you can get this song."

Mitch hummed the opening melody and waited for an answer.

"It's 'Oh Pretty Woman' by Roy Orbison," answered Carl. "The title starts with 'Oh'. Most people don't know that."

The man's wife started laughing and he soon joined in.

"I guess because we're old that don't mean we know everything," admitted the man.

Will walked over and slammed a fairway metal all the way to the front of the green.

"What, are you guys like musicians on the side or something?" asked Budgie as he and Mitch walked a couple of steps behind their golfers.

"No, we just like to try and stump each other with tunes, and while we were waiting we started talking to those old timers. The guy said we couldn't stump him, so I pulled a technicality on him. They were pretty cool about it. I'm surprised Carl knew the answer to that one."

The four of them enjoyed each other's company for the rest of the round. They argued sports among themselves and the fans as they stood on the tee waiting for the group ahead of them to clear. Will and Carl were both fast players, so there was a lot of waiting. It didn't seem to bother either of them.

On number ten, Will hooked his drive over by the cart path where a lot of people were walking. Needing to lay up on the par five, he stood there with a 6-iron in hand, waiting for Mitch and a volunteer to drop the rope that was right behind him. The volunteer had put his sign down and was in the process of picking it back up when Will stepped up and hit. People were still walking only a few feet behind him when he made his stroke. After his shot, he stood by the people waiting for Carl, who was across the fairway, to make his play.

"Why didn't you wait for the people to stand still?" asked a young boy who was standing within a few feet of him.

Will turned and addressed the boy. The young man and the people around him were surprised when Will took the time to give him more than a short answer.

"It's all about focus, son. Those people were walking behind me and talking, but I just shut them out. To me, they weren't even there. I really don't care what you do while I hit, unless you're trying to take a leak on my ball. That would be distracting."

Mitch looked over at the boy's mom, thinking maybe Will had crossed the line of decency. Her eyes went wide, and then she started to laugh. Mitch reached in the bag and gave the kid a signed golf ball. As he walked away, he looked over his shoulder to see the woman and her son explain what had just happened to a small group of fans that had gathered around but weren't privy to the conversation.

The Michigan hustler wasn't tearing up the course the way he did the previous day, but he was holding his own. His two under round took a turn for the better when he birdied fourteen through seventeen. A three-putt bogey on eighteen left him at five under for the day and sixteen under for the tournament. The Green/Cummings group had one of the largest followings for the day. The buzz around the course was that the kid could not only play, but he and his caddy were quite the characters—especially after the incident on fifteen fairway.

* * *

Will and Mitch were standing over by the right side of the fairway in the shade of one of the large trees by the cart path. As usual, he and Carl were waiting for the group ahead to clear the green. Will looked over at a high school age kid who was eating a hot dog.

"Hey, kid," said Will. "What do you want for the rest of that dog?"

"Are you serious?" came the reply.

"Yeah, I'm starving."

"Twenty bucks."

"C'mon, man, it's already half gone."

Sensing some more excitement, the people began to crowd around.

"Okay, how about your glove then."

Will took off the glove and handed it over. Then he held the end of the dog and told the kid to tear it apart right behind where he had taken a bite. The crowd went nuts, clapping and laughing. This guy from Michigan was hilarious. After eating his half of the dog, Will and his caddy headed back out toward the middle of the fairway to his ball. While Mitch got his yardage, he rummaged through his bag for another glove, only to find that he had just given away his last one. He played the shot without one.

When they got to sixteen tee, the same kid was standing behind the rope. He noticed that Will didn't have a glove on his left hand. He reached over the rope and handed it back to Will.

"You forgot to sign it," said the kid. "You can give it to me when you finish."

"Deal," said Will as he slipped it back on his left hand.

"Are you sure that isn't a rule infraction?" questioned Mitch.

"It's okay," answered Will. "Let's just say I let the kid carry my glove for half a hole. He didn't alter it in any way, so we're cool."

Budgie heard the conversation and shook his head in agreement.

* * *

Will walked out of the scorer's trailer after signing his card. Carl shook his hand and told him that he had just played one of the most enjoyable rounds that he had ever experienced on Tour. Will reciprocated the feeling. Carl told him to come back to the locker room and he'd set Will up with a few gloves and balls. Since he didn't know any of the pros, the rookie had spent only a few minutes in the players' locker room. He didn't realize that if he left a note stuck to his locker for some balls and gloves, the company rep would have left them for him.

* * *

After regaling Herman with the particulars of the last few holes, Eddie, Ronnie, and Tina headed over to Hot's for a little celebration. They each put half of their earnings in their golf bags. When they let themselves in, they heard some familiar wailing and moaning sounds coming from Hot's bedroom. Tina stood there with a shocked expression on her face.

"It's what he does," explained Ronnie. "Have a seat, Tina. Eddie and I are going to stash the other half of our cash in our room, then we'll go out for a little celebration."

One half of their security team sat on the sofa and took in the sounds coming from Hot's bedroom. Ronnie and Eddie went into their room and took out their plastic bags that held their dirty clothes. They both wrapped $125k in their underwear. Their thinking was, no respectable thief would go through a guy's underwear looking for anything of value.

Tina hopped up quickly when they came out of their room. She seemed to be in a hurry to vacate the premises. Ronnie was about to pull away from the curb when he looked over at the muscular but lovely woman next to him. She appeared to be lost in her own thoughts and was staring blankly out the front window.

"Everything okay?" asked Ronnie.

"I'm not sure what was going on back there, but it sounded like something that I'd be willing to pay for."

That was all it took to set the stage for the rest of the evening. It didn't take them long to find themselves at Harrah's Sports Book checking out the baseball games. The three of them sat there smoking cigars and drinking whiskey. Eddie had his usual Johnnie Walker while Ronnie sipped on his Jameson. Tina raised her glass of Chivas, offering a toast.

"Gentlemen, great job this week. It's always exciting when you guys are involved. It's too bad we live half a country apart. I wouldn't mind hangin' with a couple of dapper looking dudes like you two. And with your wives, of course."

"You got a boyfriend, Tina?" asked Eddie.

"Actually I do. He's an actor that I met when we were working on a movie. He's more of a bit player, and seems to be satisfied with the small parts. He's a great guy with a good head on his shoulders. He's also a physical trainer, so we've got a lot in common."

"Good for you, doll," said Eddie getting up. "Excuse me, guys. I'm heading to the restroom."

Eddie had walked to the edge of the room when a guy stepped in front of him blocking his path. He looked calmly into the man's eyes. It was obvious that he'd had a few cocktails.

"Slick move, buddy," said the man with a slight slur. "What did you and your partner do, go halfies on a hooker? That's the only way a couple of old birds like you would be with a good lookin' dame like that."

Eddie grinned at the man.

"Normally I'd bet you a hundred bucks that you wouldn't go over there and tell her what you just told me."

"Well, what's stoppin' you then?"

"Two things: One, I have to piss real bad. And two, I don't want to be responsible for what she would do to you. Hospitals are expensive. Look at her arms, dude. That woman can probably take any man in the place. And believe me, I ain't exaggerating. She's our bodyguard, man. Now step aside before I call her over."

"Why do a couple of jamokes like you need a bodyguard?"

"My friend's a famous actor. What, don't you recognize him?"

The man's stupid expression disappeared as he tried to get a closer look at Ronnie. Eddie just shook his head and went about his business. Idiots, they were everywhere. West coast, east coast, it didn't matter. When he got back to his seat, he saw that fresh drinks had arrived. He told them about his encounter with the drunk. Tina and Ronnie just laughed it off.

"I gotta ask," inquired Tina. "How are you two going to get all that cash home? And how do you think the Russian got his money into the country in the first place?"

"I'm not gonna speculate on his operation, but Ronnie and I are heading for the book store tomorrow. We buy a few books, pack them along with most of the cash, and mail them home."

"Why not just get a cashier's check made out to yourself?"

"Too many questions. 'Wow, you must have been incredibly lucky, sir. Can I see the IRS form that you have to fill out when you win this kind of cash? You don't have one? Maybe we better bring someone else in to discuss how you came by all this money. I hope it wasn't selling drugs or some other illegal activity.' It's a little risky sending it in the mail, but there are no questions to answer. Besides we'll send it in two or three boxes. Spread out the risk, so to speak."

"It sounds like you know what you're doing. I suppose you're going to take out your wives for a big celebration when you get home?"

"Actually, we're going to fly home and then drive immediately to Silvis, Illinois. Ronnie's grandson is playing in the John Deere Classic. He's up among the leaders."

"Damn, you guys do get around," said Tina.

They looked up when the man that Eddie had encountered on the way to the restroom wobbled up and stood in front of them. He swayed back and forth as he held out a small pad and a pen to Ronnie.

"Excuse me, sir," he said, trying to sound respectable. "I'm a big fan. Can I get your autograph?"

Ronnie took the pen and paper and looked over at Eddie. His partner turned and looked the other way. Ronnie signed and handed the pad back.

"Who did you say I was?" asked Ronnie as they watched the man lurch away.

"I told him you were the guy that played George on *Seinfeld*. You do look a little like him, you know."

"Like I said," remarked Tina as she stood up. "You two always have something going on. It's time to get this girl back to her friends' house. I leave in the morning for L. A. We start filming stunts on a new movie in two days, and I've got a few things to tend to. The doc says you can have Herman tomorrow morning. Please give him my best. I love working with him."

CHAPTER TWENTY-TWO

–Unorthodox Behavior

This kid from Michigan is really something. He's got no advertising on his shirt or hat, and he talks to the fans like they're his friends and not just faces in the crowd. We need more professional athletes like him. With all the money they make, you'd think they would be a little more grateful to the people that are footing the bill.

—-Hod Harrelson, bartender, golf fan

Will, Mitch, and Luke sat at a small restaurant eating breakfast only a few blocks from their motel. They grabbed a paper on the way in to check the tee times and pairings for the final day of the tournament. Luke spent an hour the night before interviewing both of them. He told his boss back at the Telegraph Herald that he was going to have an exclusive interview with the guy that was the talk of the sports world.

"Here it is," said Mitch, laying the paper on the table so they all could see it.

12:30   Mike Denard -13
        Roger Kruk -14

12:40   Will Green -16
        Brian Fitzpatrick -16

12:50   Brady Frazier -16
        Connor Edwards -17

1:00   Jason Capelle -18
        Don Schumacher -18

"When you hit your first shot of the tourney on Thursday morning, did you expect anything like this?" asked Luke.

"Actually, we did," answered Mitch. "On the drive down here we talked about our goals for this week. Will is giving up his anonymity by playing well and showing his face all over the television. We decided if our cover was going to be blown, then we might as well get as much cash as we can. Plus, the real reason for getting into this whole thing is to qualify for the U. S. Open."

"You've certainly opened a lot of eyes this week."

"For more reasons than just playing good golf," continued Mitch as he shoveled scrambled eggs into his mouth. "I'll take some of the credit for Will not going to the interview room after his great round on Friday. Some dude told me that they wanted to talk to Will when he was in signing his card, but we decided to plead ignorance and just bolt. I should have insisted, but my boy was being somewhat of a hothead, saying he didn't want to go in and answer a lot of questions about how excited he was to be rubbing shoulders with the game's best. I don't think the sports reporters were very happy about it, and we'll probably hear about it from a Tour official."

"Don't print this, Luke," added Will, "But the reason I was a little down after my Friday round was because my playing partners, Spangler and Charles, told me they were going to lodge a complaint about Mitch and me. They called it 'behavior unbecoming a Tour participant' or something like that. I guess they didn't like some of the stuff we did, like talking and joking with the fans. Those people paid a lot of money to see us play, and it didn't feel right to me to ignore them. What were we supposed to do, act like they weren't there? I can't play like a robot, and he can't caddy like one either. That's all I'm saying. Back home, when we're playing for more than a few dollars, which is most of the time, we laugh and kid with our opponents. It helps to keep us loose, and the guys we play don't seem to mind. The game is supposed to be fun, no matter what the stakes are."

"To elaborate a little further on your question," explained Mitch. "Tons of guys play incredible golf at their home courses. They can stand on their practice range and stripe ball after ball right where they are aiming. But as soon as you put a thousand people down each side of the hole, then put tens of thousands of dollars on the outcome of each stroke, their swings get a little shorter and a little quicker. Add to that the television cameras and all the BNP's walking around. I'm just saying it's a whole lot different out here."

"How did Will adapt so quickly if it's a totally different ball game?"

"He's used to playing for more than just cigar and whiskey money," answered Mitch. "And, if you haven't noticed it, the guy can focus like nobody else. It wouldn't bother him if the fans hollered like they were at a baseball game during every shot."

Luke looked over at Will for confirmation.

"I have to admit, it would take a hell of a loud noise to throw me off. It's just how I was trained."

"Speaking of your training, are you going to tell me about these mysterious guys that prepped you for all this?"

"Sorry, man, we can't do it."

"I'm going to add one more thing about the jump up to this type of competition," explained Mitch. "One of his mentors is a real good poker player, and one day he was explaining how tough it is to go out to Vegas, or anywhere they play high stakes cards, and duplicate what a guy does with his regular poker group back home. It's like going from the minor leagues to a pennant contender. He once told me that he knew this guy who thought he had a foolproof blackjack system. He sat at home and played for toothpicks at the kitchen table until he swore he couldn't lose. After one hour in Vegas, at a fast-moving game with tons of distractions, he was pretty much tapped out."

"I've got another question," offered Luke. "You both use the term 'tons' a lot. Why is that?"

Will and Mitch looked at each other, somewhat confused. They both grinned when they came to the same conclusion at the same time. Will answered this one.

"My other mentor is a horseplayer. It's a term he uses all the time—this horse has tons of closing speed or that horse has tons of early foot. I guess we picked it up from him."

"What's your take on all the stupid stuff that you hear the fans holler right after a guy hits his shot?" inquired Luke, changing the topic.

"I don't get that part of it," answered Will. "I try to ignore that stuff, but it's impossible to totally shut it out. If they did it while I was hitting a shot, I probably wouldn't hear it. Yesterday, right after I hit my drive on number nine, the long par four, some clown hollered 'get in the hole'. The hole is like 500 yards long. What he screamed didn't make sense."

"I heard it too," added Mitch. "The dude looked like he had a few beers in him. The strange thing was, there was a decent looking girl standing next to him, holding his hand. If I hollered something as stupid as that, with tons of people around, Gloria would disown me. At least he didn't holler 'mashed potatoes' or something just as idiotic. It seems like they're trying to outdo each other to see who can sound more ridiculous."

"My fiancé, Chip, would probably just smack me upside the head if I did something like that," said Luke.

"Your girl's name is Chip?" asked Mitch.

"It's a long story, man. She's pretty feisty, so I'm always on my best behavior around her. Why go looking for trouble, you know what I mean?"

"We hear you," echoed Mitch as they got up from the table. "We're thinking of leaving around ten, Luke. Are you riding with us, or are you driving your beast?"

"I'll drive too. There's no reason for me to get there any earlier. You're my story anyway. How many of the other reporters know what you had for breakfast? If I were a regular at the paper, my piece would probably get me a huge bonus. Your story might be the biggest scoop I ever come across."

"I'm thinking you've got a great future as a sportswriter ahead of you," predicted Will. "If I ever write my life story, I'll look you up to do the ghostwriting."

"I won't forget you said that, and Mitch is my witness. See you at the course."

Luke watched them pay the bill at the cashier's counter. Mitch turned and motioned that they had paid his bill too. The reporter waved his thanks and took his phone out. Something they had said about qualifying for the U. S. Open intrigued him. He was the first to admit that he didn't know a whole lot about golf, so he did a little research right there on his phone. When he got up to leave the table he had a real dilemma on his hands. If Will won the tournament today he would not automatically qualify for next year's U. S. Open. He would qualify to play in next year's Masters Tournament as the winner of a PGA Event that awarded full FedEx points but not the Open. Were they confusing the two tournaments? The dilemma that he faced was;

should he tell them before or after the tournament was over? Either way, they were sure to be disappointed.

Will and his caddy made their appearance on the practice tee exactly forty-five minutes before their tee time. The John Deere Classic was known for its hot temperatures and stifling humidity, so today's weather was definitely an exception and a welcome relief. The thermometer was at a steady eighty degrees with low humidity. It reminded them of a typical Michigan summer day. Being situated between the two big lakes usually kept the humidity at a tolerable level in the Wolverine State.

When Will went into the locker room to change his shoes, there were a dozen gloves of various sizes and two dozen balls sitting on the bench in front of his locker. A Post-It note from Carl Cummings was stuck to the top of the ball boxes wishing him good luck. Budgie added, *Hey, Nacho and Herd. You dudes suck!* Mitch laughed when Will showed him the note.

Will took the four gloves that were his size and put them in the bag. He signed the rest of them intending to give them away as souvenirs. When he got to the practice range, he walked along the rope at the back handing them out to the kids that were standing there. He was one glove short which disappointed an eight-year-old girl who had been patiently waiting to get a glimpse of her new favorite golfer. She looked like she was about to cry. Will squatted down in front of her.

"Listen," he explained in a soft voice. "Meet me at the eighteenth green, and I'll give you the ball that I finish with. How's that?"

She perked up immediately and turned to her dad who was standing right behind her. They both said thanks and that they were pulling for him to win. The young fan was thinking where she was going to keep the ball in her room as Will went back to the tee to warm up. The fans that saw what had happened clapped and whistled their approval.

"Shit," complained Will's pairing for the day. Brian Fitzpatrick had a few wins under his belt, but he wasn't considered a household name. "Who gets an applause on the practice tee? I can't wait to see this guy's game. I'm guessing he's been one lucky son-of-a-bitch so far. It won't take but a couple of holes to see if he's got what it takes."

Brian's caddy, Carney Mathewson, nodded his agreement. "He's done pretty good so far, but Sunday afternoon is a whole different ball game. I just hope he and his boy, Mitch, don't pull their circus act today. The sports channels are raving about them and their unorthodox behavior out here. Some of the pros don't appreciate it, while others claim they are a breath of fresh air. I hope they realize that this is more than just payday. There's a lot more at stake here than a big check."

"I'm gonna do my best to ignore them," said Brian. "Let's just do our thing and let them do theirs. If they get too distracting, we'll say something to them and maybe to a rules official."

* * *

"Here we go," announced Max Worth, looking at one of the Golf Channel monitors. "God's gift to golf has just shown up on the practice tee. Look at that. He went right over to the fans and started giving them stuff. What is he, a politician?"

"I'd say the kids and the adults love this guy," offered Denny Holmes. "He's one of the only pros out there that acknowledges them. The rest of them are so serious. And before you tell me that this is serious business, I will tell you that these guys are still just playing a game. A game that was created so men could enjoy each other's company, place a few bets, and have a few drinks out in the fresh air enjoying Mother Nature's gift to us humans."

"Give me a break," grumbled Max. "What are you, a golf historian now? It's crash and burn time for this rookie. I can feel it. His twenty minutes of fame are over."

Denny winked at his coworker sitting beside him.

"If the boss doesn't settle down, he's going to have a heart attack. I've never seen him get so worked up. Why do you think he doesn't like this guy, Green?"

"I don't have the foggiest," answered Angela. "I wouldn't antagonize him. If he did have a heart attack, it would be on your conscience."

Mitch and his player walked out onto the first tee to a monstrous reception from the fans. Brian and Carney were already there talking to the official starter. Mitch admitted to his fiancé later that when he heard that applause the hair on the back of his neck stood up. He was only twenty-three years old, and this was more than he had ever dreamed of. He looked over at Will and saw him bantering with the starter.

"You going to hit before I can give you a proper introduction?" asked the starter.

"It depends on how fast you can get it done," joked Will. "I don't like to burn daylight standing around talking when we can be playing golf."

"You have the honors, so I'll do my best. In the interest of professionalism, I try to give each golfer the same courtesy. It doesn't matter if you're number one on the money list or dead last."

"Where are you on that list Will?" asked Brian.

"I'm not even on it," admitted Will laughing.

"Where did you play college golf?"

"Never played college golf."

"Ask him where he played high school golf," interjected Mitch.

Will shook his head and laughed again. "Didn't play high school either."

"You didn't even play in high school?" asked Carney. "Where have you been, man?"

"To tell you the truth," said Will as he walked over and teed his ball up, "Mitch and I were just driving around the area one day, and we saw a sign that said there was going to be a tournament here. He volunteered to caddy for me if I wanted to give it a try. So here we are."

The people nearest to the tee caught most of the conversation. They were still laughing when Will stepped up to his ball. The volunteers with the "quiet" signs raised them in the air and gave a few stern looks to the fans to get them settled down.

"Ladies and gentlemen. Introducing the 12:40 tee time. Please welcome from Hickory Corners…"

That's as far as the starter got. Will ripped his drive down the left side straight at the fairway bunker. The crowd cheered when they saw the ball carry the sand. It nestled down in the thick rough about 80 yards from the green. Fitzpatrick and Mathewson had heard about Will's first tee behavior, but this was the first time they had experienced it. They looked at the starter, and he was laughing right along with the fans. Apparently he also thought the Michigan entry was a breath of fresh air.

CHAPTER TWENTY-THREE

-The Sound of Doom

I'll tell you one thing about Davis and Green. They're straight shooters when it comes to golf. They never lie about their games. Of course, they might bend the truth a little when it comes to the peripherals, but hell everybody does that. It's like this: If you ask me how I've been playing, I might say, "Not as good as I was playing a month ago. I played a few holes yesterday, and it was so bad I had to quit." True statement. I am not obligated to explain that I've been sicker than a dog the past few days. To the guy asking the question, it might appear that I'm in a slump. Now, he thinks I'm a soft target and wants to play for some serious coin. We'll get together next week, and I'll drop the hammer on him. Stinkin' chump. Tryin' to take advantage of a sick guy.

—Jerry "Snakeyes" Clausen, hustler wannabe, dice cheat, former city councilman

Honor. It seems that the younger crowd doesn't place as much value on this trait as the generations before them. In school, they can be seen with their thumbs in their pockets and a disgusted look on their faces as the class recites the Pledge of Allegiance. How dare someone asks them to stand and recite at such an early hour! Check out the crowd at any ball game, and you will see several hats sitting on the heads of the younger generation as the national anthem is played. When they are reminded that out of respect they are expected to remove their hats, they will often shrug their shoulders saying it's no big deal.

It's going to take some doing to change these attitudes. Hopefully, the awakening won't be the result of a major conflict or some sort of internal disaster. It would be refreshing for teachers to hear, 'yes sir' or yes 'ma'am' in the classroom again. This might be too much to ask for, but it would be a start.

Ronnie and Eddie were cruising west on Interstate 80 with Melissa, Suzanne, and Kathy in the back seat. The mood was quite jubilant due to the guys' victory in Las Vegas. Both of the wives had been pestering their husbands to tell them how much they had won, but the hustlers wouldn't divulge the actual number. They decided to wait until the book packages showed up. Their wives would both be at work when the mail arrived, which gave them the option of declaring all or part of their winnings.

Charise was waiting for her husband at O'Hare when their plane landed in Chicago. Herman still had a big lump on his head, but he said he felt fine. Buck was relieved of his security duties as soon as the travelers arrived home. Doc said he would hang around and watch the house while the Davis's were away. After that, he was heading to Chicago to talk to Herman about gainful employment. For him, it was a win/win situation. After the shooting exhibition by Dennis and his buddies, the Trentons and their hired goons decided they would back off and wait for the Ronnie and Eddie to get back. They weren't privy as to what was happening in Las Vegas with the Karpovs.

The girls wanted to know all the particulars of the Vegas trip. The golfers took turns lauding the others contributions to the match. They decided they would leave out their experiences at the house of their host.

"So, Melissa, how excited are you that your husband is making all this news in the golf world?" asked Suzanne.

"It's exciting, of course, but some of the sports announcers have been saying some mean stuff about Will and Mitch. I'm not too crazy about that."

"I wouldn't worry about those media people," said Ronnie. "They're always trying to come up with a story. They blow a lot of things way out of proportion just to stir things up. You know how our guys operate. They like to have a little fun, and there's nothing wrong with that. I can't believe they would do something that would bother another player. That would fall into the category of gamesmanship, and that's just poor sportsmanship."

"So you guys don't do the gamesmanship thing when you're playing?" asked Kathy.

"We do it all the time," said Ronnie. "But with us, it's all in fun. And it was part of Will's training. Obviously we were quite successful preparing him for this moment. I think we should ask for a forty percent cut of his winnings—twenty for Street and twenty for me."

"Why not ask for half?" asked Kathy.

"It wouldn't be right to ask for half," said Ronnie. "That would be just plain greedy. Suzanne, you should have seen my man here on the last day of our match. He was a combination of Superfly and Shaft all rolled into one. Street, you were the epitome of cool."

"Who is Superfly?" asked Suzanne.

"Yeah, and who is this Shaft guy?" added Kathy.

Ronnie looked in the rearview mirror at Melissa who was sitting in the middle. She just smiled and shrugged her shoulders signaling that she didn't know who Ronnie was referring to either. Eddie just chuckled.

"I have a little story for you," volunteered Melissa. "I was sitting in the lunch room at the hospital yesterday with my advisor when two doctors asked if they could join us..."

* * *

"You ladies don't mind if we join you, do you?" asked Dr. Blanchard, holding a tray full of food.

"Have a seat, gentlemen," answered Vickie Holt, Melissa's advisor.

The conversation revolved around their patients until Dr. Blanchard changed the subject.

"So, Melissa, I hear your husband is quite the golfer."

Melissa had been schooled by Will to be evasive when his golf game came up. Anybody and everybody was a potential opponent in a money match. His advice was never to tip her hand and to give ambiguous answers whenever possible.

"Yeah, he plays a lot. He works on the grounds crew at Stonehedge. He likes the game, but he doesn't practice much. He says he doesn't like practicing. I played golf in high school, but he didn't."

She also knew the rules when it came to the three hustlers. They never lied about golf. Saying that Will was just a mediocre player or a ten handicapper would be a gross misrepresentation of the truth. That was something they just didn't do. No respectable guy would lie about his game just to win a few dollars. Ronnie and Eddie knew several guys that would lie if there was a chance that it might put some cash in their pocket, but that wasn't the way they did things. It was all about one's honor and one's integrity. If you gave up either trait, the two most valuable ones a human could possess, then there wasn't much left.

"I heard he is pretty good and likes to play for a little money from time to time," continued Dr. Blanchard.

"Who told you that?" asked Melissa feigning innocence.

Vickie was getting a kick out of the whole conversation as she was watching the television screen that was on the far wall behind the two doctors.

"The pro at Stonehedge. Do you think your husband would play my nephew for, say a hundred bucks a hole? Even up, of course. He doesn't like to give strokes."

"Watch him, Melissa," said the other doctor. "His nephew plays number one for Michigan State."

"I don't know," said Melissa, weighing this new information. "If he's that good, and doesn't like to give any strokes, what about odds?"

"What kind of odds?"

"Let's say you put up $150 per hole to Will's $100. If your nephew plays at MSU, he must be real good. Like I said, Will never played high school or college golf."

"That sounds fair," said Dr. Blanchard with a satisfied look. He reached across the table and shook Melissa's hand. "My nephew is off on summer break. When do you think Will could play?"

"Uh, Doc," interrupted Vickie, "you better turn around and look at the television."

Will's image filled the screen. He was putting on the eighteenth green. The caption said he was seventeen under and was putting for a par. His putt looked good a foot from the hole, but like so many of them, it veered off line at the last second and lipped out. He walked up and tapped in to a thunderous applause.

"That's your husband!" exclaimed the doctor. "What are you doing here while he's in contention for a Tour victory?"

"I was afraid to ask for the weekend off," she admitted. "I didn't want to ask someone to cover for me so I could watch my husband play golf."

"Take tomorrow off. We'll get someone to cover."

They got up and took their plates and silverware to the dishwashing area. The doctors started to walk away.

"Hey, Doctor Blanchard," said Melissa. "Can your nephew play sometime next week? I'm pretty sure my husband will be home by then."

"I'll let you know," said the doc over his shoulder.

* * *

"You're learning, girl," said Ronnie. "Damn, Street, we've got the whole family in on the act."

"So, Eddie, are you still thinking about writing a book about your exploits?" asked Suzanne. "You could start out before you and Ronnie met, tell both of your stories, then bring it all together."

"I've thought about it, but who would want to read about a couple of Links Lizards like us? There are tons of golf books out there written by some real accomplished players."

"Links Lizards?" asked Kathy. "I've never heard that term before."

"Probably because he just made it up," added Ronnie. "I will tell you guys, when Eddie laid out the format for our half of the tie-breaker, it was one dramatic moment. If it was a movie, there would have been some cool music playing in the background."

"Like what?" asked Suzanne.

"Like "Barracuda", by Heart. Yeah, that would have been the perfect song. You ladies have heard of that one haven't you?"

"Yes," they all said in unison.

* * *

Several hundred miles to the east, Anthony Trenton entered his father's study. The family patriarch was intently reading a newspaper. Anthony sat down in a leather recliner similar to the one his father was sitting in. He waited for his father to put down the paper. That would be his cue to start the conversation. Alfonz Trenton carefully folded the paper and laid it on the end table next to his chair.

"Damn amateurs!" were the first words out of his mouth. "These stupid gang bangers are riding around shooting at each other like a bunch of buffoons. They know nothing about style, and they know nothing about guns or gun safety. Last night one of these idiots took a shot at someone and hit a little five-year-old girl instead. A five-year-old girl! It's sad and disgraceful at the same time. What is it, Anthony?"

"Father, I talked to you a while back about two golfers that had set up a match with the Karpovs out in Las Vegas. I didn't think their scheme had much of a chance, but apparently they knew what they were doing. I sent a man out there to keep an eye on things. After the first round, old man Karpov began shooting his mouth off to anyone who would listen that they, mostly due to his son's talents, were unbeatable. The Vegas and Los Angeles papers picked up on the match and sent reporters to cover it. He even did a short radio interview touting his boy's eventual goal of playing the U. S. Tour. I can't believe they gave him some actual airtime. Not much must be happening out there because of the heat. Anyway, the two old guys from Michigan ended up winning the match, totally embarrassing the Karpovs. They're a couple of hustlers that like to play high stakes golf. And here's the kicker—they're both older than Alexei Karpov. Right now he looks like an absolute fool to anyone that follows the game."

Alfonz picked up the glass of beer that was sitting on the table to his right. He drained the rest of the liquid and looked at his son.

"This is good news. These two golfers have done us a service. A small service, but a service nonetheless. And now they want us to call off your cousins? Is that the favor they expect?"

"Yes sir, that's it."

"Get a hold of your cousins and tell them I want them to cease and desist their vendetta against the two golfers. Then bring them in. I want to have a talk with those two."

"I'll relay your request."

* * *

Will looked at his lie on the left side of number one fairway. The ball was down in the thick grass with only the top showing. Normally, he would hit a sand wedge from this distance, but he decided to chop down with his pitching wedge. The sole of a pitching wedge is designed to cut into the turf, while a sand wedge is designed to slide through the sand. His aggressive swing sent the ball right at the flag. With less than half the backspin of a fairway shot, his ball landed in the middle of the green and rolled all the way to the back. From there, he three-putted for a bogey. Not a good start. The first hole was playing as one of the easiest par fours on the front side.

"Don't worry about it," consoled Mitch as they stood on the second tee. "We'll get it back right here."

Number two was a hole that most pros counted on birdying. Mitch read the plaques that adorned some of the holes when they played their practice round. He found the number two plaque quite interesting. A guy named George Davenport was an early settler and the co-founder of Davenport, Iowa, just across the river. He was murdered by a gang of outlaws. They escaped across the Mississippi, only to hide in the barn behind number two green. Later, they escaped from the barn and crossed the nearby Rock River by ferry. They were finally caught with the help of a detective named Edward Bonney.

Will, determined to get back the stroke he had just given away, nuked a drive out to the 320 mark. From there, he hit his number four hybrid, hoping to find the putting surface. An easy two-putt birdie would settle him down and maybe provide some momentum. Player and caddy watched as his shot flew toward the hole. The elderly couple behind him in their lawn chairs clapped as soon as the ball left the clubface. Will got every bit of it and watched in horror as the ball landed in the back fringe and bounced toward the famous barn. Mathewson looked at his player and raised his eyebrows as if saying, 'I knew it. There's no way he can hold it together.'

"Check it out!" exalted Max Worth back in the Golf Channel trailer. NBC was doing the main broadcast for the weekend, but his network was doing highlights and was prepared to take over if NBC had difficulties or the tournament ran long. "He's going down. He bogeys the first hole, then misjudges his second shot on number two. He's in over his head, and he knows it. Now he's almost up against that old barn back there. Does he even have a shot?"

"I don't think he's got enough room to swing the club, Chief," acknowledged Denny Holmes. "And it looks like two of his three options for an unplayable lie can't be used. Two club lengths no nearer the hole will still not give him room to swing. And if he goes behind the barn, the tall grass will be a major problem. If he drops it down in that stuff, getting the club cleanly on the back of the ball would be just about impossible. And, he would have to go over the top of that huge thing without being able to see where he's aiming. I wouldn't be surprised if he goes way back up the fairway and hits four from the spot of his previous shot. That's what most pros would do. Even if he doesn't hit his next one on from way back there, he should be able to get up and down for a bogey."

Will stood looking at his lie by the old barn. The stone base of the building went up several feet before the wooden sides started. The grass was trampled a little, but it was still long. If he aimed at the green and stabbed at his ball, he couldn't take the club back far enough to move it more than about five yards. That would leave him ten yards short of the putting surface and a long chip to the hole from the thick stuff. Hitting the shot sideways also didn't seem to be an option.

"We going back, boss?" asked Mitch. "If we hit over from back there, there's a good chance we can still make a bogey."

"Hold on a sec," said Will. "Will you check what's on the other side of this building? Maybe we can drop back there and go over the top."

His caddy set the bag down and jogged around behind the barn. He came back shaking his head.

"It's no good back there," explained Mitch. "You'd have to go far enough back to make sure there was enough distance to get it up over the building. There's hazard stakes back there, and the grass is real long."

"That settles it," said Will with conviction. "I'm going to bank it off the stone."

"That stuff's pretty uneven, and you've got no room for a follow through."

"We'll take our chances on the surface, and I don't need any room for a follow through. I'll just let the ground stop my club. That way I can go aggressively into the ball without worrying about what happens after I make contact."

"Sounds good," agreed Mitch, moving the bag off to the side. "Believe in the shot before you hit it."

His mind made up, Will looked the shot over one last time. There was a lot of whispering among the gallery and some negative head shaking. Mitch asked the fans to move further back in case the ball didn't come off the stone the way they were hoping. Will played the ball back in his stance and struck sharply down on the ball with his 6-iron. The ball slammed off the hard surface, bounced once on the slope behind the green and hopped onto the putting surface, ending up twenty-five feet from the hole. The crowd gave him a loud ovation. His two-putt par was not what he had envisioned back on the tee, but he had avoided disaster with his creative bank shot.

Will knew he needed to get back into his rhythm. The bogey on one and the subsequent par on two, kept him from gaining on the leaders. The two groups behind him were sure to fare better than ten strokes on the first two holes. He also sensed that his opponent and his caddy were enjoying his current situation. So much for the camaraderie of the Tour. It was more of a cut-throat business out here than some let on. Mitch tried to calm him down by walking and talking a little slower than normal. Will appreciated his caddy's efforts. His iron shot to the uphill par three third hole was just short of the green—short enough so he had to chip it. His 7-iron bump and run went four feet past the hole, and he missed the par putt coming back. Three holes played and he was two over par, heading in the wrong direction.

"Can you hear it?" asked Max Worth. "It's the sound of doom. The boy's rattled, and it's only going to get worse. The NBC announcers agree with me. He was the big story coming into the weekend, and now he's going to be an even bigger story. He's going down like the Hindenburg."

His people seated in front of their monitors turned and gave the boss doleful looks. They were all rooting for the kid from nowhere. He was a great story even if Max didn't think so. How often does a guy that no one had ever heard of step up and compete on the big stage? He was like the 'Rocky Balboa' of golf, out there slugging it out with the big names in the sport.

"Don't give me those looks," continued Max. "You all knew that he couldn't hold up under the pressure. The glass slipper doesn't fit, people. Tell you what. If he finishes in the top ten, I'll buy everyone here a steak dinner. That makes it a win/win deal for you. Top ten, he makes a big check and he can go home feeling like a world-beater, and you're eating a free steak on the boss."

When the people in the room didn't show any enthusiasm for his offer, he softened his delivery.

"Look, I'm not rooting against the guy. He has provided us with some genuine excitement. But he's playing with the big boys now, and he's been acting like he's playing a Saturday morning round at the club—joking with the fans and goofing around. If he were Trevino or Rodriguez, it would be different. Those guys paid their dues and had a right to be the life of the party. He's just another really good golfer who has wandered into a nest of cobras, that's all. And now he's snakebit."

Max chuckled as he headed out the door for a smoke. He thought his little analogy back there was quite clever.

CHAPTER TWENTY-FOUR

The Pursuit of Excellence

I don't know much about golf, but I've been around sports enough to know a gamer when I see one. Will Green is not a choker like some of the fans are saying.

—-Luke Slowinski, sportswriter

A true sports fan appreciates the opportunity to watch excellence in action. Larry Bird hitting a game saving three-pointer. Ted Williams hitting a home run on his last time at the plate before he retired. Walter Payton pass blocking for three counts then slipping out into the flat for a short toss, and then performing his own kind of magic as he eludes would-be tacklers. Or how about Nicklaus bouncing a 1-iron off the flag on number seventeen at Pebble Beach? There is special and then there is "unbelievably special". One wonders what goes through the minds of the truly gifted. Do they see the game several moves ahead of their opponents, does the action appear to move in slow motion, or are they just acting on instinct with very little conscious thought? Whatever they are thinking, people are willing to pay to watch them do what very few humans on the planet are capable of.

Golfer and caddy looked up at the scoreboard. Capelle, playing behind him, was one under for the day, putting him at minus nineteen. Schumacher and Connor Edwards were at minus eighteen. It was another picture perfect day, which meant the scores were liable to keep heading south. The man from Hickory Corners needed to steady the ship and get it headed in the right direction. Unfortunately, his troubles continued.

Solid ball striking resulted in pars on holes four and five. Their best chance for birdies on the front nine were behind them, but holes six and eight were still possibilities. Will hit a slider off the tee at the left fairway trap on number six, leaving him with a wedge to the green. A straight shot off the tee would have served him as well, but he wanted to work the ball, hoping to get his mojo back. He wouldn't admit it, but Fitzpatrick's caddy was impressed with the shot. His guy didn't have that one in the bag. When they got to his ball, hustler and caddy couldn't believe their luck. It was in a divot that hadn't been replaced. Mitch did a good job of keeping his cool. Up to this point in the tournament, he had replaced at least twenty divots that needed attention. Did the guys up ahead not care because they were done with the hole? It made him wonder.

"Not a problem, Will," observed Mitch with an upbeat tone. "Just play it back and be aggressive. You've hit out of worse lies than this one."

"I know, but this cuts down on my chances of sticking it in there tight."

"Remember our rule on lies like this. Go for the middle of the green and rely on your putting skills to do the rest. We're not desperate here. We're just having a run of bad luck. It happens to all golfers. Think positive and play the shot."

Will played the ball further back than he normally did and swung a little more upright. The ball squirreled off the clubface and landed in the right greenside trap—the only greenside trap on the hole. A mediocre explosion and a missed ten footer resulted in his third bogey of the round. The guys could actually feel the disappointment in the crowd. He was like a balloon that was leaking air and losing its shape. Most of the shouts were encouraging with a few catcalls mixed in. With bogeys on seven and nine, Will made the turn in forty strokes, five over par. He was totally embarrassed by his play.

The two of them walked slowly over the entrance road that separated the front and back nines. A couple of fans offered positive words, and to his credit, Will stopped and talked to them for a few seconds. Even though he was having a bad day, that was no excuse to withdraw into himself and ignore the people that had paid to see him and the other pros perform. Especially when there were so many young kids around. There was a backup on number ten tee, which gave them a little time to discuss the situation. They walked over to the far side of the tee next to the range building.

"All right," said Mitch with a voice full of emotion. "Let me explain this so even you can understand it. You know how much I love sports. I never saw Bird, Jordan, or Magic play ball—Musial, Mays, or Ted Williams either. Add to that, Hogan, Nicklaus, Palmer, Trevino. They were all before our time. Are you following me?"

"Yeah, sort of. We're too young, and we never got to see some of the greatest players ever. My grandpa loves baseball, and he never got to see Ruth or Gehrig play. So what?"

"It's all about pursuit of excellence, man. Those guys were like geniuses in their field. From my college philosophy class I remember a saying by a German philosopher, Arthur Schopenhauer. He said, *'Talent hits a target that no one else can hit, but genius hits a target that no one else can see'*. The 61 you shot on Friday was the work of a genius. A lot of the "experts" said it was a fluke and that you would fade into obscurity before the week was over. You had a bit of an attitude like you didn't care what everyone else thought—not the fans, the reporters, the TV announcers, or the other pros. It was just you and me, the hustler and his caddy, taking on the golf world and screw them if they didn't think we belonged. You laughed off the bad breaks and just kept on playing like we were playing a fifty-dollar Nassau back home. Now you're just playing scared."

"Hell of a pep talk, Mitch. I'm not playing scared; I'm just being realistic. If you haven't noticed, these are the best players in the world with tons of titles to their names. Like they've been saying, I'm just a two-bit hustler from Hicksville."

"What, now you think that 61 was luck? I saw it as a guy who was thumbing his nose at the golf establishment. All those media dudes who said you didn't belong, and maybe they should change the qualifying process to keep guys like you out. I can't believe that I stayed up late listening to all that crap on the Golf Channel and ESPN last night. They didn't see you hit that 7-iron under one tree limb and over the next, six feet from the cup in the qualifying round. They weren't there when you needed to make bird on the last two holes to get in. All I'm saying is, right now, this week, you are the best player in the tournament. And I ain't walkin' up eighteen with my head down looking like we got caught crashing somebody else's party. I don't care if we win, Will. Just play your game. I've had a chance to see the best this sport has to offer this week, and you're one of them.

You have a chance to make history here. When Ouimet won his Open, he wasn't a complete unknown. He was the Massachusetts State Amateur Champion! People knew who he was. You, on the other hand, **are** the kid from nowhere. And you and I know you ain't no Cinderella story, like they're saying. I see you play several times a week, and it doesn't cost me a nickel, unless I'm on the losing end of the game, but my point is I'd still pay to see you tee it up against these guys at the John Deere or any other tournament. Hell, I'd fly half way around the world just to see you do what you do. You're so damn good; I can't even be jealous of you."

Will looked over his shoulder and saw his opponent teeing his ball up. The group ahead had finally moved out of range.

"I hear what you're saying, man, but with all the commotion out here I'm not sure I can get back into my zone. You can't just turn it on and off at this level. There's such a fine line between mediocre and championship form. I have to admit that I've gained a lot of respect for these guys this past week. Traveling around and playing a course they will only see once a year and sleeping in strange beds all the time is tougher than it looks."

Mitch decided that since they were trying to accomplish something that had never been done before; a guy who has never won a single tournament of any kind stepping up and winning the first Tour event he ever played in, something totally unconventional was in order.

"Okay, let's try something that will hopefully get you back on track. Take the bag for the next couple of holes. Give yourself a good talking to as you play ten and eleven. When I come back, I want to see the guy that shot 61 against those two college hacks last year. Remember, they played a best ball on the front and when you were three up they wanted to quit, so you let them play a scramble on the back? You took $250 from them, and then you gave them each $50 to keep quiet about you breaking the course record. And what about the 58? The 58, man! Only you, Gloria, and I saw it, but I'll tell you I was so excited that I went home and had a dream about it. Do you think any of these other chops has ever carded a 58? C'mon, if you don't win this thing, at least beat the arrogant son-of-a-bitch you're paired with today. Respect them all you want, but do it after the tournament is over. Like the song says—-*It's a good day to whup somebody's ass.* Now go out and tackle these last nine holes like you're Secretariat on the back stretch."

"Where are you going?" asked Will as he shouldered his bag and headed over to the tenth tee where his opponent was waiting impatiently.

"I'm heading for the can, and then I'm gonna grab a brat and a soda. If anyone asks, tell them I took sick. See you on twelve."

Will received some questioning looks when he sat his bag down on the tenth tee and pulled out his driver. Fitzpatrick had already hit. The tees were up from the previous two days, making the hole play a few yards shorter.

"Caddy isn't feeling very well," he explained to his opponent and his caddy. "Guess I'm on my own for a while."

Fitzpatrick's caddy gave his man a subtle fist bump as Will teed up his ball. This was going to be some combination of beautiful and ugly at the same time. Whatever, the kid from nowhere had had his brief moment of glory, and he was not their problem. They were still trying to win a title here. Mathewson looked over at Will as he stared in the direction of the green, 586 yards away. *Get on with it, dude. Miss 'em quick and stay out of our way!* The hustler's drive flew Fitzpatrick's ball by fifteen yards and bounded down the fairway. Will shouldered his bag to several looks of dismay. One fan offered to carry it for him, but he politely declined.

Mitch's strategy had the desired effect. The adrenaline flowing through him made him want to sprint down the fairway, bag and all. He reminded himself to slow down and to stay under control. He felt like giving a two-fingered salute, but there was no one to give it to. *Damn*, he thought. *I know I'm letting Mitch down and when Melissa finds out how I tanked the front side she's gonna feel sorry for me, telling me it's only my first tournament, and there will be better days ahead once I gain some experience. And what about grandpa and Eddie? It'll be a major let down to them. They have given me everything I need to be a success at this game. All right, the pity party is over. Let's forget about what happened back there on the front side. This is a fresh nine, and I need to play every shot to perfection. Now it's all about character and pride. It's time to show everyone what Robbie Green's son can do. I know my dad can't be here, but hopefully grandpa and Eddie will make it to see Mitch and me walk up eighteen. And like Mitch said, we need to hit the final hole with our heads held high.* Unbeknownst to him, a half a mile away, "The Grip" and "The Street", each puffing on a Macanudo, had just entered the grounds.

Mitch went over to a shaded spot to eat his brat and drink his soda. He hoped his ploy with Will would produce the intended results, otherwise he and his partner would be the butt of a few jokes among the golfers and the announcers. Worse than that, he might have put their friendship in jeopardy. Naw, Will would respond and finish the round like the champion he was, win or no win. He wiped his mouth on a napkin and looked up to see Luke Slowinski heading his way with a mini tape recorder in his hand.

"Hey, Mitch, did you lose your guy?" asked Luke looking around.

"No, I'm giving him some personal time to figure out who he really is."

"And who is he?" asked the reporter with a concerned smile, holding his recorder up to get the caddy's answer.

"This weekend he's the best damn golfer here, even if he doesn't know it. You can quote me on that, Luke. He's only a few strokes off the lead, and we've had some terrible breaks, all the way back to the lost ball on number four earlier in the week. It was probably the only lost ball of the tournament. I'm not complaining. I'm just making an observation here. These fans have no idea how good he really is. Hell, he has no idea how good he is. Right now he's supposed to be out there figuring it out."

They both turned their heads in the direction of the tenth green when a huge roar went up. They gave each other a look of astonishment.

"Shit, my horse is starting to run," said Mitch as he stood and threw his brat wrapper and soda bottle into the trashcan.

"What?" asked Luke.

"I think our boy has just figured it out, and I need to be out there with him. How in the heck do I get to number twelve tee from here? Do you know a shortcut?"

"I'd only be guessing," answered Luke. "I think the best way is to follow up ten and eleven until we catch up with them. If we don't make it to twelve on time, they'll be coming back at us when they play thirteen, so we'll definitely catch them there. It's going to be slow going with all these people in the way. Maybe we can find a rules guy to give us a ride in his cart."

"Yeah, maybe. C'mon, Luke, let's get to hoofin'. The battle rages on, and I can't let him go it alone much longer. Hey, if that roar was for him, it sounds like my strategy worked. When we win this thing, I'm going to ask for a bigger cut."

Win this thing? thought Luke. *That front nine forty knocked him way back in the pack. It's going to take a miracle back nine just to be within shouting distance of the leaders.*

Reporter and caddy made their way through the massive crowd coming back at them as they moved up number ten. The fans were permitted to walk on the left side of the hole only, which slowed everyone's progress. They dodged around people trying to get as far up the fairway as they could, stopping as the last group hit their second shots into the par five. Frazier ripped his second about thirty yards short of the green, while Edwards parked his in the greenside trap. Mitch thought both shots were gutsy plays. If you wanted to win out here in the big time, a guy couldn't play conservative and hope his competitors would fade back into the pack. He looked up at the scoreboard when they reached the vicinity of the green and saw that Will had indeed eagled the hole to get back to minus thirteen, only five shots back of Schumacher and six shots behind Capelle. There was a group of five at minus sixteen. The crowd was holding them back. There was a huge mass of bodies, which made it impossible to move forward until everyone started moving. Mitch received some odd looks as they walked by spectators with his caddie's bib on.

They decided to wait for Will's group to play back up thirteen. They crossed the rough alongside number eleven green and stood behind the rope where they thought Will's drive would end up. A ball landed in front of them and rolled into the left fairway trap. It settled right next to the lip—borderline unplayable. The ball's owner, they assumed it was Will, didn't have much of a chance to get home in regulation. Mitch didn't want to walk out until after Fitzpatrick had hit. An elderly gentleman camped in a lawn chair looked at him, and seeing his caddy attire, let out with a low chuckle. He waved his mini binoculars at Mitch.

"Go ahead, son. Your guy is way down the fairway. Longest drive I've seen on this hole today. Where have you been? I've never seen a player carry his own bag at a pro tournament."

"I get a break every couple of hours," said Mitch as he ducked under the rope and walked out onto the fairway. "It's in my contract."

Luke and the man both laughed, and then they were swallowed up by a huge contingent of spectators coming at them, hurrying to get to a spot where they could see the golfers' second shots. The amount of people flowing by was incredible. This was a totally different experience for Luke who had covered mostly baseball in his internship. Most of the time, those fans just stayed in their seats. Out on the golf course you had to be fast on your feet if you wanted to follow a particular player. Luke decided to backtrack up eleven and ten. Maybe he could catch them on the par three sixteenth. That's when the action would reach a crucial point anyway. As it was, he missed a classic moment in tournament golf, and it didn't involve a club striking a ball.

"There's my guy," exclaimed Will as he approached with his bag slung over his shoulder. "Where have you been, man? This is just getting good. I thought Fitzpatrick was going to take a swing at a guy back on eleven. The dude didn't get his sneeze stifled enough. Fitzy had just put his club behind the ball, and the guy tried to muffle it, but it wasn't good enough for the superstar. They had words, and a few of the fans actually booed Fitzpatrick. It was obvious that the guy couldn't help it and was trying to do his best to keep quiet. These guys are really pampered out here, and they expect the royal treatment."

They stood and watched as Fitzpatrick explored his options. It was obvious that he was still agitated. He finally took a wedge out and advanced his ball about 50 yards up the fairway, ten yards behind Will's drive.

"There's a break," observed Mitch. "We can watch his ball flight into the green. So, you eagled ten?"

"Yeah. Side door. Almost didn't make it to the cup. But as Ronnie told me at least a thousand times, 'it doesn't matter how it got there, in is in'. A lady back there on the tee handed me her phone number. What do you think I should do with it?"

Mitch looked around and saw the strange guy that had been following them most of the round. On the front nine, he had hollered some bizarre things right after Will had hit his shots. They had discussed this type of fan before. He wasn't sure what "meatloaf" or "ba ba booey" had to do with tournament golf. Mitch chuckled to himself, thinking that some of these guys were straight out of *Happy Gilmore*. He motioned for Will to give him the number, then went over to the stranger and handed it to him. He told the guy to tell the woman on the other end that they had met at the tournament. The guy looked at the piece of paper and gave Mitch a sick looking grin with a few teeth missing.

"Good move," said Will as they arrived at his ball. "Okay, caddy, what have we got here?"

"You've got 92 to the flag. There's only about fifteen feet of green behind it, so let's stay underneath the hole. Remember how this green has held the first three rounds? Knock it down with dead hands, and we're lookin' straight at the back of the hole."

"I like the 'we' part. Let's hit the nine and run it back there. I wish Street were here to see this one."

Mitch grinned and pulled the bag away. Will took little time to line up the shot. His caddy looked over at the on-course commentator and signaled that his guy was hitting a 9-iron. The ex-tour player flashed him his thanks. He appreciated the old school approach, especially after watching Fitzpatrick land his third shot ten feet short of the pin, only to watch it spin back fifteen more feet. Will softened his hands and hit a low boring shot right at the flag. The ball landed about fifteen feet short of the stick, hopped twice, checked its momentum, and then rolled up to the cup, stopping two feet short. The crowd responded with an ovation that told Schumacher and Capelle back on number twelve green that the kid from Hicksville was back on track. Whatever, they assumed that his front nine 40 had put him in an untenable position. It would still take a miracle for him to make up the shots he had lost on the front side. As Mitch hustled to replace the divot, Will tossed his club ten yards back up the fairway and winked at a ten-year-old boy standing behind the ropes next to his parents. He smiled and waved at him as the crowd laughed. The kid was back!

Frazier and Edwards saw Mitch hustle back toward them to get the thrown club. It only took him about ten seconds to retrieve it and get back to his bag, but they still didn't appreciate it. They decided to lodge a complaint as soon as the tournament was over. Guys like this Green character should not be allowed out on tour with serious golfers who were trying to make a living. He was making a mockery of the game.

Back in the Golf Channel trailer, the producer was telling anybody and everybody who would listen what he thought of Will.

"This guy has to be the luckiest golfer alive! He all but shoots himself out of the tournament and all of a sudden his rabbit's foot kicks in, and he's back near the lead."

"What's the matter, Chief?" asked one of his staff. "You got money on Capelle or Schumacher?"

"Hell no, I don't have a cent on anyone. What I'm talking about is his behavior—him and his stinking caddie. Throwing clubs back up the fairway and talking to the crowd like he's playing at a local club member/guest outing. This is a serious PGA event, and he should be showing some respect."

"Respect or no respect," added one of his assistants, taking off his headphones. "I just heard from the network, and they say the ratings are going through the roof. Willy Green is drawing them in, Chief. I bet the sponsors are loving it."

"Agghh, I'm gonna take a leak. When I get back, tell me he just bogeyed fourteen."

The producer visited the port-o-potty, then smoked half of a cigarette. He knew smoking was bad for his blood pressure, but this kid was driving him crazy. He also knew he would have to give the kid an interview after the round. Green had probably committed more violations of tournament protocol than any five of the Tour's "bad boys". He entered the trailer just in time to see Green miss a slick downhill ten-footer on fourteen green.

"Ha, not birdying fourteen on the last day is a sure sign of a choke job. Just like I predicted. It's the easiest par four on the back side."

"Actually, Chief, that was for a deuce," came the response. "That was his drive. This guy is phenomenal. You should have bet on him."

"I didn't bet on anybody!" hollered the producer as he watched the action on fourteen green. "I told you that. Alright, everyone, let's get focused and do our jobs, no matter how much this guy is making a joke of everything."

Will walked over and waited for Fitzpatrick to putt for his bird. The crowd voiced its approval when Fitzpatrick's putt found the bottom of the hole. Will turned to see the little girl that had been following him with her dad for most of the back nine. She was the one that he had promised to give the ball to when he holed out on the last green. It was obvious that she was distressed, so he crouched down in front of her once everyone had cleared the green. Mitch had walked on ahead with the rest of the group.

"What's the matter, sweety?" asked Will.

"I can't find my dad," she said sobbing. "I was supposed to wait for him while he went to the bathroom, but all the people came by and pushed me out of the way."

"Why don't you walk with me," explained Will, offering her his hand. "We'll be inside the ropes away from all the people, and that will make it easier for your dad to see you. The television people will see you too, and they can talk to the guys with the radios. I'll bet your dad will show up in a few minutes. What's your name?"

"It's Sharon," she said still sniffing.

Will walked her to the tee on fifteen and gave her one of his small towels so she could blow her nose. The immediate crowd went ballistic when they saw what was happening.
Will walked out and teed up quickly. He went through a hasty pre-shot routine, and as he started his backswing, Sharon clapped her hands encouraging him. He stopped his swing and gave her a stern look. The camera zoomed in on his face sensing there was going to be an incident. Will walked over to her and put his hands on her shoulders. Then he did something that made the producer want to throw up—he kissed her on top of the head.

"You can say anything you want when I'm hitting, but you have to be quiet when the other guys are playing, okay?"

"Okay," beamed Sharon. "I just wanted you to hit a good one."

"So does my caddy," responded Will. "He's up to his neck in college loans and gambling debts."

This time the crowd outdid itself. It took a whole minute for them to settle down. Will hit his tee shot while there was a lot of murmuring and while the people in front were explaining to the people in the back what had just occurred. The noise and the commotion didn't bother him one bit.

CHAPTER TWENTY-FIVE

Max Comes Around

I'll be honest. I didn't like him at first. It's not that he was too cocky or anything. He was just different than what I was used to seeing out on the Tour. I think his behavior was just his way of dealing with all the pressure that a golfer goes through during his first professional event. That, and he was just a talented young man enjoying himself doing what he does best.

—-Max Worth, Golf Channel producer

Max looked at the electronic scoreboard on one of the monitors.

Score	Thru
Capelle -19	13
Schumacher -18	13
Edwards -16	14
Green -16	14
Frazier -15	14
Denard -15	15
Kruk -15	15

He finally softened his attitude toward the first-timer and his caddy. He wasn't sure why. Maybe it looked like the kid was out of it. He looked at the monitor and saw the little girl walking on number fifteen along with Winston, Green's caddy, holding on to the bag's bootstrap. She looked over at the crowd and let out with a squeal when she saw her dad. She let go of the bag and ran over to him. Max got a little misty eyed when the man picked up his daughter and gave her a big hug. The dad looked out at Mitch and Will and gave them a big thumbs up. The on-course reporter had relayed to the dad that his daughter was fine, and she was walking along with Green's caddy. Again, the crowd gave them a huge ovation. Fitzpatrick and Mathewson did their best to ignore them. Fitzy was two over for the day and had dropped to minus fourteen. After shooting his abysmal forty on the front side, Will had actually caught and passed him. In his heart, he knew it wasn't the newbie's fault. As in the past, when he was in contention, he could feel himself tighten up which caused his swing to get a littler quicker and out of sync. It was a tough habit for him to break.

Fitzpatrick was the first to play his second shot into fifteen. The pin was tucked in behind the left trap. He had some ground to make up, so with his caddy in agreement, he decided to go for it. He caught his 8-iron a tad thick and watched in dismay as it plunked down in the sand. Will walked forward to his ball. With no wasted effort, he hit his full wedge to a spot six feet right of the hole. The fans on the last four holes knew something big had just transpired. There was a lot of commotion over by fifteen. When it was his turn, Will wasted little time converting his birdie putt. He was now six under on the back and two behind the leader.

Capelle and Schumacher were standing back on fifteen tee. They assumed that the new "crowd favorite" had just made another birdie, but with only three holes to go they figured he still didn't have a chance. They were both Tour veterans, and they had never seen another player come from as far back as Will was with only nine holes to go, especially after a total tank job on the front nine. They were both counting on making four on the par five seventeenth. Capelle figured a four there would lock up his win.

Eddie, Ronnie, and the girls sat in one of the refreshment areas up the hill from the eighteenth green. The guys were drinking beer and the ladies were drinking diet sodas.

"Tell me again why we're not out there cheering him on?" asked Kathy.

"The dude's got enough going on without us showing up out of the blue and surprising him," explained Ronnie. "We'll watch him finish on eighteen. By then, the extra pressure of seeing us shouldn't make a difference. Besides, I told him on the phone that we'd be here to celebrate when it was over. He's expecting us, but later, not sooner."

The Michigan contender made a routine par on sixteen. It was Will's second par of the nine. They walked over to seventeen tee to find Denard and Kruk still standing there. They told the recent arrivals that there was some kind of medical emergency with one of the fans up ahead on the right side of the hole. Mitch sat the bag down and parked himself on the bench. Will walked back and rummaged around the sweater pocket until he found what he was looking for. He pulled out the miniature football that he and Mitch used to toss around when they had to wait for a slow group ahead of them. He walked back by the rope and waved to a couple of boys who were anxiously standing there.

"Come over on this side of the rope, guys. Let's play 'monkey drop'. We toss the ball back and forth until someone drops it. The one that drops it is the monkey, okay?"

The boys ducked under the rope and took up positions about fifteen feet away. They started with easy tosses until they figured out that no one was going to drop a soft one. Will threw one high in the air and was surprised when the boy on the right signaled for a fair catch. He caught it easily. The other three pros stood in a group away from them discussing the situation. This guy was an absolute embarrassment.

The medical carts started to clear the area, so Will told each boy they had to run a straight route down the right side of the tee. He threw a perfect pass to the first one, but he couldn't handle it.

"All right, this is for all the marbles," he challenged the second boy.

The crowd was loudly rooting for the boy not to drop his pass. Will hit him right in the numbers, and he held on. He got a nice ovation from the crowd as he walked back to Will holding the ball high above his head. Will turned and motioned to Mitch. His caddy was way ahead of him. He tossed the Sharpie marker over. Will signed the ball and gave it to the boy. He turned and looked at Mitch, and sure enough, he was waiting with a golf ball in his hand. Will signed that one and gave it to the boy that had dropped the pass. The two boys were patted on the back when they ducked back under the ropes.

"Hey, Will," one of them said. "Why is your bag so much smaller than the other guys' bags? And why does it have legs on it?"

"Look at my caddy, son," answered Will. "Does he look like a guy that can carry one of those big staff bags for eighteen holes? I had to carry this small one myself on ten, eleven, and twelve earlier. There's a lesson there for you young people. Stay in shape and stay away from those donuts."

The crowd laughed, and Mitch just shook his head. The players and caddies walked over to the right side of the tee when one of the volunteers told them it was time to resume play. Denard and Kruk both hit acceptable drives and left the tee. Will went back and sat on the bench and struck up a conversation with the fans that were close enough to hear.

"So, you're not actually a pro, are you?" asked one fan.

"Technically, no," answered Will. "But if I want to win any money, I have to declare myself a professional, or they will skip me and give what I would have made to the next guy. Then everyone behind me will move up one slot in the money department."

"You gonna take the money?" asked another.

"Let me think about it for a minute. Uh, yeah. If I don't, my caddy will mutiny."

As they talked, Frazier, Edwards, and their caddies walked up on the tee and joined them. They ignored Will and Mitch, walking over to talk to Fitzpatrick and Mathewson. Mitch overheard enough of the conversation to ascertain that Schumacher had dropped a shot. The leader was still minus nineteen, and Schumacher was now minus seventeen. That put Will in a tie with Schumacher, only two shots back.

Will's group was finally waved to the tee. The fans calmed down and watched their new favorite golfer as he pounded out a 300-yard drive right down the middle. Fitzpatrick's 280 follow-up wasn't quite as impressive but a quality shot nonetheless. Will gave the crowd a parting wave and headed up the fairway.

"Most of these fans are pretty nice," commented Will as Mitch caught up with him.

"You gave away our football," said Mitch.

"Dude, I'm sure we'll win enough to buy another one."

"I want a football, a new set of clubs, some skis, and a motorcycle."

"You'll get nothing, and you'll like it," responded Will, mimicking Judge Schmails from *Caddy Shack*.

"I loved that movie. Did you know that the critics had nothing good to say about it when it came out? Now it's one of the most quoted movies of all time. Heck, even Gloria knows some of the lines."

"That's probably because you are always repeating them. Guys will do that when they can't come up with anything clever to say."

"I can be clever," protested Mitch. "After a few beers, I'm a stinkin' riot."

Carney Mathewson was listening to the two rookies as they walked up the fairway. It was like they were some kind of comedy act. How did Will concentrate with all the nonsense going on? Then again, maybe there was something to it. His guy was falling further back, and Will was now in contention. They stopped at Fitzpatrick's ball. After some discussion, they decided to lay up with a 6-iron between the fairway traps. Fitzy hit a smooth shot to about the 100-yard marker.

Will had about 270 yards to the green. The pin was on the right side of the green with the trap partially guarding it. He pulled his 3-metal out of the bag and grinned at his caddy.

"You're going to have to get every bit of it if you cut it in there," advised Mitch. "The upside is, if you're on line and a little short, we should have an easy chip."

"That's what I'm thinking," added Will. "If I catch it solid, it might just run up there."

Will stepped up to his ball. This was what he had been trained to do. He told himself he was back home playing for a hundred a hole, and this was the make or break shot that determined if he was going home a little richer than when he started. No worries. Just trust his swing and make a smooth pass at it. He was in perfect balance when he swept the club back across the grass tops. As he came back into the ball, he held off his release for a millisecond. The result was a rocket fade that started out at the left side of the green.

Player, caddy, and opponents watched in suspense as the little white sphere flew toward the intended target. The fans behind the green in the luxury boxes screamed their approval when his ball hit a few yards short of the putting surface, then kicked up onto the green, stopping twenty feet from the hole.

Max Worth was speechless for the first time all week. He just stared at the monitor and shook his head in disbelief. The kid had just pulled off the shot of the tournament under unbelievable pressure.

"Holy shit!" exclaimed Max. "Who shoots five over on the front, then plays the back like he owns it?"

"If you're looking for an answer," responded Denny Holmes, "it's the kid from nowhere. And he's serving notice that he thinks he intends to win this thing. Are you a believer yet, boss?"

"Yeah, Denny, I'm a believer," admitted Max in a hushed voice. "I know I've been a little biased against this kid, but he pulled off a miracle shot just when he needed to. How does he stand for this nine?"

"If he makes this putt, he'll be eight under for eight holes. Unbelievable."

Will received a huge ovation when he walked up onto the seventeenth green. He waved and smiled at them.

"Don't get too excited, jerk," said Mitch. "They're clapping for me. They've never seen a caddy with so much style and class. You are just a means for me to gain the fame I rightfully deserve."

They waited for Fitzpatrick to mark his ball. His sand wedge from 100-yards out flew the trap and stopped fifteen feet from the hole. Will crouched down and looked his putt over. It wasn't supposed to happen to a highly trained hustler with a near perfect golf swing, but nonetheless the emotions came crashing down on him. Out of nowhere, an image of a little boy flashed into his head. The boy was hitting a soda can around the back yard with a cut down golf club his mother had bought for him at a garage sale.

Then he was older, hunting golf balls in the woods so he could sell them to the golfers at GLV. Eddie and Ronnie walked up and gave him twice what the balls were worth, and Eddie bought his bottle of homemade insect repellent. The next image to flash by was one of him angrily hitting balls on the Stonehedge range. He remembered that day. Thoughts of Troy holding Melissa's hand in the hallway had enraged him. Mitch leaned over his shoulder and looked at the twenty-foot putt.

"It's going to break the same way it did in our practice round," he said. "Get the speed right and it has to drop."

Will looked up at his good friend and partner with tear-filled eyes. Mitch's eyes went wide. In a split second he figured out what was happening.

"No, no, no," he scolded in a hushed tone. "Don't do this. Not now. We're about to make history here. Think of all the kids that are here and are at home watching. They need somebody to believe in. Someone they can look up to. Damn, Will, do it for me. I'm your biggest fan."

"Get a grip, dude, you're starting to ramble," said Will as he stood, still looking at his line. He wiped his eyes with the back of his hand and took his position. Mitch stepped away. The cup was a little blurry, but he remembered the putt from his Tuesday practice round. He only looked up once after he went into his putting crouch. He took the putter back and gave the ball a solid rap. The line was good, but the speed was in question. The ball looked as if it was rolling in slow motion. Fans were glued to the luxury box windows behind the green. The people standing behind the green stood on their toes trying to get a glimpse of the rolling ball. For the first time all day the vicinity around the seventeenth green was totally silent. Will never stood up. He just watched from his bent over position. The ball got to the front edge and hesitated—then it toppled into the cup. Eight holes. Eight under. The roar could be heard on the sixteenth and eighteenth greens. Thirty seconds later, another roar erupted at the eighteenth green as Will's score was posted on the scoreboard.

Score	Thru
Green -19	17
Capelle -18	16
Schumacher -17	16
Edwards -16	16
Denard -16	17
Kruk -16	17
Frazier -15	16

CHAPTER TWENTY-SIX

"It's What I Do"

Humility. I guess I didn't truly understand the word, or the value of the trait, until I played eighteen holes with a kid that was loaded with it. There was nothing fake about him. He was the old, "what you see is what you get" kind of guy. There are a whole lot of us out here on Tour that could learn something from this guy. I know I did.

—Brian Fitzpatrick, Tour pro

What would you be like if you were a pampered athlete from middle school through college and beyond? Would you be an unassuming, humble sort of guy or gal, or would you behave like the world owed you because of your special gifts? There seems to be way too many of the latter types that don't realize that their monster paychecks come from the fans who buy tickets and jerseys with their names plastered on the back.

One can only wonder what would happen if Wrigley Field's or the Boston Garden's attendance dropped to fifty percent of capacity for an entire season—a season where both teams were playoff contenders. What if huge numbers of fans decided that they didn't want to subsidize another collection of Lamborghinis and Maseratis? Larry Bird reportedly said, after his first contract negotiation, "The joke was on them. I would have played for nothing." An attitude like that would obviously be viewed as naïve today, but it would also be refreshing in a world where money talks and everything else walks.

"What is happening here?" asked Max in a state of disbelief. "This kid has more guts than anybody I've ever seen. He's playing his ass off in front of millions, and last week he was riding a mower and playing for beers at his local club. Who is this guy?"

"Things are going to get really interesting, boss," remarked Denny. "Did you see him wipe his eyes before he hit that putt? I hope he's not starting to crack. You're supposed to cry after your first win, not before you've finished the round."

"Show me," ordered Max. "Have them back it up."

Denny spoke into his mike and the action on his monitor reversed itself until he said "freeze it", then "step it forward". Green was kneeling behind his putt, then he looked up at his caddy. The caddy's expression gave them an idea what was transpiring. Then it looked like he was lecturing his man. Green stood and Mitch walked away from him. Then he wiped his eyes with the back of his hand.

"Freeze it," commanded Denny. "There you go, tears."

"How did he make that putt if he had trouble seeing?" asked Max.

"I think it was by pure feel," remarked Denny. "He must have had a similar putt earlier in the week. He barely looked at it just before he putted. So now you're rooting for him, Chief?"

"Hell yes, I'm rooting for him. A guy can change his mind, can't he? Angela here probably changes her mind several times a day."

"I do," she giggled. "I tried on three pair of shoes this morning before I decided which ones to wear. Even then, I was second-guessing my decision on the way here."

"So there, wise guy. I'm allowed to see the error of my ways. I am now officially on the Willy Green bandwagon."

"You and several million others," remarked Denny.

"I want to see what's going on," said Melissa. "Let's see if we can get close to the landing area on eighteen. If he hits the shot of his life, that's where it will happen, and I want to be there to witness it."

"I thought the shot of his life was when he hit that first 5-iron fade to impress you," said Kathy.

"Okay, the second most important shot of his life," admitted Melissa as she stood and headed for the exit. "Who's coming with me?"

"Tell me you're cool with what's going on," demanded Mitch as they stood on eighteen tee. "We've got one hole to go, and it's going to be absolutely crazy up there by the green. Tell me that the guy standing here is going to play like the player I've known for years— fearless and confident with the best damn swing I've ever seen. And believe me, I've seen a lot of good swings this week."

Will refused to look at his caddy. He was staring at the trees across the cart path behind the tee. Images were still running rapidly through his head. They began to slow down. He saw Melissa in the high school hallway coming at him with a big smile on her face. Then he saw himself admitting to his grandfather that the clubs he and Eddie had bought him had been stolen. The next image lingered in his mind. He was standing before the picture of his father on Ronnie's wall. Then Ronnie walked up and told him he was his grandfather, and they hugged. The next image was him paying Ronnie on the ninth green at Stonehedge North after he had lost the one club par bet on a technicality. Eddie was standing behind his grandfather in the background looking away, trying not to laugh.

The last image was the most touching. He was still a teenager. The Grip and The Street were standing over on the right side of the tee waiting for him to hit. They both had on tan shorts. Ronnie was wearing an orange shirt, and Eddie was wearing a light blue one. Two self-pro-claimed Divot Dogs. All he ever wanted to be was just like them. He thought back to the first time he saw them at the GLV East course. There was something about the two of them that told him they were not just two ordinary guys that played a lot of golf together. They occupied his thoughts as he rode his bike home that day. He hoped he would see them again. He had a few golf questions, and he was pretty sure they would know the answers. Of course, that was before he found out that one of them was family. And now, here he was, on the brink of a Tour victory. He heard Mitch talking, but it didn't register. He recognized Luke standing with the crowd at the back of the tee.

"Bet me," he said quietly as he acknowledged Luke with a small wave.

"What?" asked Mitch, glad to get any sort of response out of his guy.

"Bet me I can't birdie this hole."

"Okay, I'll bet you twenty bucks you can't birdie this hole. Even money."

The fans that could hear the strange conversation between player and caddy looked at each other in confusion. Will offered his hand to his caddy. Mitch took it and held it a little longer than a normal handshake. A similar feeling passed between them. Their old saying, 'it was time to get to the gettin' was never more appropriate. Ahead of them, Denard and Kruk were now out of range. The hustler stepped to the tee and hit his drive. It came a little off the heel and, as a result, only traveled about 265 yards, starting out toward the left fairway trap, then curving back to the middle of the fairway. Fitzpatrick blew his drive twenty yards closer to the green on the same line.

Will stood beside Mitch as Fitzpatrick hit his drive. When his caddy shouldered the bag, Will grabbed him by the arm and stopped him from walking off the tee.

"Partner, I think I need a little help here."

Mitch looked his friend in the eye and gave him a reassuring smile.

"Just take a hold of the bootstrap like Sharon did," explained Mitch in a calm voice. "We'll stroll down this fairway like we own the place. Don't look left or right. Just focus on the shot you are about to hit. It's what you do, man. It's what you do."

The sight of caddy leading player down the fairway was a little odd, but then again, these two already had a history of doing some strange things. Fans shouted encouragement as the two of them walked down eighteen. Will gave them a little wave from time to time. His main concern at the moment was just putting one foot in front of the other and not falling on his face. When they got to his ball, Mitch sat the bag down and went about getting the yardage. Up ahead at the green, they could see Denard playing his third shot out of the back right bunker. Will was informed that he was 211 out—just a smooth 5-iron for him.

Mitch attempted to get his guy's mind off all the pressure of the situation by discussing dinner plans and the drive home. They were surprised when they heard a loud moan up by the green. Denard had played his difficult shot a little too aggressively out of the trap, only to see it roll into the water hazard on the other side of the green. Mitch told him to forget about what the other guys were doing. His goal was to win the twenty-dollar bet he had made back on the tee. Will looked up at Mitch, and over his caddy's shoulder he saw his wife, "The Grip" and "The Street", and their wives, standing in back of the rope under the trees that lined the right side of the hole. He wanted to walk over and talk to them but decided that it wouldn't be a wise thing to do. He smiled and gave them a wave.

"Do you know him?" asked a fan standing next to Melissa.

"Yes," she beamed. "He's my husband."

"Why aren't you waiting for him over by the scorer's tent like the other Tour players' wives do? You shouldn't have to stand out here like a common fan."

"Thanks, but this is fine with us," said Melissa. "Do you know why he has all those marks all over his shirt?"

"Yeah, before the round, he all but waded into the crowd signing autographs and shaking hands. The people were holding out their pens for him to sign their stuff. Your husband is one of a kind, ma'am. I've never seen anything like him. And the people here are crazy about him. He sure has a way with the young ones."

"We think he's pretty special too," she said, motioning toward the rest of the group.

"He's about 210 out," said the man. "Do you know what he'll hit here for his second shot?"

"He'll hit one of the best 5-irons you've ever seen," said Melissa with a tinge of pride in her voice.

"Are you sure about that?" asked the man. "There's a lot of pressure on this shot. It could decide the winner."

"Oh, I'm sure. He hits his 5-iron like he owns it. In fact, the first shot I ever saw him hit was with that club."

Denard finally holed out, making a disappointing double bogey, dropping him back to minus thirteen, shrinking his winnings substantially. He and Roger Kruk shook hands and walked off the green with their caddies. Kruk looked up at the big scoreboard behind the green and decided to stand in the walkway for a minute to watch Will's second shot come in.

Will took his time pulling his 5-iron out of the bag and walked over to his ball. The small bag with legs on it looked out of place with all the big "staff bags" that the regular pros used. He placed his hands on the full cord grip like he had done thousands of times before. There was more pressure on this shot than he had ever experienced in the ten years he had been playing the game. He walked back over to his bag and rubbed the grip down with a towel. His caddy gave him a reassuring look.

"Stick it, partner, and let's get out of here," said Mitch in a quiet voice. "I'd be more than happy to lose twenty bucks here."

He went back to his ball and took his address position. He took one more look at his caddy. Then he did something that mystified the fans on the right side of eighteen and at home watching on their televisions. He looked at two guys standing over by the rope and put two fingers to the brim of his cap. The two men repeated the gesture back at him. Then a striking young lady and two beautiful older ladies standing along side the men repeated the same two-fingered gesture.

"What was that?" asked Max. "Did you see that little two-finger thing and the people it was aimed at? They did the same thing back to him."

"I think it was some kind of secret sign, Chief," said Denny. "Maybe they're a team of assassins or even worse, government agents."

"You used to be somewhat funny. Now you're just weird. Remind me again why I keep you around."

"Because I married your daughter, and she'd be brokenhearted if you fired me," said Denny with a straight face.

"I knew it had to be something like that," conceded Max. "Pass the word. When we interview him, ask him about the gesture he just made. It has to mean something."

Will took his stance and waggled the club. His 5-iron was always one of his favorite clubs. He could hit it high or low, and he could fade it or draw it on command. The present shot called for his standard ten feet of draw—a shot he could hit right after jumping out of bed with only one practice swing. He looked at his target twice and slightly adjusted his stance. The pin was back left—perfect for his preferred shot shape. The ball left the clubface like a bullet from a .22 rifle. Halfway there it was fifteen feet right of the hole. Then it started to turn slowly toward the flag. The fans in the vicinity of the green went berserk when the ball landed twenty feet short of the pin and then checked up after twelve more feet of roll, leaving him with an eight foot putt to get to minus twenty.

He tipped his cap to acknowledge the applause and started toward the green. He glanced over to the spot where his friends and family were standing. They were nowhere to be seen. Mitch replaced Will's divot and hustled to catch up with him. The caddy walked along staring at the side of his player's face. After several paces, Will looked over at his best friend.

"What, you were surprised? Like you said, it's what I do."

"You're a real piece of work, man, you know that?" said Mitch as he threw his left arm over Will's shoulders.

"I've been called that before. You love it and you know it."

"You're damn straight I love it," admitted Mitch. "If I can't be out here playing, and you and I both know that's never going to happen, then there's no place I'd rather be than lugging your equipment around a beautiful course like this, watching you kick everybody's ass. I gotta tell you, man, this is as good as it gets for a golfaholic like me."

They stopped to watch Fitzpatrick hit his approach shot.

"Uh, Brian," said Krusty, as his man stood behind his ball picturing the shot. "I'll bet you a hundred dollars you can't get it inside Green's ball."

Fitzpatrick looked at his caddy like he was deranged.

"And I'll give you three-to-one odds," added Krusty.

"You're on, man," said a determined Brian.

He pulled out his 6-iron and hit one of the sweetest irons that he had hit in the entire tournament. His ball stopped three feet closer than Will's on the opposite of the hole. They hi-fived each other, then were surprised when Will and Mitch walked over and raised their hands to be slapped. As they walked together to the green, Will showed his maturity by telling Fitzpatrick he could putt first if he wanted to. If Will putted and made it to twenty under, it would be almost impossible to get the crowd to quiet down. As they approached the green, the onlookers showed their appreciation for two of the finest shots they had seen on eighteen all day. Brian looked at his caddy and smiled.

"We've been making fun of these guys all tournament long, and what we should have been doing was taking lessons from them. This back nine has made me a believer. That son-of-a-bitch can really play. I don't care if this is his first tournament. After his horrible front nine, he's played like a real champion on the back side."

"True that," echoed Krusty.

Fitzpatrick made short work of his five-footer to get back to minus fifteen and a top ten finish. His round had its ups and downs, but he was pleased with the way he had played. He walked off to the side of the green to give Will center stage. The Michigan hustler walked around the hole checking out all the angles. If his opponent's ball had been on the same line as his ball, Will wouldn't have offered to let him putt first. That might have been construed as a player aiding his opponent by showing him the line.

He walked back and conferred with Mitch about the pace of his putt. They both knew that to leave it short would be inexcusable. Will stepped up and the crowd went deathly silent. It was as if all breathing around the green had stopped, anticipating something marvelously historic was about to happen, and they were all part of it. Will put a smooth stroke on his ball and watched it roll toward the hole. He definitely did not leave it short. It hit the back of the cup dead center, hopped up a couple of inches, and disappeared from sight. Nine holes. Nine under. The eighteen green and surrounding area was pure bedlam.

"I don't believe it!" hollered Max looking at the screen. "That crazy kid just shot 40, 27. He turned a five over round into a minus four. His twenty under could win this thing. That had to be one of the greatest nine holes in the history of golf. He's going to do an interview if we have to tie him down. This day will be remembered for a long time to come."

"Man, when a zebra changes his stripes, he really changes them," whispered Denny to Angela.

"What was that?" asked Max.

"Nothing, boss, nothing."

After shaking hands, Will's group headed up the hill between the ropes. Fans were reaching out to get the pros and caddies to touch them. Will and Mitch were walking behind Fitzpatrick and his caddy. They were interacting with the fans, and the people were loving it. Halfway up the hill, he stopped and walked back a few paces. There, standing in front of her dad, with the biggest smile imaginable, was Sharon, the girl he had promised his finishing ball to. He took it out of his pocket and asked for a felt tipped pen to sign it. A pen was thrust into his hand, and he signed the ball and handed it over.

"She'll remember this for the rest of her life," shouted her dad over the din.

"Her and me both, sir," agreed Will, shaking his hand.

"That kid is a class act, Sharon," said the dad as Will and his caddy continued on up the hill. "The game of golf could use more like him, don't you agree?"

Sharon shook her head, signaling an emphatic yes, while she held on tightly to her golf ball.

Melissa was waiting at the top of the hill. He gave her a big hug and shook hands with his two mentors and received hugs from Suzanne and Kathy. The television people couldn't believe how calmly Will, and the people he had just interacted with were behaving. Their demeanor was quite different than what they had seen in the past. Normally there was a lot of enthusiastic hugging and a few tears. These people seemed to be taking it all in stride.

"How can I get a decent gig after this?" asked Will.

"You're going to have to be creative, that's for sure," said Eddie. "Go sign your card, and we'll watch the last two groups come in."

CHAPTER TWENTY-SEVEN

Two Very Cool Guys

There was this guy, Eddie Davis from Detroit, that could play the game as well as anyone I ever saw. Once in a while, he would join our regular bunch for a round. We all knew who he was, so the bets were always minimal. The cool thing about Eddie was that he didn't take advantage of us. Money traded hands, and in the long run I think we were all pretty much even. He always helped us with our game if we asked. I have a lot of respect for the guy. It's too bad he's not with us anymore. I refused to go to the course the day I heard that he died. The guy was one of a kind, that's for sure.

—-Bruce Sims, CPA, scratch golfer

Indecision, to some athletes, is like a strange sound in the middle of the night. To others, it's like watching a horror movie, not knowing when the next shocking moment will present itself and elicit a little girly scream from a 200-pound man sitting in the back row of the theatre. The strain of the unknown causes the biological functions of the body to become erratic. Breathing intensifies and sweat glands go into overdrive. Imagination goes wild with possible scenarios. The really good ones can calm themselves and go about their business. The great ones welcome the feeling and feed off of it.

As expected, Capelle, playing in the last group, birdied seventeen drawing even with Will. His drive on eighteen was close to where Fitzpatrick's ball was a few minutes earlier. He also had a 6-iron in his hand, making slow practice swings while he waited for Frazier and Edwards to take care of their business up on the green. A par would get him into a playoff with the kid from Hicktown, and a birdie would win it outright. He decided that he would play it conservative. He had been in three playoffs in his career and had won two of them. The kid would be at a huge disadvantage if it were just the two of them. He could taste victory, and it was like a medium rare steak fresh off the grill.

Will was in the scoring area going over his card when he heard the commotion around eighteen green. Capelle had just blocked his approach shot, and it ended up in the same back bunker that Denard was in twenty minutes earlier. It was all on Capelle's shoulders now. After signing his card, Will walked out and stood with the others. He decided to call his mother back in Michigan. Ronnie had called her the day before, telling her of their plans to drive to the tournament and asking her if she wanted to go along. She refused his invitation, stating that she had to work and that Sundays were usually big days for tips.

The crowd watched intently as Capelle surveyed his shot. The green ran slightly away from him toward the pond on the other side. Knowing Denard's outcome from the same location might or might not have been helpful. The ball was sitting up on top of the sand. All he had to do was fluff it out of there about ten feet onto the green and then watch it roll down toward the hole. Or, since it was sitting up so nice, he could just clip it out of the sand with some decent backspin. He would have to carry the shot a little further if he went that route. As he wiggled his feet into the soft sand, he hadn't fully committed to the type of shot he wanted to hit. Indecision, in a situation like this one, was like a huge dragon looking over his shoulder. At least, that was the way he had once explained it to his caddy. His solution to the dragon thing was to say, "slay the dragon" to himself in his backswing. His caddy, Arnie Swift, gave him a strange look when informed of this little peculiarity. It didn't matter to him if his guy thought about poodle skirts or muscle cars when he hit his shots. Results were all that mattered out here on the circuit.

The shock of what happened next could be heard as the crowd collectively gasped their disbelief. Capelle, an experienced Tour pro who had been in this position before, hit his shot so heavy that it barely made it out of the trap and ended up only a few feet onto the green. Eddie raised his right eyebrow at the group, indicating his shock at this turn of events. Will calmly stood between his grandfather and his wife, with an arm around both of them. He knew the normal thing to do was to go to the practice area to hit a few balls, anticipating a playoff, but he wasn't a normal Tour pro. At this moment, in the eyes of the golf world, he wasn't even a pro.

Capelle, disgusted with himself, and more than a little embarrassed, followed up his trap miscue with a putt that stopped two feet short of the cup, giving the kid from nowhere the victory. Will had just won the first tournament that he had ever played in. The kid that no one had ever heard of wasn't a BNP, but the golf world now knew who he was. There were more handshakes and hugs all around. Luke was standing off to the side with his recorder when Will saw him.

"Get over here, Luke," invited Will. "I want you to meet my family."

Luke took a couple of steps and did a double take when he recognized Eddie. Eddie's reaction was the same.

"What, do you two know each other?" asked Mitch.

"Sort of," said Luke, shaking Eddie's hand. "I'm pretty sure I saw you a couple of years ago at my fiancé's high school softball game back in Texas."

"Yup, that was me. Small world, huh?"

"How is that possible?" asked Will.

"We'll explain it to you later, champ," answered Eddie, motioning to the television people that were heading their way. "Right now you have to talk to your fans. Let's go get a beer while he does the interview thing. Do us a favor and don't mention any names, kid. Just 'cause your cover is blown, you don't have to drag us down with you. C'mon, Luke, you can tell me how Chip and Annie are doing."

* * *

The sun was much lower in the sky when Will walked over to the parking lot where his people were waiting. Mitch and Luke were over on the practice green putting for quarters. The others were sitting in Will's car discussing the day's events. On the ride down in Suzanne's car, they had listened to the tournament on Sirius's PGA Tour radio. Will was going up nine fairway when they found a parking spot in a resourceful entrepreneur's front yard across from the course's main entrance. By the time they had bought their tickets and had passed through all the displays, Will was on the tenth green, and Mitch was enjoying his brat and soda.

They decided to grab a light supper, then head for home. Luke declined their invitation to join them, as he had to get back to the office to put the finishing touches on his article. He bade them farewell and promised to keep in touch. It was amazing how they had become such good friends in such a short period of time.

They all piled into Will's car for the short ride down the drive to the tournament's main entrance. Ronnie and Eddie sat by the back seat doors with their wives on their laps. Melissa sat on Will's lap in the front passenger seat and Mitch drove. One of the competitor's and his caddy watched them pile into the car and head back down the entrance road.

"Stinkin' hillbillies," he observed.

"I don't know if you noticed," said his caddy. "But those hillbillies had three of the best looking women I have ever seen. We should be so lucky."

"Whatever. Let's get outta farm country. All these tractors around here make me want to puke."

"You can't be serious. Without these tractors, we don't eat. This is farm country, man."

* * *

Herman's secretary took a call from an area code that she didn't recognize. It was a short call from a man named Anthony. He informed her that the Trenton family had no further business with Herman Wakefield's two clients. She thanked the caller and hung up the phone. Like her boss, she loved it when a plan came together.

* * *

The group sat at a local Mexican restaurant waiting for their food.

"It's about time we had something with a little spice in it," said a satisfied Mitch as he pushed his empty plate off to the side. "All week we've been avoiding foods that had anything more than just salt and pepper for seasoning."

"Don't forget, dude, you owe me twenty bucks," said Will, winking at his wife.

"What, now the caddy has to pay the player?" asked Melissa.

"Nope. We made a little bet on the last hole, and he lost," explained Will.

"I'll pay as soon as I get my caddy fee," said Mitch with a satisfied grin. "By the way, do you know exactly how much you just won?"

Will looked around the table at the smiling faces. He actually didn't know what the winner's share was. He was so intent on qualifying for the U. S. Open, the money for this tournament never entered his mind. He knew there was a lot at stake but wasn't aware of the actual figure.

"It's about 850 grand, hotshot!" said Mitch with a fist out.

They all put their fists in the middle and then "exploded" them as they drew them back.

"Street, the kid caught up with our whole career winnings in one day," said Ronnie feigning remorse.

"You've won over 800 thousand dollars playing golf?" asked Kathy.

"Uh, probably not," stammered Ronnie. "It was just a figure of speech."

It was a running gag with the two hustlers that whenever they pulled out their money clips to pay for something, they turned away from their spouses so they couldn't see how much they were carrying. In truth, the two wives did not know exactly how much their husbands were worth. Gaining knowledge of that figure would have surprised them both.

"Of course, that's before taxes and caddy fees," added Mitch. He decided it was time to pass on the information that Luke had given him as they were catching up to Will out on the back nine. "On top of that news, Will, I have one more piece of information, and you're not going to like it."

The table was silent as they looked at Mitch, waiting for him to continue.

"With this win today, you did not qualify for the Open. The Masters, yes, but not the Open. Luke told me. We should have looked it up. He said he found the Open qualifying procedure in less than a minute on his phone. He didn't tell you because he thought you might be disappointed and that it might affect your round today. Sorry, buddy. You still have to play in the qualifier events if you want to get into the big one."

"I was going to say we drove all the way down here for nothing, but that would sound a little ungrateful, with the huge check I've got coming," admitted Will, trying to disguise the disappointment he was feeling.

"And just in time, too," beamed Melissa, changing the subject. "I hear that diapers and formula are getting real expensive."

No one said anything until her comment soaked in. Kathy and Suzanne rose and came around the table to hug Melissa. Will just looked at her in shock. Mitch clapped him on the back.

"Well, Street," offered Ronnie, "it looks like we're going to have to train another little one in the family business."

"I hope we can still hold a club by the time he or she is old enough," said Eddie as they got up to leave.

"One more thing," added Ronnie in a low voice, attempting to keep it between him and Eddie. "You know that the four thousand we won at the Vegas sports book betting on the champ here will also come in the form of a check. That means the casino will take a huge chunk out for taxes."

"You two really made four thousand on me at a Vegas sports book?" asked Will.

"We would have if we had bet a hundred skins on you," whispered Eddie.

"Well, how much did you bet?"

"Ten large," answered Eddie as he turned to get into his car.

Will just stood and stared at his two mentors. Ronnie told him how much the two of them had taken off the Russians, and on top of that they had just won four hundred grand betting on him. Together they won more than he did. The two hustlers and their wives got into Suzanne's car, while Melissa joined her husband and his caddy. Will looked over at the other car with the two old guys in the back seat. Ronnie put his window down and signaled for the other car to lead the way. Will was in the back seat with his arm around Melissa. He looked at his caddy and best friend sitting behind the wheel.

"Mitch, there goes two of the coolest guys walking the planet today. Someone should write a book about them."

"If they do, what are the chances of us being in it?" asked Mitch, looking in the rearview mirror.

"I'd say our chances are pretty good, buddy. Like I said, we're all just a bunch of Links Lizards at heart."

Monday morning—-

Complete Unknown Takes Top Prize at John Deere Classic
By Luke Slowinski

Yes, Virginia there is a Cinderella. And he's from Hickory Corners, Michigan. For the past few days I had the privilege of experiencing my first PGA Tour event up close and personal. I happened to meet the eventual winner on my way back to the motel after the first round of the tournament. My car broke down and Will Green and his caddy, Mitch Winston, stopped to lend a hand. I knew who they were, as I had spoken to them briefly while they were experiencing some trouble of their own on the fourth hole of the Deere Run Golf Course. This itself is an exception to the norm. Tour professionals rarely talk to the spectators while they are playing. But then again, Will and Mitch are not your average tour participants. Much to the chagrin of several participants and broadcasters, the two friends from southwest Michigan went about their business in their own special way.

The spectators at the JDC found out how special these two were when Green fired a 61 on Friday in some pretty intense winds. Any golfer that kept it close to par under those conditions was rewarded by leapfrogging the players who lacked the ability to negotiate the fierce conditions. Green's fans grew in number when word got out that there was a fresh face on the course attempting something that had never been done before. Will Green was playing in his very first tournament, ever! That's right. Up until this past Thursday, Will had never played in an organized golf event, including junior high or high school. The Stonehedge Golf Course employee was definitely venturing into uncharted waters. Add to that, a caddy that had never caddied in a pro tournament, and you have a recipe that would normally end up being a learning experience for the two of them and nothing more. It should have been a humbling exercise for two dreamers that happened to find themselves on the big stage. But these two turned the tables on the nonbelievers.

Fans flocked to Green's group on Saturday, and he did not disappoint them. Green carded a five under 66 to get to sixteen under for the tournament. During the round, Green and his caddy had song guessing contests with the fans, bought half a hot dog from another fan, and gave away his last glove only to get it back on the next hole. Golf fans, at the tournament and at home, couldn't wait for Sunday to see what Team Green would do next. Their behavior was one of the main topics of conversation in the press tent. Right before he was scheduled to tee off on Sunday, Will pulled another unorthodox maneuver: he gave this reporter an interview while he was on the practice green.

Some of his comments were off the record, but he did say that he had been playing for ten years, and he had two of the best instructors that a young man could have. Their teachings were paramount in the shaping of the golfer and the man. I got the impression that I would be prying if I tried to delve any deeper into this subject.

Sunday had the makings of pure disaster. Green, playing only two groups behind the leaders, was tied for fourth, trailing by two shots. The weather was perfect, and if one expected to be in there at the end, he needed to get off to a hot start. Wilson Green decided to take a different approach. He went out in forty strokes, giving back five shots to par. The majority of golf fans were disappointed, feeling that the young man that no one had ever heard of had had his moment of glory and was now going to be an afterthought. Mr. Green and his caddy had other ideas.

To say that the spectators on hole number ten were shocked at the sight of a tournament participant carrying his own bag would be understating the situation. Green carried his bag on holes number ten, eleven, twelve, and half of thirteen until he hooked up with his caddy again. At the time, I was informed that this was a special kind of therapy reserved for extreme situations such as this. Apparently it worked, as Green played ten through twelve in three under par. Don't be surprised if you see this approach being used at a later date if a pro tanks the front nine on the final day of a tournament. It might result in a win, then again the caddy might find himself looking for another bag in future tournaments.

Will Green and his caddy continued to shake up the golf world with his play and their actions on the back nine. Before he hit his first shot of the round, Will was at the back of the practice tee talking to the fans and giving away souvenirs. Once on the course, they helped a little girl find her father. Then Green tossed a football around with a couple of young fans while they waited on seventeen tee. Oh yeah, they did all this while shooting nine under for the last nine holes!

Will told me afterward that he got a little misty on seventeen green while he was lining up his birdie putt. He started having flashbacks of some of the events that led up to his being at the tournament. That's when his caddy stepped in and took control of the situation. His steady guidance was there when needed, and his man responded like a true champion. They were a team from start to finish, and golf is all the better for it. Hopefully, Mr. Green and Mr. Winston will grace us with their presence on the links at some future date. Golf fans all over the world are anticipating their return.

Tuesday morning—-

Eddie Ferguson, aka Eddie Davis, sat by the window seat as the airliner flew over Tennessee en route to Florida. He was on his way to visit his oldest daughter and his grandkids. The $25,000 in cash that he had mailed on his way to the airport would arrive a few days after he did. His daughter would make a huge fuss about not wanting to take his money, but would eventually give in, after he suggested that she deposit it bit by bit into the kids' college fund. He looked over at the passenger with a Titleist hat on sitting next to him.

"Judging by your hat, I'd say you're a golfer," commented Eddie.

"Yup," answered the man. "And a pretty fair one. I'm a four-handicapper back at my home course. You play?"

"I do. It's a great game no matter how well you play. I know some people that regularly shoot over a hundred for eighteen holes, and they seem to enjoy it as much as an accomplished golfer. Of course, like in any sport, the better you play, the more satisfying it is. At least there are fewer frustrating moments."

"I suppose you're right," agreed the man. "Did you hear about the kid that just won the John Deere Classic? They said it was his first official tournament of any kind. Imagine that."

"Yeah, I read about it."

"I'll tell you one more thing," offered the man, lowering his voice. "I've got a friend out in Las Vegas, and he told me that he saw two big-time hustlers take a half a million off a couple of Russian mobsters last week. I wish I could have been there to see that. You don't see something like that happening in any other sport."

"You're right about that," agreed Eddie, looking out the window. "A lot of cash can change hands on the links if you run into some guys that know what they're doing."

About The Author

Tom Hoch is a retired golf professional, teacher, and coach. He lives in northwest Illinois with his wife. His two daughters and five grandchildren live close by. This is his fifth sports novel.

CPSIA information can be obtained
at www.ICGtesting.com
Printed in the USA
FFOW01n1119260916
27946FF